The Observers Series
CARS

About the Book

An enthusiast's quick reference guide to cars, for people of all ages and experience, provided they are interested in cars and motoring – that sums up the scope of this book. Whatever you want to know about a car, you are likely to find it here – except the price, which obviously cannot be included because of the frequency with which prices change.

Within the familiar format of one car to each page, a recent picture gives instant recognition and is supported by brief notes putting the car into perspective – how you can recognise it, when it was introduced, and other general helpful information.

The specification paragraphs give all essential details about the model, from a concise, factual description of the engine to a run-down on transmission, suspension, steering and brakes, plus all key dimensions. Such questions as whether a catalyst is fitted or not, whether anti-lock brakes are available, and what is the size of the fuel tank, are also answered. Of special importance is the snappy section on performance, which gives top speed, acceleration and fuel consumption. The concise summary which follows gives a thumbnail sketch of the car.

Completely updated for 1992–93, this edition includes many cars that were new at the Brussels and Geneva shows at the beginning of the year, and features a number of special high-performance models, such as the Chrysler Viper, Ferrari 512tr, Jaguar XJR-S, RJD Tempest, TVR Griffith and Venturi 260 Coupé. In total, more than 180 cars are covered.

About the Author

Stuart Bladon completes ten years of writing this annual publication with the 1992–3 edition: he took over from the previous editor, John Blunsden, to produce the book for 1983. At that time, he had just left *Autocar* to become a freelance motoring writer.

His interest in cars started as a boy in the early years of the war when he was evacuated to North Wales. He used to walk miles along the deserted roads to meet an aunt returning each day from war work at Cook's Explosives at Penrhyndeudraeth, so that he could steer her Morris 8 back to home at Llanbedr from the passenger seat.

National service in the RASC gave the opportunity for more motoring when he ran a platoon of staff cars and ambulances based in Kent, and used a Vauxhall Velox army car to visit detachments. On completion of the obligatory two years' service he joined the staff of what was then known as *The Autocar* – now *Autocar & Motor* – in 1955.

In compiling the material for this book, he has the advantage of having driven most of the cars it covers. Indeed, where there are one or two omissions (such as the new Mazda 626), they have been left out because of lack of information and personal experience of them.

The *Observer's* series was launched in 1937 with the publication of *The Observer's Book of Birds*. Today, over fifty years later, paperback *Observers* continue to offer practical, useful information on a wide range of subjects, and with every book regularly revised by experts, the facts are right up-to-date. Students, amateur enthusiasts and professional organisations alike will find the latest *Observers* invaluable.

'Thick and glossy, briskly informative' – *The Guardian*

'If you are a serious spotter of any of the things the series deals with, the books must be indispensable' – *The Times Educational Supplement*

O B S E R V E R S

CARS

Stuart Bladon

BLOOMSBURY BOOKS
LONDON

PENGUIN BOOKS

Published by the Penguin Group
Penguin Books Ltd, 27 Wrights Lane, London W8 5TZ, England
Penguin Books USA Inc., 375 Hudson Street, New York, New York 10014, USA
Penguin Books Australia Ltd, Ringwood, Victoria, Australia
Penguin Books Canada Ltd, 10 Alcorn Avenue, Toronto, Ontario, Canada M4V 3B2
Penguin Books (NZ) Ltd, 182–190 Wairau Road, Auckland 10, New Zealand

Penguin Books Ltd, Registered Offices: Harmondsworth, Middlesex, England

First published 1955
Thirty-fifth edition 1992

This edition published by Bloomsbury Books, an imprint of
The Godfrey Cave Group, 42 Bloomsbury Street, London, WC1B 3QJ,
under licence from Penguin Books Limited, 1993

  3 5 7 9 10 8 6 4 2

NOTE

The specifications contained in this book were collated on the basis
of material available to the compiler up to the start of 1992.
All information is subject to change and/or cancellation during the course
of the model year. Although every effort has been made to ensure
accuracy in compiling this book responsibility for errors and omissions
cannot be accepted by the compiler and publishers.

Printed and bound in Great Britain by
BPCC Hazell Books Ltd

ISBN 1 85471 199 7

CONTENTS

COUNTRY OF MANUFACTURE

After each make, the letters in brackets show the country of origin, using the abbreviations established by International Convention. We have a new one this year: the Sao Penza, from South Africa (ZA). In some cases several letters are given, indicating the main countries of origin for a car such as the Ford Fiesta which has multiple sourcing.

B	Belgium	K	Korea
CS	Czechoslovakia	MAL	Malaysia
D	Germany	NL	Holland (Netherlands)
E	Spain	S	Sweden
F	France	SU	Russia
GB	Great Britain	USA	United States of America
I	Italy	YU	Yugoslavia
J	Japan	ZA	South Africa

AMERICA'S SMALLER GALON

Over the years, this publication has looked at numerous explanations for America's galon (spelt with single 'l') to be smaller than the Imperial one, in contradiction of the trend for almost everything else American to be bigger and better. I feared we had exhausted all possible explanations – some plausible, some highly dubious – until I heard from Mr I. M. A. Tallboy of Illinois. It's all to do, he says, with the nip.

Apparently the nip is or was a measure of beer, with four nips to the pint and 32 to the English gallon. A little-known clause of the American Act of Independence allowed a free nip in every eight, from which, he says, comes the expression 'one over the eight'. I attach little credence to this explanation, which would seem to leave them with a very odd-sized gallon. Perhaps more important is the comment of Mr G. E. Titright who points out that I am quite wrong in saying that it's 1.2 US galons to 1 Imperial one. The actual conversion factor, he tells me, is 1.20095.

I stand corrected here, but still feel that Americans who multiply tank capacity by 1.2 will not be far out. Similarly, mpg figures should be divided by 1.2 to see how far a car will go at 75 mph on an American galon, if not stopped for speeding first.

Even stranger, perhaps, is British obstinacy in persisting with mpg at all in an era when nearly every service station sells fuel by the litre, and the younger generation hardly knows what a gallon is.

1992—THE THIRTY-FIFTH EDITION

Changing times bring different requirements: at one time it was necessary to answer the question, 'Will it run on unleaded fuel?' Now, of course, every car has to be able to do this, and the question is 'Does it have a catalyst?' Soon, this enquiry will also be redundant, since every new petrol car from 1993 onwards must be catalysed. The format for the specification details provided in these pages thus changes slightly from year to year, but this is the first year in the ten that I have been responsible for *Observers Cars* that I felt no major changes were needed. The format now well-established covers all the key points of information required for any car, up to the limits possible in the format of one car per page, in a layout that can be consulted easily and quickly.

Perhaps the most important data about any car concerns its performance: how fast it will go, how well it accelerates, and how much fuel it uses. I am grateful again to the Editor of *Autocar & Motor* for permission to quote key figures from the journal's weekly road tests. Although manufacturers are usually reliable in their claims, there is no substitute for independent testing. Use of *Autocar & Motor* figures also makes it possible to quote acceleration from rest to 80 mph through the gears—a figure which is still not quoted by most manufacturers.

Last year's edition introduced the 0 to 80 mph figure, which gives a much more significant idea of a car's acceleration, since it is high enough for aerodynamics to be able to show up, and eliminates the anomaly that sometimes results when a car will just make 60 mph in second gear. It would be good to see 0 to 80 mph adopted as the international yardstick for acceleration, instead of the present over-rated 0 to 60 mph time, because the metric equivalent of 130 km/h is very close (80.8 mph). With 0 to 60 mph, there is a slight difference, and when a Continental manufacturer quotes 0 to 100 km/h it has been necessary to draw attention to the fact that this is the time to 62 mph, not 60.

Fuel consumption is shown as the overall figure returned in *Autocar & Motor* road tests, and the DoT 'official' figure for consumption at constant 75 mph is also given. The other DoT figures (urban and at a constant 56 mph) are deliberately omitted as being potentially misleading.

Where no test data is available, the term 'Works' shows that the figures are the manufacturer's claim, and in the case of some American cars, it has been necessary to give estimated results. Things are improving, though, and Americans – anxious to try to establish markets for their cars in Europe – are beginning to show a more realistic attitude to performance details.

Introduction dates are usually expressed as the International Motor Show at which the model was first exhibited; the word 'show' is omitted throughout to save space. Usual motor show dates are: Brussels and New York, January; Amsterdam, February; Geneva, March; Turin, April; Frankfurt, September; Paris and Birmingham or Motorfair in October.

CHALLENGING TIMES

Last year's issue recorded 1990 as a 'setback year'; would that 1991 had been no worse. In the event, the slide in car sales was given a further downhill shove by the March Budget and its imposition of VAT at 17½ per cent instead of 15 per cent. Manufacturers and importers had pleaded for a cut in the Special Car Tax, which adds 10 per cent to all new car prices in Britain before the VAT calculation is made, but to no avail. Businesses had also asked for anomalies in Company Car Tax to be sorted out; instead, the same old formula was retained, with a further increase in the rates.

At the time of writing, the 1992 Budget was eagerly awaited, with its expected help for an industry plunged into decline. The year's new car sales were 1,592,326 – a terrible figure when it is remembered that they had been at the 2.3 million level two years earlier.

Ford held on to its position at the head of the league table, with over half a million cars sold during 1991 and things looking good on the surface, as Fiesta and Escort held the top two places. Worrying times are ahead, however. Already the Vauxhall Cavalier has established itself as a better-selling car than the Ford Sierra. With more versions of the new Astra coming on the market during 1992, Ford management must be deeply concerned as to whether the Escort will be overtaken by its rival, the Vauxhall Astra.

More credit deserves to be conceded to Rover's success with the 200 and 400 series, which are still proving very popular; they were given a big boost in 1991 by addition of 2-litre petrol and 1.8-litre diesel versions. Little noticed was the fact that – no doubt helped by a big sales campaign – the Rover 200 was Britain's best-selling car in December 1991. If the two models are taken together, the 200 and 400 were fifth best-sellers in Britain in 1991. This was achieved in spite of the lack of publicity resulting from Rover's decision not to be represented at Motorfair in London in October.

In these challenging times, when buyers are fewer in the showrooms and more cautious with their fleet orders, manufacturers cannot afford to slacken off. The impetus of new model announcements to draw attention to the marque and stimulate interest is vital. So perhaps it is no surprise that it was a record year for new models, with a total of 113 major new car announcements. These vary in importance, from minor additions such as a new diesel version of an existing model to a completely new range like the Vauxhall Astra. There is also some duplication, as the more important models may have their international launch first and then appear in Britain at a later date, and so tend to be counted twice. In spite of this, it was still a remarkable achievement.

First major event of the year on the international scene was the launch of Citroën's very pleasing new ZX range at the Geneva Show. For many at that show, however, the highlight was revealed when Rolls-Royce took the wraps off the magnificent Bentley Continental R. Such luxury may be only for a few, but it cannot help to interest all who are fascinated by superb cars.

A number of models which had been unveiled abroad in 1990 had their UK launch at the beginning of the year, among them being the Mitsubishi Sigma with its ingenious anti-slip control, the extremely fast Audi Coupé S2, Lancia's also very quick Dedra Turbo, the Renault Clio, Alfa Romeo 33 with four-wheel drive, and the BMW 3-Series, which I am able to include at last, albeit a year late.

May's releases brought the Mitsubishi Shogun (which other countries call the Pajero), SEAT's promising new Toledo, Audi S4, and Renault's stylish new Convertible based on the 19. Interest in June was kept up by British launch of the Citroën ZX, the first application of the 16-valve 2-litre engine to the Rover 200-Series, the 220 GTi, and the arrival of the competitively priced Sao Penza from South Africa. Most important news of the summer was undoubtedly the new small-medium car from GM, launched in July in Germany. It was given the name Astra for the first time – previously it had always been called the Opel Kadett – and was known in Britain as the Vauxhall Astra. This was the most important new model at Motorfair in October.

More big news came in August with a completely new Golf range, including one version with a big V6 2.8-litre engine, from Volkswagen, the new Audi 80 from the same VAG concern, and Peugeot's promising new 106 model. But my personal top memory of August remains a journey to Sweden to drive what I consider the best Saab yet—new 9000CS.

It's always in September that a motoring writer tends to be busiest, jetting from one new model launch to the next and wondering whether it wouldn't be easier just to camp down at the airport; the month brought a flurry of activity at the Frankfurt Show. Among the most important of the new models were the quiet and refined Toyota Camry, estate car versions of the Audi 100 and Citroën XM, the new Honda Civic, Mitsubishi Space Runner and Space Wagon, Mazda MX6, and the Mercedes-Benz 300 convertible. BMW unveiled new diesel models and an estate car version of the 5-Series, expected in the UK in 1992, and Opel showed a four-wheel drive turbocharged version of the Calibra.

Back at home I enjoyed a splendid drive in the north of England in Ford's new Escort RS2000, but I do question the thinking which seems to argue that a sporting car must offer soaring acceleration even in fifth gear, with the result that the gearing is too low for refined fast cruising. I would have thought that sporty drivers should be prepared to use the gears properly and hence have a good high gear for efficient cruising. One of the most important figures in these data pages, I believe, is the top gear speed at 1,000 rpm in the 'Transmission' section, revealing how high- or low-geared a car is. It's incidentally one of the most difficult figures to obtain from manufacturers, and most of these entries have had to be individually calculated.

October brought us the 'on and off' Motorfair exhibition at the now revitalised and extended Earls Court building in London. It was often presumed that the show was going to be cancelled when some manufacturers and importers decided not to take part, but as far as the organisers were concerned, it was always 'on'. It proved in fact to be one of the best British motor shows in London that I can recall. In passing, I noted that it was exactly 40 years since I first went to the Motor Show.

Although they would never admit it, those who were absent must have regretted their decision not to participate. In particular, Rover seemed ill-advised to stay away, as the new 800-Series was all ready to be launched and could have 'stolen' the show. As it was, we had to wait for November to reveal the new 800. With minimal publicity, Rover also announced more 2-litre additions to the 400 range.

Last launch of the year was the British introduction of the Renault 19 convertible and an impressive new turbocharged diesel version of the 19, for release in January 1992; both are covered in this edition. The pace continued in 1992, which looks like going down as an even more fruitful year for new model developments, with the Toyota plant at Derby coming on stream, Honda starting to build a completely new car at Swindon, and Nissan adding a Micra replacement to the cars being built at Sunderland.

As the year rolls on, I try to feature as many as possible of the latest releases, to ensure topicality, and justify the dateline on the cover that this is the 1992–93 edition; but sooner or later – usually later than it should be – the curtain has to come down to meet the press date.

1991 was also a fascinating year for the launch of a number of very high performance cars, regardless of the world recession. Although these inevitably come under the heading of 'playthings for the rich and few', they are of great interest to the enthusiast, and I have included as many of these exciting but impractical cars as possible. Among them are the Bugatti EB110, the Chrysler Viper, the Ferrari 512tr which replaced the Testarossa at the Brussels Show, and the Venturi 260 Coupé. Decidedly in this category, too, is the exciting RJD Tempest which featured also in the 1991 edition.

Development of the fast car has moved far ahead of the roads on which to exploit its speed potential or, indeed, the ability of drivers of ordinary skill to handle such performance. That does not make the sheer technical achievement and design ingenuity any less exciting.

As usual, some of the entries are carried over from last year, but the number of repeats has diminished as more and more new models came crowding in, deserving space. All have been checked for current specification and addition of test data where this has become available since the previous edition. Well over half of the 181 cars featured are entirely new, and the intention as always is that the book should be kept and used for reference in conjunction with those of earlier years, so that if you can't find the car you are looking for in this edition, you may well find it in the 1990 or 1991 volumes. Complete sets of *Observers Cars* and the former *Observers Book of Automobiles* are even now becoming of value, so – keep on taking the mixture as before!

Identity: Latest version of the Alfa 33, launched Brussels 1990, has a more modern look, with traditional Alfa Romeo grille continued back into the bonnet swage lines and 16-valve engine available. The eight-valve engine continues, and a 1.5-l injection engine was added September '90.

Engine: Front-mounted longitudinal four-cylinder with horizontally opposed pistons and twin ohc per bank working four valves per cylinder; Bosch Motronic ML 4.1 injection and ignition. Bore 87.0 mm, stroke 72.0 mm; capacity 1,712 cc. Power 139 PS (102 kW) at 6500 rpm; torque 119 lb ft (164 Nm) at 4600 rpm. Compression 9.5-to-1. Catalyst: not available.

Transmission: Front-wheel drive; five-speed manual gearbox. Automatic, not available. Top gear speed at 1000 rpm: 19.9 mph (32.0 km/h).

Suspension: Front, independent, MacPherson struts, anti-roll bar. Rear, dead beam axle on trailing arms with coil springs and Panhard rod.

Steering: Rack and pinion. Power assistance: standard. **Brakes:** Vented discs front, solid discs rear. ABS: not available. **Tyres:** 185/60 HR 14. **Fuel Tank:** 10.9 Imp. gall (50 litres). **Unladen weight:** 2138 lb (970 kg).

Dimensions: Length 160.4 in (4075 mm), width 63.5 in (1614 mm), height 53.1 in (1350 mm), wheelbase 97.4 in (2475 mm).

Performance *Autocar & Motor* test: Maximum speed 128 mph (206 km/h); 0 to 60 mph (97 km/h) 8.9 sec; 80 mph (130 km/h) 15.0 sec. Fuel consumption at constant 75 mph (120 km/h): 35.8 mpg; overall test, 29.7 mpg.

Features: Rear spoiler and aerodynamic sills identify the Boxer 16V, which also has alloy wheels as standard; but sunroof is an extra on both models. **Summary:** Although much improved, including a neater instrument layout, I still felt that the 33 was a dated design, with too much of its original Alfasud parentage. Still, it performs well and the standard power steering makes it much lighter to drive.

Identity: New top version of the Alfa Romeo 164 was introduced December 1990 and provided some superb motoring over the Yorkshire moors just before Christmas. Power is increased to the 'magic' 200 bhp, and the Cloverleaf has special equipment and additional aerodynamic skirts and spoilers.

Engine: Front-mounted transverse V6-cylinder with all-alloy construction and single ohc each bank; 12 valves. Bosch Motronic ML4.1 fuel injection/ignition. Bore 93.0 mm, stroke 72.6 mm; capacity 2959 cc. Power 203 PS (149 kW) at 5800 rpm; torque 198 lb ft (274 Nm) at 4400 rpm. Compression 10.0-to-1. Catalyst: standard.

Transmission: Front-wheel drive; five-speed manual gearbox. Automatic, not available. Top gear speed at 1000 rpm: 23.0 mph (37.0 km/h).

Suspension: Front, independent, MacPherson struts, anti-roll bar. Rear, independent, MacPherson struts with double transverse links and trailing arms.

Steering: Rack and pinion. Power assistance: standard. **Brakes:** Vented discs front, solid discs rear. ABS: standard. **Tyres:** 195/60 VR 15. **Fuel tank:** 15.5 Imp. gall (70 litres). **Unladen weight:** 3152 lb (1430 kg).

Dimensions: Length 179.5 in (4560 mm), width 69.0 in (1760 mm), height 55.1 in (1400 mm), wheelbase 104.7 in (2660 mm).

Performance *Autocar & Motor* test: Maximum speed 143 mph (230 km/h); 0 to 60 mph (97 km/h) 7.8 sec; 80 mph (130 km/h) 12.7 sec. Fuel consumption at constant 75 mph (120 km/h): 30.4 mpg; overall test, 21.4 mpg.

Features: Automatic suspension control is standard, responding to speed and driving conditions; also fitted are air conditioning, electric sunroof and audio with compact disc unit. **Summary:** Standard 164 3.0 V6 continues, but this new Cloverleaf addition brings a more sporty concept. Hence no automatic version and slightly lower gearing. An extremely enjoyable high-performance car.

ALFA ROMEO (I)   164 Twin Spark

Identity: Additional version of the 164, first introduced with V6 engine Frankfurt 1987, came to the UK market in 1990 in less expensive form with an under 2-litre engine. Alfa's ingenious dual-ignition system allows the engine to run efficiently on weak mixtures.

Engine: Front-mounted transverse four-cylinder with twin overhead camshafts, eight valves, and Bosch Motronics with dual ignition. Bore 84.0 mm, stroke 85.5 mm; capacity 1962 cc. Power 150 PS (110 kW) at 5800 rpm; torque 137 lb ft (189 Nm) at 4000 rpm. Compression 10.0-to-1. Catalyst: not available.

Transmission: Front-wheel drive; five-speed manual gearbox. Automatic, not available. Top gear speed at 1000 rpm: 23.8 mph (38.3 km/h).

Suspension: Front, independent, MacPherson struts, anti-roll bar. Rear, independent, MacPherson struts, anti-roll bar.

Steering: Rack and pinion. Power assistance: standard. **Brakes:** Vented discs front and rear. ABS: optional. **Tyres:** 185/70 VR 14. **Fuel tank:** 15.4 Imp. gall (70 litres). **Unladen weight:** 2646 lb (1200 kg).

Dimensions: Length 179.5 in (4560 mm), width 69.0 in (1760 mm), height 55.0 in (1400 mm), wheelbase 105.0 in (2660 mm).

Performance *Autocar & Motor* test: Maximum speed 126 mph (202 km/h); 0 to 60 mph (97 km/h) 9.5 sec; 80 mph (130 km/h) 16.4 sec. Fuel consumption at constant 75 mph (120 km/h): 33.2 mpg; overall test, 23.4 mpg.

Features: Impressive interior styling and quite good standard equipment, especially on the Lusso version, which includes sunroof and ABS.
Summary: In this form the 164 lacks the effortless performance of the V6, but it's still a very pleasant car to drive, with particularly crisp engine response, while handling benefits from the smaller engine.

Identity: First launched at Geneva 1966 as the Duetto, the pretty little Alfa two-seater reappeared in updated, but still classic, form at the same show 24 years later. More practical bodywork and 2-litre engine. No rhd model is available from the factory, but in late 1990, a very well-engineered rhd conversion was developed by Seaking.

Engine: Front-mounted longitudinal four-cylinder with twin chain-driven ohc and Bosch Motronic ML 4.1 ignition/injection system. Bore 84.0 mm, stroke 88.5 mm; capacity 1962 cc. Power 128 PS (94 kW) at 5800 rpm; torque 123 lb ft (170 Nm) at 4200 rpm. Compression 10.0-to-1. Catalyst: optional.

Transmission: Rear-wheel drive; five-speed manual gearbox. Automatic, not available. Top gear speed at 1000 rpm: 21.8 mph (35.0 km/h).

Suspension: Front, independent, wishbones and coil springs; anti-roll bar. Rear, live axle on longitudinal links with central wishbone.

Steering: Recirculating ball. Power assistance: not available. **Brakes:** Solid discs front and rear. ABS: not available. **Tyres:** 195/60 R 15. **Fuel tank:** 10.1 Imp. gall (46 litres). **Unladen weight:** 2447 lb (1110 kg).

Dimensions: Length 167.6 in (4258 mm), width 64.2 in (1630 mm), height 50.8 in (1290 mm), wheelbase 88.6 in (2250 mm).

Performance Works: Maximum speed 118 mph (190 km/h); 0 to 62 mph (100 km/h) 9.4 sec. Fuel consumption at constant 75 mph (120 km/h): 32.5 mpg.

Features: Classic styling of the 60s is retained but cleverly brought up to date, and the Spider now features such items as electrically adjusted mirrors. **Summary:** Some of the 1960s features may be less desirable, such as the rather crude ventilator outlets, but the Spider is certainly a most eye-catching shape. The Seaking conversion to right-hand drive is well engineered, except for too-tight – and hence jerky – throttle cable action.

ASTON MARTIN (GB)　　　Virage Volante

Identity: It took well over a year from the Birmingham 1988 launch of the Virage to get the car into production, but everything started happening in 1990, including launch of the convertible model, Volante, at Paris. Magnificent for high-speed grand touring, but not so good at lower speeds. This 2 + 2 Volante was launched at Geneva 1991.

Engine: Front-mounted longitudinal V8-cylinder with twin chain-driven ohc; four valves per cylinder. Weber Marelli fuel injection. Bore 100.0 mm, stroke 85.0 mm; capacity 5340 cc. Power 334 PS (246 kW) at 6000 rpm; torque 343 lb ft (475 Nm) at 3700 rpm. Comp. 9.5-to-1. Catalyst: standard.

Transmission: Rear-wheel drive; five-speed manual gearbox. Automatic, three-speed optional extra. Top-gear speed at 1000 rpm: 27.1 mph (43.7 km/h).

Suspension: Front, independent, wishbones and coil springs; anti-roll bar. Rear, de Dion axle with Watts linkage and triangulated radius arms; dual rate springs and damper units.

Steering: Rack and pinion. Power assistance: standard. **Brakes:** Vented discs front, solid discs rear. ABS: not available. **Tyres:** 225/60 ZR 16. **Fuel tank:** 26.0 Imp. gall (118 litres). **Unladen weight:** 3946 lb (1790 kg).

Dimensions: Length 186.8 in (4745 mm), width 72.8 in (1849 mm), height 52.0 in (1320 mm), wheelbase 102.8 in (2611 mm).

Performance *Autocar & Motor* test (saloon): Maximum speed 157 mph (252 km/h); 0 to 60 mph (97 km/h) 6.8 sec; 80 mph (130 km/h) 10.5 sec. Fuel consumption, overall test, 15.6 mpg.

Features: Superb finish and luxurious leather trimming, but a little short on modern refinements. Neatly trimmed power hood. **Summary:** An all too brief one-day drive with the Virage was most exhilarating, especially at higher speed. Less good aspects are the big turning circle and difficulty of driving smoothly at low speeds, but it is certainly a most exciting and rewarding machine.

AUDI (D)

Identity: New Audi 80 range was launched Frankfurt 1991, and on British market from February 1992. Family styling, with bonnet and radiator grille integral, identifies the new model, and smallest engine is now this 2-litre, although there are also two 1.9-litre diesels.

Engine: Front-mounted longitudinal four-cylinder with alloy head and single ohc; eight valves. Single point injection or digitally mapped (details follow). Bore 82.5 mm, stroke 92.8 mm; capacity 1984 cc. Power 115 PS (85 kW) at 5400 rpm; torque 119 lb ft (165 Nm) at 3200 rpm. Compression 10.3-to-1. Catalyst: standard.

Transmission: Front-wheel drive; five-speed manual gearbox. Automatic, optional extra, four-speed. Top gear speed at 1000 rpm: 20.8 mph (33.5 km/h).

Suspension: Front, independent, MacPherson struts, anti-roll bar. Rear, torsion beam on trailing arms, with V-shaped transverse beam; coil springs.

Steering: Rack and pinion. Power assistance: standard. **Brakes:** Vented discs front, solid discs rear. ABS: standard. **Tyres:** 195/65 R 15 91V. **Fuel tank:** 14.5 Imp. gall (66 litres). **Unladen weight:** 2711 lb (1230 kg).

Dimensions: Length 176.4 in (4482 mm), width 66.7 in (1695 mm), height 55.4 in (1408 mm), wheelbase 102.8 in (2612 mm).

Performance Works: Maximum speed 118 mph (190 km/h); 0 to 62 mph (100 km/h) 11.8 sec. Fuel consumption at constant 75 mph (120 km/h): 38.2 mpg.

Features: Major improvement over the previous 80 is the much bigger boot, achieved without reducing size of the generously big fuel tank.
Summary: Handling better than before, with less prominent understeer. Such a smooth, quiet engine and high level of refinement that I was tremendously impressed by this new 80 when I drove it in Germany last August.

AUDI (D)   **80 V6 quattro**

Identity: As well as the 2.0-litre four-cylinder and 2.3-litre five-cylinder engines, the new 80 gets the superbly smooth and quiet V6 2.8-litre. Standard front-wheel drive available, or this top model with four-wheel drive, under the usual quattro name. Manual transmission only, for quattro.

Engine: Front-mounted longitudinal V6-cylinder with aluminium block and heads; electronic multi-point injection and multi-path intake manifold. Bore 82.5 mm, stroke 86.4 mm; capacity 2771 cc. Power 174 PS (128 kW) at 5500 rpm; torque 177 lb ft (245 Nm) at 3000 rpm. Compression 10.3-to-1. Catalyst: standard.

Transmission: Four-wheel drive; five-speed manual gearbox. Automatic, not available. Top gear speed at 1000 rpm: 22.6 mph (36.4 km/h).

Suspension: Front, independent, MacPherson struts, anti-roll bar. Rear, independent, wishbones and track control arms; coil springs.

Steering: Rack and pinion. Power assistance: standard. **Brakes:** Vented discs front, solid discs rear. ABS: standard. **Tyres:** 195/65 R 15 91V. **Fuel tank:** 14.0 Imp. gall (64 litres). **Unladen weight:** 3150 lb (1430 kg).

Dimensions: Length 176.4 in (4482 mm), width 66.7 in (1695 mm), height 55.4 in (1408 mm), wheelbase 102.8 in (2612 mm).

Performance Works: Maximum speed 137 mph (220 km/h); 0 to 62 mph (100 km/h) 8.0 sec. Fuel consumption at constant 75 mph (120 km/h): 28.8 mpg.

Features: With the extra space taken by the independent suspension it has been difficult to achieve same capacity of fuel tank, but by using a complex moulded structure, Audi has managed it—almost. **Summary:** Very quiet car, with wonderfully smooth engine and drive-line, but it didn't seem to give the performance one might have expected for a 2.8 in this compact body. Perhaps this was a deception, and the car was going faster than it seemed.

AUDI (D)   80 2.3E Cabriolet

Identity: Although it was not ready in time for the international Press launch in August 1991, by the time the Frankfurt Show doors opened, the Cabriolet was revealed, with delightfully sleek appearance. It follows the format of the previous Cabriolet, but offers a bigger boot. Available only with 2.3-litre engine. On UK market summer 1992.

Engine: Front-mounted longitudinal five-cylinder with aluminium head, single ohc and ten valves; multi-point fuel injection. Bore 82.5 mm, stroke 86.4 mm; capacity 2309 cc. Power 98 PS (133 kW) at 5500 rpm; torque 134 lb ft (186 Nm) at 4000 rpm. Compression 10.0-to-1. Catalyst: standard.

Transmission: Front-wheel drive; five-speed manual gearbox. Automatic, optional extra, four-speed. Top gear speed at 1000 rpm: 22.0 mph (35.4 km/h).

Suspension: Front, independent, MacPherson struts, anti-roll bar. Rear, torsion beam on trailing arms, with V-shaped transverse beam; coil springs.

Steering: Rack and pinion. Power assistance: standard. **Brakes:** Vented discs front, solid discs rear. ABS: standard. **Tyres:** 195/65 R 15 H. **Fuel tank:** 14.5 Imp. gall (66 litres). **Unladen weight:** 3050 lb (1383 kg).

Dimensions: Length 176.4 in (4482 mm), width 66.7 in (1695 mm), height 55.4 in (1408 mm), wheelbase 102.8 in (2612 mm).

Performance Works: Maximum speed 124 mph (200 km/h); 0 to 62 mph (100 km/h) 9.8 sec. Fuel consumption at constant 75 mph (120 km/h): 33.2 mpg.

Features: A lot of attention was paid to reinforcement of the chassis and to making the Cabriolet accident-safe. All windows are electrically operated, and sports suspension is fitted. **Summary:** Very attractive open car, with careful tailoring of the hood to eliminate draughts when closed, and there is neat provision for it to fold away electrically into the well behind the rear seat.

AUDI (D)   Coupé S2

Identity: Added to the Audi range in August 1990, the Coupé S2 is the natural successor to the Quattro, having four-wheel drive and 20-valve turbocharged engine. In one of these I enjoyed magnificent motoring to Geneva and back in 1991, and appreciated its superbly balanced and controllable handling over the mountains.

Engine: Front-mounted longitudinal five-cylinder with alloy head and twin ohc working four valves per cylinder. Bosch Motronics and turbocharger with intercooler. Bore 81.0 mm, stroke 86.4 mm; capacity 2226 cc. Power 220 PS (162 kW) at 5900 rpm; torque 223 lb ft (309 Nm) at 1950 rpm. Compression 9.3-to-1. Catalyst: standard.

Transmission: Four-wheel drive; five-speed manual gearbox. Automatic, not available. Top gear speed at 1000 rpm: 24.7 mph (39.7 km/h).

Suspension: Front, independent, MacPherson struts, anti-roll bar. Rear, independent, wishbones and coil springs; anti-roll bar.

Steering: Rack and pinion. Power assistance: standard. **Brakes:** Vented discs front, solid discs rear. ABS: standard. **Tyres:** 205/55 ZE 16. **Fuel tank:** 15.4 Imp. gall (70 litres). **Unladen weight:** 3130 lb (1420 kg).

Dimensions: Length 173.3 in (4401 mm), width 67.6 in (1716 mm), height 54.1 in (1375 mm), wheelbase 100.4 in (2549 mm).

Performance *Autocar & Motor* test: Maximum speed 148 mph (238 km/h); 0 to 60 mph (97 km/h) 5.9 sec, 80 mph (130 km/h) 10.5 sec. Fuel consumption at constant 75 mph (120 km/h): 30.4 mpg; overall test, 18.2 mpg.

Features: Comprehensive equipment includes 'one touch' electric sunroof. Permanent four-wheel drive with Torsen centre diff. and lockable rear diff. Procon-Ten safety system standard. **Summary:** An extremely fast and very safe car, able to cruise at 130 mph with excellent stability and brakes, plus very high standards of cornering.

AUDI (D)

Identity: Audi's industrious engineering team brings out new models almost faster than one can keep pace with them, and at Frankfurt 1991 the elegant and functional Avant version of the 100 was launched. It was added to the British market from Motorfair, though without the Avant name.

Engine: Front-mounted longitudinal five-cylinder with alloy head and single ohc; ten valves. Electronic multi-point fuel injection. Bore 82.5 mm, stroke 86.4 mm; capacity 2309 cc. Power 133 PS (98 kW) at 5500 rpm; torque 135 lb ft (186 Nm) at 4000 rpm. Compression 10.0-to-1. Catalyst: standard.

Transmission: Front-wheel drive; five-speed manual gearbox. Automatic, optional extra, four-speed. Top gear speed at 1000 rpm: 22.0 mph (35.4 km/h).

Suspension: Front, independent, MacPherson struts, anti-roll bar. Self-correcting steering geometry. Rear, dead beam axle on trailing arms with Panhard rod; coil springs.

Steering: Rack and pinion. Power assistance: standard. **Brakes:** Solid discs front and rear. ABS: standard. **Tyres:** 195/65 R 15 H. **Fuel tank:** 17.6 Imp. gall (80 litres). **Unladen weight:** 3130 lb (1420 kg).

Dimensions: Length 188.5 in (4790 mm), width 70.0 in (1777 mm), height 56.3 in (1431 mm), wheelbase 105.8 in (2687 mm).

Performance Works: Maximum speed 121 mph (194 km/h); 0 to 62 mph (100 km/h) 10.5 sec. Fuel consumption at constant 75 mph (120 km/h): 28.0 mpg.

Features: Easy action tailgate opens down to bumper level, and rear seat is divided 40/60 and folding for extra load space. Folding rearward facing back seat for two children is optional. **Summary:** Comfortable and roomy load carrier, offered with wide choice of engines from 2-litre to V6 2.8, as well as the 2.3-litre turbo S4 and two diesel versions. Four wheel drive quattro also available.

Identity: In addition to the familiar four- and five-cylinder engines, Audi launched a delightfully smooth V6 to go with the new 100, giving high torque output, while enhancing the quietness of the car. It is available with front-drive or in quattro form (details follow).

Engine: Front-mounted longitudinal V6-cylinder with alloy heads and single ohc each bank. Ingenious multi-path intake manifold achieves high torque without spoiling peak power. MPI electronic fuel injection. Bore 82.5 mm, stroke 86.4 mm; capacity 2771 cc. Power 174 PS (128 kW) at 5500 rpm; torque 181 lb ft (250 Nm) at 3000 rpm. Compression 10.0-to-1. Catalyst: standard.

Transmission: Four-wheel drive; five-speed manual gearbox. Automatic, optional extra, four-speed. Top gear speed at 1000 rpm: 22.1 mph (35.6 km/h).

Suspension: Front, independent, MacPherson struts; anti-roll bar. Self-correcting steering geometry. Rear, independent, four-joint trapezium arms with transverse links. Coil springs and anti-roll bar.

Steering: Rack and pinion. Power assistance: standard. **Brakes:** Vented discs front, solid discs rear. ABS: standard. **Tyres:** 195/65 R 15V. **Fuel tank:** 17.6 Imp. gall (80 litres). **Unladen weight:** 3307 lb (1500 kg).

Dimensions: Length 188.6 in (4790 mm), width 70.0 in (1777 mm), height 56.3 in (1431 mm), wheelbase 105.8 in (2687 mm).

Performance *Autocar & Motor* test: Maximum speed 135 mph (217 km/h); 0 to 60 mph (97 km/h) 9.0 sec; 80 mph (130 km/h) 15.5 sec. Fuel consumption 75 mph (120 km/h): 29.4 mpg; overall test, 23.9 mpg.

Features: Six flap valves in the engine intake system open at 4,000 rpm to re-route the mixture path, giving better power. Comprehensive equipment and lockable centre differential. **Summary:** With this engine, the new Audi 100 is an outstanding car, providing effortless performance and high standards of quietness and refinement, especially with the smooth, snatch-free power train of this four-wheel drive version.

Identity: Performance version of the new 100, added to the range at Frankfurt 1991, using the 2.2-litre turbocharged five-cylinder engine familiar from the quattro. The S4 is an important executive car rival to such models as the BMW 735i, with the advantage that it has four-wheel drive as standard.

Engine: Front-mounted longitudinal five-cylinder with alloy head and twin ohc working 20 valves. Bosch Motronics and turbocharger with intercooler. Bore 81.0 mm, stroke 86.4 mm; capacity 2226 cc. Power 230 PS (169 kW) at 5900 rpm; torque 253 lb ft (350 Nm) at 1950 rpm. Compression 9.3-to-1. Catalyst: standard.

Transmission: Four-wheel drive; five-speed manual gearbox. Six-speed optional; automatic not available. Top gear speed at 1000 rpm: 23.8 mph (38.3 km/h).

Suspension: Front, independent, MacPherson struts, anti-roll bar. Self-correcting steering geometry. Rear, independent, four-joint trapezium arm with transverse links; coil springs.

Steering: Rack and pinion. Power assistance: standard. **Brakes:** Vented discs front and rear. ABS: standard. **Tyres:** 215/60 ZR 15. **Fuel tank:** 17.6 Imp. gall (80 litres). **Unladen weight:** 3550 lb (1610 kg).

Dimensions: Length 188.5 in (4790 mm), width 70.0 in (1777 mm), height 56.3 in (1431 mm), wheelbase 105.8 in (2687 mm).

Performance Works: Maximum speed 152 mph (244 km/h); 0 to 62 mph (100 km/h) 6.8 sec. Fuel consumption at constant 75 mph (120 km/h): 29.7 mpg.

Features: The optional six-speed gearbox does not change the overall ratio in top, which could usefully be higher. Generous equipment and interior furnishing. **Summary:** An extremely capable and comfortable long journey express with very high safety standards because of its terrific acceleration and braking, in conjunction with the security of four-wheel drive.

AUDI (D) V8

Identity: Although the V8 already seemed impressively fast when I used it to go to the 1989 Frankfurt Show, at the same show in 1991 its V8 engine was increased from 3562 cc to 4172 and 280 PS. The V8 was first launched Paris 1988; on British market from 1990. Magnificent specification.

Engine: Front-mounted longitudinal V8-cylinder with alloy block and heads; four ohc working 32 valves. Bosch Motronics. Bore 84.5 mm, stroke 93.0 mm; capacity 4172 cc. Power 280 PS (206 kW) at 5800 rpm; torque 289 lb ft (400 Nm) at 4000 rpm. Compression 10.6-to-1. Catalyst: standard.

Transmission: Four-wheel drive; six-speed manual gearbox. Automatic, four-speed, no cost option. Top gear speed at 1000 rpm: 25.4 mph (40.9 km/h).

Suspension: Front, independent, MacPherson struts, anti-roll bar. Self-correcting steering geometry. Rear, independent, four-joint trapezium arm with transverse links; coil springs.

Steering: Rack and pinion. Power assistance: standard. **Brakes:** Vented discs front, vented rear. ABS: standard. **Tyres:** 215/60 ZR 15. **Fuel tank:** 17.6 Imp. gall (80 litres). **Unladen weight:** 3900 lb (1770 kg).

Dimensions: Length 191.9 in (4874 mm), width 71.4 in (1814 mm), height 55.9 in (1420 mm), wheelbase 106.4 in (2702 mm).

Performance Works: Maximum speed 155 mph (249 km/h); 0 to 62 mph (100 km/h) 7.0 sec. Fuel consumption at constant 75 mph (120 km/h): 26.4 mpg.

Features: Torsen centre and rear differentials. Top equipment including air conditioning with reduced power consumption and more sensitive control. **Summary:** Superbly comfortable, safe and extremely fast car. The V8 is also available with long wheelbase; the 3.6-litre saloon remains in production and is also available with six-speed manual gearbox.

BENTLEY (GB)　　　　　　　　　Continental R

Identity: An unusually well-kept secret was Bentley's surprise announcement of a new model at Geneva 1991—the Continental R: familiar running gear, but entirely new body, owing much to the Project 90 special shown at Geneva 1985. It is the first uniquely styled Bentley since 1952.

Engine: Front-mounted longitudinal V8-cylinder with all-alloy construction and hydraulic tappets. Two valves per cylinder; Bosch K-Motronic fuel injection and Garrett TO4 turbocharger. Bore 104.1 mm, stroke 99.1 mm; capacity 6750 cc. Power and torque: no data released. Compression 8.0-to-1. Catalyst: standard.

Transmission: Rear-wheel drive. Automatic, four-speed, standard, with mode control. Top gear speed at 1000 rpm: 28.7 mph (46.2 km/h).

Suspension: Front, independent, coil springs and wishbones with electronically controlled dampers; anti-roll bar. Rear, independent, coil springs and semi-trailing arms; electronically controlled dampers and hydraulic self-levelling; anti-roll bar.

Steering: Rack and pinion. Power assistance: standard. **Brakes:** Vented discs front, solid discs rear. ABS: standard. **Tyres:** 255/60 ZR 16. **Fuel tank:** 23.5 Imp. gall (107 litres). **Unladen weight:** 5340 lb (2420 kg).

Dimensions: Length 210.3 in (5342 mm), width 80.5 in (2044 mm), height 57.6 in (1462 mm), wheelbase 120.5 in (3061 mm).

Performance Works: Maximum speed 145 mph (233 km/h); 0 to 60 mph (97 km/h) 6.6 sec. Fuel consumption at 75 mph (120 km/h): 19.3 mpg.

Features: Luxuriously trimmed and extravagantly equipped two-door coupé, most beautifully fitted out inside, with console flowing through from front into the rear compartment. **Summary:** The elegant new body of the Continental R is in steel with integral bumpers and front air dam. Flush glazing, but wipers are still visible, and the round headlamps look a bit dated. Nevertheless, the launch of the Continental R certainly caused a stir at Geneva that year.

Identity: On the British market, this model of the new 3-series costs £6,400 less than the 325i—a lot to pay for two more cylinders! The 318i is more reasonably priced, but the 1.8-litre engine has to be worked hard for reasonable performance.

Engine: Front-mounted longitudinal four-cylinder with alloy head and single ohc; eight valves. Bosch DME electronic fuel injection. Bore 84.0 mm, stroke 81.0 mm; capacity 1796 cc. Power 113 PS (84 kW) at 5900 rpm; torque 119 lb ft (162 Nm) at 3000 rpm. Compression 8.8-to-1. Catalyst: standard.

Transmission: Rear-wheel drive; five-speed manual gearbox. Automatic, optional extra, four-speed. Top gear speed at 1000 rpm: 20.5 mph (33.0 km/h).

Suspension: Front, independent, MacPherson struts, anti-roll bar. Rear, independent, trailing arms with transverse and diagonal links; coil springs and anti-roll bar.

Steering: Rack and pinion. Power assistance: standard. **Brakes:** Solid discs front, drums rear. ABS: optional. **Tyres:** 185/65 HR 15. **Fuel tank:** 14.3 Imp. gall (65 litres). **Unladen weight:** 2775 lb (1260 kg).

Dimensions: Length 174.5 in (4433 mm), width 66.8 in (1698 mm), height 54.8 in (1393 mm), wheelbase 106.2 in (2700 mm).

Performance *Autocar & Motor* test: Maximum speed 122 mph (196 km/h); 0 to 60 mph (97 km/h) 10.2 sec; 80 mph (130 km/h) 17.7 sec. Fuel consumption at constant 75 mph (120 km/h): 36.2 mpg; overall test, 27.6 mpg.

Features: Saloon body only available initially, coupé added this year. Equipment not very generous, with extra to be paid for sunroof, radio and other items normally standard at this price level. **Summary:** Good handling, and the 318i performs better than might be expected on only 1.8-litre capacity and eight valves, but the engine gets rather harsh and noisy if worked hard. Economy poor for a 1.8.

Identity: Replacement for the former model of the same name, launched December 1990, and on British market March last year. 325i is the top model of the range with six-cylinder 2.5-litre engine. Four-door saloon body of more aerodynamic shape than before.

Engine: Front-mounted longitudinal six-cylinder with alloy head and twin ohc working four valves per cylinder; digital fuel injection. Bore 84.0 mm, stroke 79.0 mm; capacity 2494 cc. Power 189 PS (139 kW) at 5900 rpm; torque 177 lb ft (245 Nm) at 4700 rpm. Compression 10.0-to-1. Catalyst: standard.

Transmission: Rear-wheel drive; five-speed manual gearbox. Automatic, optional extra, five-speed. Top gear speed at 1000 rpm: 23.1 mph (37.2 km/h).

Suspension: Front, independent, MacPherson struts, anti-roll bar. Rear, independent, trailing arms with transverse and diagonal links; coil springs and anti-roll bar.

Steering: Rack and pinion. Power assistance: standard. **Brakes:** Vented discs front, solid discs rear. ABS: standard. **Tyres:** 205/60 ZR 15. **Fuel tank:** 14.3 Imp. gall (65 litres). **Unladen weight:** 2962 lb (1330 kg).

Dimensions: Length 174.5 in (4433 mm), width 66.8 in (1698 mm), height 54.8 in (1393 mm), wheelbase 106.2 in (2700 mm).

Performance *Autocar & Motor* test: Maximum speed 141 mph (227 km/h); 0 to 60 mph (97 km/h) 7.3 sec; 80 mph (130 km/h) 12.0 sec. Fuel consumption at constant 75 mph (120 km/h): 33.6 mpg; overall test, 26.6 mpg.

Features: Special equipment model available, but very expensive, and even then it does not include such items as an electric sunroof. **Summary:** Automatic is unusual in having five speeds, but control is poor and the 325i is much more enjoyable with manual gearbox, when the smoothness of the engine and drive-line can be appreciated.

Identity: Slightly lower than the saloon, and considerably restyled at the front, the two-door coupé of the 3-Series was launched Geneva 1992, and on British market from April. It looks a very shapely car, and gave me a superb drive in Spain in January 1992. Also available with 1.8- and 2.0-litre engine.

Engine: Front-mounted longitudinal six-cylinder with alloy head and twin ohc working four valves per cylinder. Bosch Motronics M3.1. Bore 84.0 mm, stroke 75.0 mm; capacity 2494 cc. Power 192 PS (141 kW) at 5900 rpm; torque 177 lb ft (245 Nm) at 4700 rpm. Compression 10.0-to-1. Catalyst: standard.

Transmission: Rear-wheel drive; five-speed manual gearbox. Automatic, optional extra, five-speed. Top gear speed at 1000 rpm: 22.7 mph (36.5 km/h).

Suspension: Front, independent, MacPherson struts, anti-roll bar. Rear, independent, central arm axle with longitudinal control arms and double track control arms; coil springs and anti-roll bar.

Steering: Rack and pinion. Power assistance: standard. **Brakes:** Vented discs front, solid rear. ABS: standard. **Tyres:** 205/60 ZR 15. **Fuel tank:** 14.3 Imp. gall (65 litres). **Unladen weight:** 2930 lb (1330 kg).

Dimensions: Length 174.5 in (4433 mm), width 67.3 in (1710 mm), height 53.8 in (1366 mm), wheelbase 106.3 in (2700 mm).

Performance Works: Maximum speed 145 mph (233 km/h); 0 to 62 mph (100 km/h) 8.0 sec; 80 mph (130 km/h) 12.7 sec. Fuel consumption at constant 75 mph (120 km/h): 33.6 mpg.

Features: Very low wind noise due to excellent window sealing. A clever technique makes the window lower automatically one inch as the door is opened; it shuts again after the door has been closed. **Summary:** Very satisfying road behaviour with excellently responsive controls, delightfully well-balanced handling and impressive performance. The coupé body provides generous four-seater space and a roomy boot.

BMW (D) 850i

Identity: Sports coupé launched Frankfurt 1989, to replace the respected 635CSi range. It appears first as the 850i, with V12 5-litre engine, but the 8-Series is expected to develop into a range, with six-cylinder engine versions later. Sleek four-seater two-door body.

Engine: Front-mounted longitudinal V12-cylinder with alloy block and heads; single chain-driven ohc per bank, and hydraulic tappets. Bosch Motronic injection-ignition system. Bore 84.0 mm, stroke 75.0 mm; capacity 4988 cc. Power 300 PS (223 kW) at 5200 rpm; torque 325 lb (450 Nm) at 4100 rpm. Compression 8.8-to-1. Catalyst: standard.

Transmission: Rear-wheel drive; six-speed manual gearbox. Automatic, optional, four-speed. Top gear speed at 1000 rpm: 34.4 mph (55.4 km/h).

Suspension: Front, independent, double-jointed spring struts with anti-dive and self compensating features; anti-roll bar. Rear, independent, five-link layout with coil springs and anti-dive, anti-squat compensation; anti-roll bar.

Steering: Ball and nut. Power assistance: standard. **Brakes:** Vented discs front, solid discs rear. ABS: standard. **Tyres:** 235/50 ZR 16. **Fuel tank:** 19.8 Imp. gall (90 litres). **Unladen weight:** 3946 lb (1790 kg).

Dimensions: Length 188.1 in (4780 mm), width 73.0 in (1855 mm), height 52.8 in (1340 mm), wheelbase 105.6 in (2684 mm).

Performance *Autocar & Motor* test: Maximum speed 157 mph (253 km/h); 0 to 60 mph (97 km/h) 7.2 sec; 80 mph (130 km/h) 11.0 sec. Fuel consumption at constant 75 mph (120 km/h): 27.2 mpg; overall test, 14.4 mpg.

Features: Many technical innovations, including six-speed gearbox, seat-belt system integrated with seats, and ellipsoid pop-up headlamps.
Summary: Worthy successor to the much-admired 635 CSi, though it's perhaps disappointing that it is again only produced as a closed car. Very high performance, and the 850i in manual form comes with automatic anti-wheelspin control. Automatic has stability control.

BUGATTI (I)   EB110

Identity: Rumours about a new car resurrecting the famous Bugatti name finally crystallised in a lavish presentation in 1991. The EB110 certainly lived up to expectations as an appropriately extravagant, enormously fast and, some might say, rather impractical coupé every bit as exciting as the name implies.

Engine: Mid-mounted longitudinal V12-cylinder with twin overhead camshafts on each bank working five valves per cylinder (total 60 valves!). Any turbochargers? Yes—**four!!** Bore 81.0 mm, stroke 56.6 mm; capacity 3499 cc. Power 551 PS (405 kW) at 8500 rpm; torque 412 lb ft (569 Nm) at 3800 rpm. Compression 7.5-to-1. Catalyst: standard.

Transmission: Four-wheel drive; six-speed manual gearbox. Automatic, not available. Top gear speed at 1000 rpm: 24.7 mph (39.7 km/h).

Suspension: Front, independent, wishbones and coil springs; anti-roll bar. Rear, independent, wishbones and coil springs; anti-roll bar.

Steering: Rack and pinion. Power assistance: standard. **Brakes:** Vented discs front and rear. ABS: standard. **Tyres:** Front, 245/40-18; rear, 325/30-18. **Fuel tank:** 26.4 Imp. gall (120 litres). **Unladen weight:** 3240 lb (1470 kg).

Dimensions: Length 172.4 in (4380 mm), width 78.3 in (1990 mm), height 43.9 in (1115 mm), wheelbase 100.4 in (2550 mm).

Performance Works: Maximum speed 214 mph (345 km/h); 0 to 62 mph(100 km/h) 3.5 sec; 80 mph (130 km/h) 4.8 sec. Fuel consumption: no data.

Features: Carbon fibre chassis, and bodywork in composite material. An 'active suspension' is being developed, which will read the road surface and position the wheels accordingly. **Summary:** Although bizarre in concept the EB110 presents many fascinating technical developments, and is a serious production venture, with output of 150 cars per year planned. Whether sufficient buyers for the car will be found, at the no doubt astronomical price, remains to be seen.

BUICK (USA)   Skylark Gran Sport

Identity: After a period when American car styling had become quite respectable, a new age of ugliness appears to be dawning, of which the all-new '92 Skylark is a hideous example. 'The car has, we hope, a shape that entertains you,' says Buick's Corby L. Casler.

Engine: Front-mounted transverse four-cylinder with alloy head and single ohc working eight valves, despite the title 'Quad OHC'. Multi-point fuel injection. Bore 92.2 mm, stroke 85.1 mm; capacity 2261 cc. Power 122 PS (90 kW) at 5200 rpm; torque 140 lb ft (194 Nm) at 3200 rpm. Compression 9.5-to-1. Catalyst: standard.

Transmission: Front-wheel drive; manual gearbox not available. Automatic, three-speed standard. Top gear speed at 1000 rpm: 24.8 mph (39.9 km/h).

Suspension: Front, independent, MacPherson struts. Rear, torsion beam axle on trailing crank arms.

Steering: Rack and pinion. Power assistance: standard. **Brakes:** Solid discs front, drums rear. ABS: standard. **Tyres:** P185/75 R 14. **Fuel tank:** 12.7 Imp. gall (57.6 litres). **Unladen weight:** 2965 lb (1345 kg).

Dimensions: Length 189.2 in (4806 mm), width 67.5 in (1715 mm), height 52.2 in (1326 mm), wheelbase 103.4 in (2626 mm).

Performance (est): Maximum speed 105 mph (169 km/h). Fuel consumption overall (est), 24 mpg.

Features: The Americans have discovered remote central locking, and the Skylark can have it as an option. Split folding rear seat standard.
Summary: Many things Europe has accepted for years are now creeping into America, like a headlamp flasher switch. Good feature is the low engine maintenance—oil, filters and plugs only need to be changed every 100,000 miles.

CADILLAC (USA) Seville

Identity: Rebodied Seville was launched August 1991, featuring the now widely used (in Europe) technique of extending the door tops into the roof, and less angular styling than before. The new Seville is longer than its predecessor, with wheelbase extended three inches.

Engine: Front-mounted transverse V8-cylinder with alloy block and heads; cast iron cylinder liners. Pushrod ohv. Sequential port fuel injection. Bore 92.0 mm, stroke 92.0 mm; capacity 4894 cc. Power 204 PS (150 kW) at 4100 rpm; torque 275 lb ft (380 Nm) at 3000 rpm. Compression 9.5-to-1. Catalyst; standard.

Transmission: Front-wheel drive; four-speed automatic, standard. Top gear speed at 1000 rpm: 24.6 mph (39.6 km/h).

Suspension: Front, independent, MacPherson struts with varying rate springs, anti-roll bar. Rear, independent, wishbones and transverse glass fibre leaf spring; anti-roll bar.

Steering: Rack and pinion. Power assistance: standard. **Brakes:** Vented discs front, solid discs rear. ABS: standard. **Tyres:** P225/60 R 16. **Fuel tank:** 15.6 Imp. gall (71 litres). **Unladen weight:** 3790 lb (1723 kg).

Dimensions: Length 203.9 in (5179 mm), width 74.4 in (1890 mm), height 54.0 in (1372 mm), wheelbase 111.0 in (2819 mm).

Performance Works: Maximum speed 112 mph (180 km/h); 0 to 60 mph (97 km/h) 8.9 sec. Fuel consumption overall (est), 25 mpg.

Features: Long-life sparking plugs are designed to go 100,000 miles without replacement. Good equipment including driver information centre. **Summary:** American cars seem to be getting bigger again, to judge from the new Seville. Sport interior is an option, and there is a choice of suspension packages. Above 60 mph (not long ago an unmentionable speed in America) the suspension goes automatically into 'firm' mode.

CATERHAM CARS (GB)   Super 7 HPC

Identity: Very high power/weight ratio of the little Caterham Seven resulted from the decision to adopt the Vauxhall 16-valve 2-litre engine in this special HPC model for 1991. The Super 7 is also available, fitted with the Rover K-Series 16-valve engine.

Engine: Front-mounted longitudinal four-cylinder with alloy head and belt-driven twin ohc working 16 valves; twin Weber 45 DCOE carbs. Bore 86.0 mm, stroke 86.0 mm; capacity 1998 cc. Power 175 PS (129 kW) at 6000 rpm; torque 155 lb ft (214 Nm) at 4800 rpm. Compression 10.5-to-1. Catalyst: not available.

Transmission: Rear-wheel drive; five-speed manual gearbox. Automatic, not available. Top gear speed at 1000 rpm: 20.2 mph (32.5 km/h).

Suspension: Front, independent, wishbones and coil springs; anti-roll bar. Rear, de Dion axle with radius arms and lower diagonal links; coil springs and anti-roll bar.

Steering: Rack and pinion. Power assistance: not available. **Brakes:** Vented discs front and rear. ABS: not available. **Tyres:** 205/45 VR 16. **Fuel tank:** 10.0 Imp. gall (45.5 litres). **Unladen weight:** 1380 lb (626 kg).

Dimensions: Length 133.5 in (3390 mm), width 62.0 in (1580 mm), height 42.5 in (1080 mm), wheelbase 88.0 in (2230 mm).

Performance *Autocar & Motor* test: Maximum speed 126 mph (203 km/h); 0 to 60 mph (97 km/h) 5.2 sec; 80 mph (130 km/h) 8.4 sec. Fuel consumption, overall test, 17.3 mpg.

Features: Weather protection is rather basic, but much better than a motorcycle, which might be the nearest comparison! Alloy wheels are standard, and there is a roll-over cage. **Summary:** The heavy fuel consumption recorded in the test is a bit alarming, but perhaps reflects a lot of use of that staggering acceleration, with 80 mph coming up in only 8.4 sec from rest, and 120 mph in 25.7 sec.

CHEVROLET (USA)   Corvette ZR-1

Identity: This car more than any other marked the return to production of high performance cars in America, after the dull period which followed imposition of very low speed limits. ZR-1 performance was demonstrated in 1990 when one of these cars raised the world 24-hour speed record from 161 to 176 mph.

Engine: Front-mounted longitudinal V8-cylinder with alloy heads and block; twin ohc each bank working four valves per cylinder. Multec fuel injection. Bore 99.0 mm, stroke 93.0 mm; capacity 5736 cc. Power 380 PS (279 kW) at 5800 rpm; torque 370 lb ft (511 Nm) at 4800 rpm. Compression 11.0-to-1. Catalyst: standard.

Transmission: Rear-wheel drive; six-speed manual gearbox. Automatic, not available. Top gear speed at 1000 rpm: 42.5 mph (68.3 km/h).

Suspension: Front, independent, wishbones and transverse glass fibre reinforced plastic leaf spring; anti-roll bar. Rear, independent, five-link layout with transverse glass fibre plastic leaf spring; anti-roll bar.

Steering: Rack and pinion. Power assistance: standard. **Brakes:** Vented discs front and rear. ABS: standard. **Tyres:** Front: 275/40 ZR 17; rear: 315/35 ZR 17. **Fuel tank:** 16.7 Imp. gall (76 litres). **Unladen weight:** 3465 lb (1571 kg).

Dimensions: Length 178.5 in (4534 mm), width 73.2 in (1859 mm), height 46.7 in (1186 mm), wheelbase 96.2 in (2443 mm).

Performance *Autocar & Motor* test: Maximum speed 176 mph (283 km/h); 0 to 60 mph (97 km/h) 5.6 sec; 80 mph (130 km/h) 9.2 sec. Fuel consumption overall (est), 20 mpg.

Features: 'Power Key' on facia gives choice of engine settings: 'Normal' restricts it to 210 PS; 'Full' makes the 380 PS available. **Summary:** Few changes are made to the ZR-1 for 1992, but the current model can be spotted by the two rectangular exhaust tail pipes instead of four square ones, and CZR1 script above the side louvres. An impressive and very fast sports car.

CHRYSLER (USA)   Grand Voyager

Identity: 'Once bitten, twice shy' is the saying, but not as far as Chrysler is concerned. Despite the collapse of the earlier effort to move into Europe, Chrysler will try again to import the Jeep to Britain later this year, and is pushing hard to sell this model, the Voyager and Grand Voyager, on the Continent.

Engine: Front-mounted transverse V6-cylinder with alloy heads, single ohc on each bank; 12 valves. Multi-point fuel injection. Bore 93.0 mm, stroke 81.0 mm; capacity 3301 cc. Power 150 PS (110 kW) at 4850 rpm; torque 174 lb ft (241 Nm) at 3750 rpm. Compression 8.9-to-1. Catalyst: standard.

Transmission: Front-wheel drive; four-speed automatic, standard; five-speed manual gearbox for 2.5-litre only. Top gear speed at 1000 rpm: 32.0 mph (51.5 km/h).

Suspension: Front, independent, MacPherson struts, anti-roll bar. Rear, dead beam axle on leaf springs; anti-roll bar.

Steering: Rack and pinion. Power assistance: standard. **Brakes:** Vented discs front, drums rear. ABS: not available. **Tyres:** 205/70 R 15. **Fuel tank:** 16.7 Imp. gall (76 litres). **Unladen weight:** 3700 lb (1680 kg)

Dimensions: Length 192.8 in (4896 mm), width 72.0 in (1830 mm), height 66.4 in (1687 mm), wheelbase 119.3 in (3031 mm).

Performance Works: Maximum speed 108 mph (174 km/h); 0 to 62 mph (100 km/h) 12.8 sec. Fuel consumption at constant 75 mph (120 km/h): 22.4 mpg.

Features: All Chryslers sold in Europe get a driver's air bag restraint system as standard. Longer than the standard Voyager by 14½ in, the Grand Voyager seats up to seven and offers generous legroom.
Summary: At Frankfurt 1991, the capacity of the V6 engine was increased to 3.3-litre, giving a bit more power and torque. Both short and long wheelbase versions are available, and the standard Voyager V6 is also offered with four-wheel drive. Base has a 2.5-litre engine.

CHRYSLER (USA) Viper RT/10

Identity: First shown as a concept car with the Dodge name at Detroit and Geneva 1989, the Viper was launched at the same shows just three years later, in 1992. Biggest engine of modern times, with unusual V10 format, and promising staggering performance. It is claimed to go from rest to 100 mph (160 km/h) and back to rest in just 14.5 sec!

Engine: Front-mounted longitudinal V10-cylinder with alloy block and heads; pushrod-operated overhead valves. Sequential multi-port fuel injection. Bore 101.6 mm, stroke 98.5 mm; capacity 7997 cc. Power 400 PS (294 kW) at 4600 rpm; torque 442 lb ft (611 Nm) at 3600 rpm. Compression 9.1-to-1. Catalyst: standard.

Transmission: Rear-wheel drive; six-speed manual gearbox. Automatic, not available. Top gear speed at 1000 rpm: 49.7 mph (80.0 km/h).

Suspension: Front, independent, wishbones and coil springs with concentric dampers; anti-roll bar. Rear, independent, wishbones and coil springs with longitudinal links and concentric dampers; anti-roll bar.

Steering: Rack and pinion. Power assistance: standard. **Brakes:** Vented discs front, and rear. ABS: not available. **Tyres:** 275/40 ZR 17 front, 335/35 ZR 17 rear. **Fuel tank:** 18.3 Imp. gall (83 litres). **Unladen weight:** 3276 lb (1486 kg).

Dimensions: Length 175.1 in (4448 mm), width 75.7 in (1923 mm), height 44.0 in (1118 mm), wheelbase 96.2 in (2444 mm).

Performance Works: Maximum speed 165 mph (266 km/h); 0 to 60 mph (97 km/h) 4.5 sec. Fuel consumption overall (est), 15 mpg.

Features: Body is in composite material on tubular steel chassis; sporty interior finish with urethane foam trim. Removable roof panel. **Summary:** A most exciting sort of car for the Americans to build, reflecting the influence of President Bob Lutz and Carroll Shelby. As well as being phenomenally fast, it is claimed to be docile, but I can't confirm, having not yet been invited to give it a bash round!

CITROEN (F)   AX 14 TZD

Identity: Many improvements to the AX range were revealed in the updated model at Frankfurt 1991, on UK market from Motorfair. The chevron badge in the centre at the front, instead of offset, identifies the latest model. The TZD is mechanically the same as the 14RD in which I set the world fuel economy record at 112.01 mpg in 1989.

Engine: Front-mounted transverse four-cylinder with alloy head and belt-driven ohc; eight valves. Ricardo combustion chambers. Bore 75.0 mm, stroke 77.0 mm; capacity 1360 cc. Power 53 PS (39 kW) at 5000 rpm; torque 62 lb ft (86 Nm) at 2500 rpm. Compression 22.0-to-1. Catalyst: not required.

Transmission: Front-wheel drive; five-speed manual gearbox. Automatic, not available. Top gear speed at 1000 rpm: 20.3 mph (32.7 km/h).

Suspension: Front, independent, MacPherson struts, anti-roll bar. Rear, independent, trailing arms and transverse links with transverse torsion bars; telescopic dampers mounted horizontally to save space.

Steering: Rack and pinion. Power assistance: not available. **Brakes:** Solid discs front, drums rear. ABS: not available. **Tyres:** 145/70 R 13. **Fuel tank:** 9.5 Imp. gall (43 litres). **Unladen weight:** 1620 lb (735 kg).

Dimensions: Length 139.0 in (3530 mm), width 61.5 in (1562 mm), height 53.5 in (1359 mm), wheelbase 90.0 in (2285 mm).

Performance *Autocar & Motor* test: Maximum speed 91 mph (146 km/h); 0 to 60 mph (97 km/h) 16.2 sec; 80 mph (130 km/h) 36.2 sec. Fuel consumption at constant 75 mph (120 km/h): 56.5 mpg; overall test, 54.7 mpg.

Features: The TZD is top model of the AX diesel range, and gets such features as electric front windows, central locking and sunroof. **Summary:** Previously the internal design and quality of the AX were not a match for its mechanical side. With the 1991 changes it becomes a much more attractive small car, while still very lively and economical.

CITROEN (F) AX GTi

Identity: At the same time as the revised AX range was introduced in September 1991, a very lively GTi model was added to the range, still with only 1360 cc, yet able to reach 114 mph. It has sports suspension and is identified by special alloy wheels and high level rear spoiler.

Engine: Front-mounted transverse four-cylinder with alloy head with belt-driven ohc; eight valves. Bosch MP3.1 fuel injection. Bore 75.0 mm, stroke 77.0 mm; capacity 1360 cc. Power 100 PS (75 kW) at 6800 rpm; torque 90 lb ft (122 Nm) at 4200 rpm. Compression 9.9-to-1. Catalyst: not available.

Transmission: Front-wheel drive; five-speed manual gearbox. Automatic, not available. Top gear speed at 1000 rpm: 18.6 mph (29.9 km/h).

Suspension: Front, independent, MacPherson struts, anti-roll bar. Rear, independent, trailing arms and transverse links with transverse torsion bars; telescopic dampers mounted horizontally to save space; anti-roll bar.

Steering: Rack and pinion. Power assistance: not available. **Brakes:** Vented discs front, drums rear. ABS: optional. **Tyres:** 185/60 HR 13. **Fuel tank:** 9.5 Imp. gall (43 litres). **Unladen weight:** 1753 lb (795 kg).

Dimensions: Length 139.0 in (3530 mm), width 61.5 in (1562 mm), height 53.5 in (1359 mm), wheelbase 90.0 in (2285 mm).

Performance *Autocar & Motor* test: Maximum speed 114 mph (183 km/h); 0 to 60 mph (97 km/h) 9.3 sec; 80 mph (130 km/h) 15.9 sec. Fuel consumption at constant 75 mph (120 km/h): 43.5 mpg; overall test, 26.0 mpg.

Features: Improved facia houses extra instruments, and there are sports seats. Generous equipment package includes remote central locking. **Summary:** Suspension was made tauter for the new range, and the extra performance of the GTi is matched by brakes with vented front discs, alloy wheels with Michelin MXV2 tyres, and sports seats, to make an attractively responsive small car.

CITROEN (F)   BX GTi 4 × 4

Identity: Important additions to the BX range in 1990 were four-wheel drive versions of the GTi and 1.9-litre estate car. I used the GTi 4 × 4 for a caravan-towing job, on which the four-wheel traction proved a great advantage, but 4 × 4 brings a slight economy penalty.

Engine: Front-mounted transverse four-cylinder with eight-valve alloy head, alloy block, and wet cylinder liners. Bosch LE 3 fuel injection. Bore 83.0 mm, stroke 88.0 mm; capacity 1905 cc. Power 126 PS (93 kW) at 5500 rpm; torque 123 lb ft (170 Nm) at 2750 rpm. Compression 9.3-to-1. Catalyst: not available.

Transmission: Four-wheel drive; five-speed manual gearbox. Automatic, not available. Top gear speed at 1000 rpm: 20.7 mph (33.3 km/h).

Suspension: Front, independent, MacPherson struts, hydro-pneumatic springs with integral dampers; anti-roll bar. Rear, independent, trailing arms with hydropneumatic spring-damper units and automatic self-levelling, height adjustable; anti-roll bar.

Steering: Rack and pinion. Power assistance: standard. **Brakes:** Solid discs front and rear. ABS: standard. **Tyres:** 185/60 R 14. **Fuel tank:** 14.5 Imp. gall (66 litres). **Unladen weight:** 2502 lb (1135 kg).

Dimensions: Length 166.5 in (4230 mm), width 65.4 in (1660 mm), height 53.6 in (1361 mm), wheelbase 104.5 in (2655 mm).

Performance *Autocar & Motor* test: Maximum speed 115 mph (185 km/h); 0 to 60 mph (97 km/h) 10.6 sec; 80 mph (130 km/h) 18.9 sec. Fuel consumption at constant 75 mph (120 km/h): 31.7 mpg; overall test, 26.3 mpg.

Features: Drive is permanently engaged to all four wheels, with Torsen rear differential. Very comprehensive equipment, plus air conditioning as an option. **Summary:** Four-wheel drive gives an even more confident feel to the GTi on the road, and makes it a very capable all-weather car with excellent handling. It is also an ideal tow-car, for which the rather low gearing is perfect.

CITROEN (F)   XM 2.0Si Estate

Identity: This very attractively styled and functional estate car version of the XM was launched Frankfurt 1991, and in UK from Motorfair the same year. The 2-litre model is available with standard or 'S' trim, and there are also turbo diesel and V6 Si or SEi models.

Engine: Front-mounted transverse four-cylinder with alloy head, eight valves and single ohc. Bosch LE2 fuel injection. Bore 86.0 mm, stroke 86.0 mm; capacity 1998 cc. Power 130 PS (97 kW) at 5600 rpm; torque 129 lb ft (175 Nm) at 4800 rpm. Compression 8.8-to-1. Catalyst: standard.

Transmission: Front-wheel drive; five-speed manual gearbox. Automatic, optional extra, four-speed. Top gear speed at 1000 rpm: 21.5 mph (34.6 km/h).

Suspension: Front, independent, MacPherson struts with hydropneumatic units and Hydractive control of spring and damper rates; anti-roll bar. Rear, independent, trailing arms with hydropneumatic units, automatic self-levelling and Hydractive control; anti-roll bar.

Steering: Rack and pinion. Power assistance: standard. **Brakes:** Vented discs front, solid discs rear. ABS: optional. **Tyres:** 195/65 R 15. **Fuel tank:** 17.6 Imp. gall (80 litres). **Unladen weight:** 3042 lb (1380 kg).

Dimensions: Length 195.4 in (4963 mm), width 70.6 in (1793 mm), height 57.8 in (1468 mm), wheelbase 112.2 in (2850 mm).

Performance *Autocar & Motor* test (saloon): Maximum speed 120 mph (193 km/h); 0 to 60 mph (97 km/h) 11.2 sec; 80 mph (130 km/h) 20.2 sec. Fuel consumption at constant 75 mph (120 km/h): 31.0 mpg; overall test, 25.8 mpg.

Features: Self-compensating ride control, with height adjustable by driver, is an ideal basis for an estate car. Longitudinal roof rack runners are standard on all models. **Summary:** With its impressive payload of nearly two-thirds of a tonne, and huge internal space, this is a very capable estate. Tail door opens high, taking the upper part of the bumper with it, revealing easy access to a flat floor.

CITROEN (F) XM Turbo SED automatic

Identity: Why not automatic with a diesel car? It goes against the general principle of having a diesel to save fuel, but in fact makes good sense, since the torque converter gives the turbo better chance to come into play, as I found when I tried this remarkable XM in mid-1991.

Engine: Front-mounted transverse four-cylinder with alloy head and single ohc working three valves per cylinder. Lucas Rotodiesel injection and Mitsubishi turbocharger with intercooler. Bore 85.0 mm, stroke 92.0 mm; capacity 2088 cc. Power 110 PS (80 kW) at 4300 rpm; torque 183 lb ft (253 Nm) at 2000 rpm. Comp. 21.5-to-1. Catalyst: not available.

Transmission: Front-wheel drive; five-speed manual gearbox. Automatic, optional extra, four speed. Top gear speed at 1000 rpm (auto): 27.8 mph (44.7 km/h).

Suspension: Front, independent, MacPherson struts with hydropneumatic units, Hydractive control and integral dampers; anti-roll bar. Rear, independent, trailing arms with hydropneumatic spring-damper units and Hydractive control; anti-roll bar.

Steering: Rack and pinion. Power assistance: standard. **Brakes:** Vented discs front, solid discs rear. ABS: standard. **Tyres:** 195/65 R 15. **Fuel tank:** 17.6 Imp. gall (80 litres). **Unladen weight:** 3042 lb (1380 kg).

Dimensions: Length 185.4 in (4708 mm), width 70.6 in (1794 mm), height 54.7 in (1390 mm), wheelbase 112.2 in (2850 mm).

Performance *Autocar & Motor* test (manual): Maximum speed 116 mph (187 km/h); 0 to 60 mph (97 km/h) 12.4 sec; 80 mph (130 km/h) 23.2 sec. Fuel consumption at constant 75 mph (120 km/h): 43.5 mpg; overall test, 32.0 mpg.

Features: Excellent selector layout gives the driver easy control over the automatic when required, and the unit is responsive, with smooth changes. **Summary:** Unusual combination of a car which is extremely comfortable, very easy to drive, yet also potentially cheap to run. The very high torque is well suited to an automatic transmission.

CITROEN (F) XM 3.0 V6 24V

Identity: At original introduction of XM range, in 1989, it was known that a 24-valve version was expected later. It came to the British market at Birmingham 1990, and offers noticeable extra punch for brisk acceleration. It is a very fast, safe and comfortable car.

Engine: Front-mounted transverse V6-cylinder with alloy heads and single ohc per bank working four valves per cylinder. Bendix Fenix 4 fuel injection. Bore 93.0 mm, stroke 73.0 mm; capacity 2975 cc. Power 200 PS (147 kW) at 6000 rpm; torque 192 lb ft (265 Nm) at 3600 rpm. Compression 9.4-to-1. Catalyst: standard.

Transmission: Front-wheel drive; five-speed manual gearbox. Automatic, not available. Top gear speed at 1000 rpm: 22.9 mph (36.8 km/h).

Suspension: Front, independent, MacPherson struts with hydropneumatic units and Hydractive control of spring and damper rates; anti-roll bar. Rear, independent, trailing arms with hydropneumatic units, giving automatic self-levelling, and Hydractive control; anti-roll bar.

Steering: Rack and pinion. Power assistance: standard. **Brakes:** Vented discs front, solid discs rear. ABS: standard. **Tyres:** 205/60 ZR 15. **Fuel tank:** 17.6 Imp. gall (80 litres). **Unladen weight:** 3245 lb (1745 kg).

Dimensions: Length 185.4 in (4708 mm), width 70.6 in (1794 mm), height 54.7 in (1390 mm), wheelbase 112.2 in (2850 mm).

Performance *Autocar & Motor* test: Maximum speed 143 mph (230 km/h); 0 to 60 mph (97 km/h) 7.5 sec; 80 mph (130 km/h) 12.4 sec. Fuel consumption at constant 75 mph (120 km/h): 27.7 mpg; overall test, 20.8 mpg.

Features: Equipment is much the same as for the SEi, but note the special sports alloy wheels, unique to the 24V. Citroën see this as the car for the performance driver, so it is available only with manual gearbox.
Summary: Occasionally the ordinary V6 lacks low-down response, a failing which the 24V corrects with vigorous answer to the throttle. But the gearing could be higher for relaxed high-speed cruising.

CITROEN (F)   ZX 1.9D Aura

Identity: 'Diesels will come later,' I was told when the ZX was first launched at Geneva 1991; they followed at Frankfurt, with UK launch at Motorfair. Only the non-turbo 1.9-litre is offered, with choice of Reflex, Avantage or this model, Aura, with top equipment: an outstandingly smooth and quiet diesel.

Engine: Front-mounted transverse four-cylinder with alloy cylinder head and eight valves; single ohc. Lucas or Bosch fuel injection. Bore 83.0 mm, stroke 88.0 mm; capacity 1905 cc. Power 72 PS (53 kW) at 4600 rpm; torque 90 lb ft (124 Nm) at 2000 rpm. Compression 23.0-to-1. Catalyst: not required.

Transmission: Front-wheel drive; five-speed manual gearbox. Automatic, not available. Top gear speed at 1000 rpm: 23.0 mph (37.0 km/h).

Suspension: Front, independent, MacPherson struts. Rear, independent, trailing arms and transverse torsion bars; programmed self-steering correction geometry.

Steering: Rack and pinion. Power assistance: standard. **Brakes:** Solid discs front, drums rear. ABS: not available. **Tyres:** 165/70 R 13. **Fuel tank:** 12.3 Imp. gall (56 litres). **Unladen weight:** 2282 lb (1035 kg).

Dimensions: Length 160.3 in (4071 mm), width 67.0 in (1702 mm), height 55.0 in (1397 mm), wheelbase 100.0 in (2540 mm).

Performance *Autocar & Motor* test: Maximum speed 97 mph (156 km/h); 0 to 60 mph (97 km/h) 14.7 sec; 80 mph (130 km/h) 30.8 sec. Fuel consumption at constant 75 mph (120 km/h): 47.9 mpg.

Features: Only the Aura diesel gets power steering, but this model also features remote central locking, alloy wheels, and electric sunroof.
Summary: Setting very high standards for mid-range diesel cars, with little to remind one that a diesel engine is under the bonnet, the ZX diesel also performs quite well, and is a pleasure to drive. Length-adjustable rear seat helps to make this a very versatile car.

CITROEN (F)   ZX Volcane

Identity: Apart from diesels, three sizes of engine are offered for the Citroën ZX, which was one of the new cars at Geneva 1991; Reflex and Avantage have 1360 cc, Aura 1580 cc, and top model is this 1.9-litre performance version, the Volcane, with multi-point fuel injection.

Engine: Front-mounted transverse four-cylinder with alloy cylinder head and eight valves; Bosch Motronic injection and ignition system. Bore 83.0 mm, stroke 88.0 mm; capacity 1905 cc. Power 132 PS (97 kW) at 6000 rpm; torque 118 lb ft (163 Nm) at 3250 rpm. Compression 9.2-to-1. Catalyst: not available.

Transmission: Front-wheel drive; five-speed manual gearbox. Automatic, not available. Top gear speed at 1000 rpm: 19.9 mph (32.0 km/h).

Suspension: Front, independent, MacPherson struts. Rear, independent, trailing arms and transverse torsion bars; programmed self-steering correction geometry.

Steering: Rack and pinion. Power assistance: standard. **Brakes:** Vented discs front, solid discs rear. ABS: not available. **Tyres:** 185/60 R 14. **Fuel tank:** 12.3 Imp. gall (56 litres). **Unladen weight:** 2326 lb (1055 kg).

Dimensions: Length 160.6 in (4076 mm), width 67.0 in (1702 mm), height 55.0 in (1397 mm), wheelbase 100.0 in (2540 mm).

Performance *Autocar & Motor* test: Maximum speed 124 mph (199 km/h); 0 to 60 mph (97 km/h) 9.1 sec; 80 mph (130 km/h) 15.5 sec. Fuel consumption at constant 75 mph (120 km/h): 36.2 mpg; overall test, 25.3 mpg.

Features: Extra spoilers and special wheels identify this high performance version of the ZX range, which comes with good equipment and sporty refinements, such as the leather-trimmed steering wheel. **Summary:** At first the Volcane seems a little fussy due to the low overall gearing, but the compensating feature is the vigorous performance available even in fifth gear. Comfortable and fast, with precise handling.

DAIHATSU (J)   Applause 1.6 GXi

Identity: Launched at the beginning of 1990, the Applause replaced the Chamade. It offers a roomy hatchback body with quite good performance for a 1.6-litre, and high specification including such features as power steering. Notchback body styling makes it look like a saloon.

Engine: Front-mounted transverse four-cylinder with block and head of alloy; single ohc working four valves per cylinder. Electronic fuel injection. Bore 76.0 mm, stroke 88.0 mm; capacity 1589 cc. Power 105 PS (77 kW) at 6000 rpm; torque 99 lb ft (137 Nm) at 4800 rpm. Compression 9.5-to-1. Catalyst: standard.

Transmission: Front-wheel drive; five-speed manual gearbox. Automatic, optional extra, three-speed. Top gear speed at 1000 rpm: 20.4 mph (32.8 km/h).

Suspension: Front, independent, MacPherson struts, anti-roll bar. Rear, MacPherson struts, anti-roll bar.

Steering: Rack and pinion. Power assistance: standard. **Brakes:** Vented discs front, solid discs rear. ABS: not available. **Tyres:** 185/60 HR 14. **Fuel tank:** 13.2 Imp. gall (50 litres). **Unladen weight:** 2205 lb (1000 kg).

Dimensions: Length 167.7 in (4260 mm), width 65.4 in (1660 mm), height 54.1 in (1375 mm), wheelbase 97.2 in (2470 mm).

Performance *Autocar & Motor* test: Maximum speed 110 mph (177 km/h); 0 to 60 mph (97 km/h) 10.1 sec; 80 mph (130 km/h) 18.4 sec. Fuel consumption at constant 75 mph (120 km/h): 39.2 mpg; overall test, 29.0 mpg.

Features: One-piece tailgate gives a large rear opening, and rear seat backrests fold down for extra load space. Electric sunroof is an option.
Summary: Deceptive body styling is quite clever, giving hatchback facility with saloon appearance, but the drawback is that it doesn't offer the total load capacity that a true hatchback body might afford.

DAIHATSU (J)   Charade GTti

Identity: With the new range launched May 1987, Daihatsu included a high performance model offering a promising specification, and a car which proved equally exciting on the road. Its near-100 bhp 1-litre engine gives phenomenal power/weight ratio.

Engine: Front-mounted transverse three-cylinder with alloy head, and twin ohc operating four valves per cyl. Electronic fuel injection and IHI RHB51 turbocharger. Bore 76.0 mm, stroke 73.0 mm; capacity 993 cc. Power 99 PS (74 kW) at 6500 rpm; torque 96 lb ft (130 Nm) at 3500 rpm. Compression 7.8-to-1. Catalyst: not available.

Transmission: Front-wheel drive; five-speed manual gearbox. Automatic, not available. Top gear speed at 1000 rpm: 18.5 mph (29.8 km/h).

Suspension: Front, independent, MacPherson struts; anti-roll bar. Rear, independent, MacPherson struts; anti-roll bar.

Steering: Rack and pinion. Power assistance: not available. **Brakes:** Vented discs front, solid discs rear. ABS: not available. **Tyres:** 175/60 HR 14. **Fuel tank:** 8.8 Imp. gall (40 litres). **Unladen weight:** 1786 lb (810 kg).

Dimensions: Length 142.1 in (3610 mm), width 63.3 in (1615 mm), height 54.4 in (1385 mm), wheelbase 92.1 in (2340 mm).

Performance *Autocar & Motor* test: Maximum speed 114 mph (184 km/h); 0 to 60 mph (97 km/h) 7.9 sec; 80 mph (130 km/h) 14.3 sec. Fuel consumption at constant 75 mph (120 km/h) 37.3 mpg; overall test 28.8 mpg.

Features: Although the other Charade models have five doors, the sporting GTti is three-door only. Electric windows, central locking and alloy wheels standard from September 1991. **Summary:** Outstandingly quick car, fun to drive with its combination of excellent handling, steering and brakes, plus outstanding performance for a small car. Test consumption a bit disappointing, but in swift driving that is not too fierce, over 35 mpg is obtainable.

DAIHATSU   (J)   Sportrak ELXi

Identity: An improved version of the Sportrak, introduced in the UK July 1990 to supplement the existing DX and EL models, the ELXi has 16-valve engine and fuel injection, with catalyst as standard. '16 valve ELXi' is lettered on the doors, and the injection engine copes much better with this tough little vehicle.

Engine: Front-mounted longitudinal four-cylinder with head and block of alloy, and single ohc working four valves per cylinder. Multipoint electronic fuel injection. Bore 76.0 mm, stroke 87.6 mm; capacity 1589 cc. Power 95 PS (70 kW) at 5,700 rpm; torque 95 lb ft (131 Nm) at 4800 rpm. Compression 9.5-to-1. Catalyst: standard.

Transmission: Four-wheel drive; five-speed manual gearbox. Automatic, not available. Four-wheel drive is selectable, with low-ratio transfer gearbox. Top gear speed at 1000 rpm: 16.9 mph (27.2 km/h).

Suspension: Front, independent, wishbones and torsion bars; anti-roll bar. Rear, beam axle on tapered leaf springs with gas-filled dampers.

Steering: Recirculating ball. Power assistance: standard. **Brakes:** Solid discs front, drums rear. ABS: not available. **Tyres:** 195 R 15 94S. **Fuel tank:** 13.2 Imp. gall (60 litres). **Unladen weight:** 2590 lb (1175 kg).

Dimensions: Length 149.9 in (3785 mm), width 64.4 in (1635 mm), height 67.7 in (1720 mm), wheelbase 85.6 in (2175 mm).

Performance Works: Maximum speed 93 mph (150 km/h). Fuel consumption at constant 75 mph (120 km/h): 23.7 mpg.

Features: Hardtop body includes a sunroof, but can also be removed altogether, leaving strong roll-over bar in place. Adjustable steering column; radio/cassette. **Summary:** With its lively performance and tidy handling, for an off-road vehicle, the Sportrak ELXi is fun to drive. It has good off-road capability, although the ride is a bit lively on bad going.

FERRARI (I)

Identity: Over the years, the V8 engine of the Ferrari coupé has increased in size, but the change to injection and emission control brought a disappointing power drop. This was made good at Frankfurt 1989, when the 348 was introduced, with power increased to 300 PS.

Engine: Mid-mounted longitudinal V8-cylinder with alloy block and cylinder heads; twin ohc each bank, operating four valves per cylinder. Bosch Motronic injection. Bore 85.0 mm, stroke 75.0 mm; capacity 3405 cc. Power 300 PS (221 kW) at 7200 rpm; torque 234 lb ft (323 Nm) at 4200 rpm. Compression 10.4-to-1. Catalyst: optional.

Transmission: Rear-wheel drive; five-speed manual gearbox. Automatic, not available. Top gear speed at 1000 rpm: 23.7 mph (38.2 km/h).

Suspension: Front, independent, wishbones and coil springs; anti-roll bar. Rear, independent, wishbones and coil springs; anti-roll bar.

Steering: Rack and pinion. Power assistance: not available. **Brakes:** Vented discs front, and rear. ABS: standard. **Tyres:** 215/50 (front), 255/45 (rear) ZR 17. **Fuel tank:** 20.8 Imp. gall (95 litres). **Unladen weight:** 3070 lb (1393 kg).

Dimensions: Length 166.5 in (4230 mm), width 74.6 in (1894 mm), height 46.0 in (1170 mm), wheelbase 96.5 in (2450 mm).

Performance *Autocar & Motor* test: Maximum speed 163 mph (262 km/h); 0 to 60 mph (97 km/h) 5.6 sec; 80 mph (130 km/h) 9.0 sec. Fuel consumption at constant 75 mph (120 km/h): 28.5 mpg; overall test, 18.4 mpg.

Features: Emphasis is very much on speed with safety, rather than luxury or extravagance of equipment. **Summary:** Extremely fast two-seater, available as the tb (Berlinetta) illustrated, or as 348ts, the Spyder with removable roof panel. Slats and scoops in the doors channel cooling air to the rear engine, but the radiator is at the front.

FERRARI (I)   Mondial t Cabriolet

Identity: Revised version of the Mondial, designated 't', was launched Geneva 1989 and shown at Motorfair. Seating four – it is claimed, though really more a 2 + 2 – the Mondial first appeared in 1980, and its V8 engine, increased to 3405 cc, now gives 300 bhp.

Engine: Mid-mounted longitudinal V8-cylinder with toothed belt drive to twin ohc each bank, working four valves per cylinder. Bosch Motronic injection. Bore 85.0 mm, stroke 75.0 mm; capacity 3405 cc. Power 300 PS (221 kW) at 7200 rpm; torque 234 lb ft (323 Nm) at 4200 rpm. Compression 10.4-to-1. Catalyst: not available.

Transmission: Rear-wheel drive; five-speed manual gearbox. Automatic, not available. Top gear speed at 1000 rpm: 19.9 mph (32.0 km/h).

Suspension: Front, independent, wishbones and coil springs; anti-roll bar. Three-position damper firmness control. Rear, independent, wishbones and coil springs; anti-roll bar. Three-position damper firmness.

Steering: Rack and pinion. Power assistance: standard. **Brakes:** Vented discs front, and rear. ABS: standard. **Tyres:** 205/55 (front), 225/55 (rear) ZR 16. **Fuel tank:** 21.1 Imp. gall (96 litres). **Unladen weight:** 3236 lb (1468 kg).

Dimensions: Length 178.5 in (4534 mm), width 71.2 in (1808 mm), height 48.6 in (1234 mm), wheelbase 104.3 in (2649 mm).

Performance *Autocar & Motor* test (coupé): Maximum speed 143 mph (230 km/h); 0 to 60 mph (97 km/h) 6.8 sec; 80 mph (130 km/h) 10.8 sec. Fuel consumption at constant 75 mph (120 km/h): 23.7 mpg; overall test, 16.8 mpg.

Features: Three-position selector switch gives choice of ride firmness; an electronic control box varies the setting according to speed and cornering forces. **Summary:** Unusual arrangement of the Mondial as re-launched 1989 was that the engine is mounted longitudinally while the transmission is transverse. In familiar Ferrari manner, the clutch and flywheel are on a shaft, the other side of the gearbox, Superb motoring.

FERRARI (I) 512 tr

Identity: Paris 1984 saw introduction of the Testarossa (redhead), recalling the great sports racing 250 GT of 1957. At Brussels 1992 this in turn was redesigned and refined, appearing with a new and less exciting name, the 512tr. Emphasis is on improved performance with emission control, and better handling.

Engine: Mid-mounted longitudinal 12-cylinder with horizontally opposed (boxer) layout; alloy cylinders and heads, and aluminium cylinder liners with Nikasil coating. Two ohc each bank, 48 valves. Bore 82.0 mm, stroke 78.0 mm; capacity 4943 cc. Power 427 PS (314 kW) at 6750 rpm; torque 360 lb ft (498 Nm) at 5500 rpm. Compression 10.0-to-1. Catalyst: standard.

Transmission: Rear-wheel drive; five-speed manual gearbox. Automatic, not available.

Suspension: Front, independent, wishbones and coil springs; anti-roll bar. Rear, independent, wishbones and coil springs; anti-roll bar.

Steering: Rack and pinion. Power assistance: not available. **Brakes:** Vented and cross-drilled discs front and rear. ABS: not available. **Tyres:** 235/40 ZR 18, front; 295/35 ZR 18, rear. **Fuel tank:** 25.0 Imp. gall (115 litres). **Unladen weight:** 3344 lb (1517 kg).

Dimensions: Length 176.3 in (4480 mm), width 77.8 in (1976 mm), height 44.7 in (1135 mm), wheelbase 100.4 in (2550 mm).

Performance Works: Maximum speed 192 mph (309 km/h); 0 to 62 mph (100 km/h) 4.8 sec; 80 mph (130 km/h) 7.3 sec. Fuel consumption (est), 16 mpg.

Features: Leather interior; air-conditioning, central locking, and electric action for windows and mirror adjustment. **Summary:** Italian specialist Pininfarina carried out the redesign in conjunction with Ferrari, and Pininfarina also builds the body. The 512tr marks further progress to make this Ferrari handle better, with more accurate steering and road behaviour, as well as having cleaner exhaust and improved performance.

FIAT (I)   Tempra 1.8ie SX Station Wagon

Identity: Following launch of the Tempra – a saloon version of the Tipo – on the British market in mid-1990, the Station Wagon was displayed at Birmingham in September, in anticipation of its arrival on the market in April 1991. It is available with seven-seater option, and diesel engine was added, December 1991.

Engine: Front-mounted transverse four-cylinder with alloy head and twin ohc working eight valves; IAW electronic injection/ignition. Bore 84.0 mm, stroke 79.2 mm; capacity 1756 cc. Power 110 PS (81 kW) at 6000 rpm; torque 103 lb ft (142 Nm) at 2500 rpm. Compression 9.5-to-1. Catalyst: not available.

Transmission: Front-wheel drive; five-speed manual gearbox. Automatic, not available. Top gear speed at 1000 rpm: 19.3 mph (31.1 km/h).

Suspension: Front, independent, MacPherson struts, anti-roll bar. Rear, independent, trailing arms and coil springs; anti-roll bar.

Steering: Rack and pinion. Power assistance: standard. **Brakes:** Solid discs front, drums rear. ABS: not available. **Tyres:** 175/65 R 14H. **Fuel tank:** 14.3 Imp. gall (65 litres). **Unladen weight:** 2513 lb (1104 kg).

Dimensions: Length 176.1 in (4472 mm), width 66.7 in (1695 mm), height 56.9 in (1445 mm), wheelbase 100.0 in (2540 mm).

Performance *Autocar and Motor* test (saloon): Maximum speed 122 mph (196 km/h); 0 to 60 mph (97 km/h) 10.6 sec. Fuel consumption at constant 75 mph (120 km/h): 34.0 mpg; overall test, 24.7 mpg.

Features: SX is top of the three trim levels available and gets good equipment, including alloy wheels and an electrically heated driving seat. **Summary:** Tailgate is horizontally divided on the Station Wagon, with the bumper integrated in the lower part, which folds down to facilitate loading. The Tempra Wagon is a spacious load carrier, but economy is poor for a 1.8.

Identity: Addition to the Tipo range, launched Motorfair 1991, with much the same 16-valve engine as fitted in the Lancia Thema. *Sedicivalvole* (Italian for 16 valves) appears on plinth above the rear number plate. Good performance, though not as quick as some rivals.

Engine: Front-mounted transverse four-cylinder with alloy head and twin ohc working four valves per cylinder. Magneti Marelli fuel injection. Bore 84.0 mm, stroke 90.0 mm; capacity 1995 cc. Power 148 PS (109 kW) at 6250 rpm; torque 125 lb ft (173 Nm) at 5000 rpm. Compression 10.5-to-1. Catalyst: standard.

Transmission: Front-wheel drive; five-speed manual gearbox. Automatic, not available. Top gear speed at 1000 rpm: 19.8 mph (31.9 km/h).

Suspension: Front, independent, MacPherson struts, anti-roll bar. Rear, independent, MacPherson struts with trailing arms; anti-roll bar.

Steering: Rack and pinion. Power assistance: standard. **Brakes:** Vented discs front, solid discs rear. ABS: optional. **Tyres:** 185/55 R 15 81V. **Fuel tank:** 11.4 Imp. gall (52 litres). **Unladen weight:** 2600 lb (1180 kg).

Dimensions: Length 155.8 in (3960 mm), width 66.9 in (1700 mm), height 56.3 in (1430 mm), wheelbase 100.0 in (2540 mm).

Performance *Autocar & Motor* test: Maximum speed 128 mph (206 km/h); 0 to 60 mph (97 km/h) 8.2 sec; 80 mph (130 km/h) 13.6 sec. Fuel consumption at constant 75 mph (120 km/h) 30.4 mpg; overall test, 25.0 mpg.

Features: Very full equipment, with such items as headlamp wash/wipe, remote central locking and electric glass sunroof. **Summary:** Catching up on the 16v at the end of the year, after a work crisis forced me to miss the launch, I concluded that this was the best Fiat I had ever driven. Responsive, lively and enjoyable; but awkward pedal layout.

Identity: Although slow to join the general move to pollution control, Italy showed signs of progress at last in 1991 with introduction of a catalyst-equipped Uno. Engine capacity goes to 1.4-litre, with fuel injection. Five-door hatchback body as revised in 1989.

Engine: Front-mounted transverse four-cylinder with alloy head and single ohc; eight valves. Bosch single-point fuel injection. Bore 80.5 mm, stroke 67.4 mm; capacity 1372 cc. Power 71 PS (53 kW) at 6000 rpm; torque 80 lb ft (109 Nm) at 3000 rpm. Compression 9.2-to-1. Catalyst: standard.

Transmission: Front-wheel drive; five-speed manual gearbox. Automatic, optional extra, constantly variable. Top gear speed at 1000 rpm: 20.0 mph (32.1 km/h).

Suspension: Front, independent, MacPherson struts. Rear, torsion beam axle with coil springs.

Steering: Rack and pinion. Power assistance: not available. **Brakes:** Solid discs front, drums rear. ABS: not available. **Tyres:** 155/70 R 13. **Fuel tank:** 9.2 Imp. gall (42 litres). **Unladen weight:** 2273 lb (1030 kg).

Dimensions: Length 145.2 in (3689 mm), width 61.3 in (1558 mm), height 56.1 in (1425 mm), wheelbase 93.0 in (2362 mm).

Performance *Autocar & Motor* test: Maximum speed 102 mph (164 km/h); 0 to 60 mph (97 km/h) 12.3 sec; 80 mph (130 km/h) 24.6 sec. Fuel consumption at constant 75 mph (120 km/h): 39.2 mpg; overall test, 32.1 mpg.

Features: Standard equipment is somewhat restricted, but electric windows, central locking and sliding glass sunroof can all be added. **Summary:** Injection compensates quite well for the power loss of the catalyst, and the Uno feels lively and responsive. Comfortable ride, but awkward driving position and unappealing interior are disappointing.

FORD (GB, B, D)   Escort Cabriolet 1.6 EFi

Identity: With the February introduction of the new 16-valve Zeta engine for top Escorts and Orions, the Cabriolet became available with a choice of 105 PS engine (details follow) or the more powerful 130 PS unit. The Cabriolet has always featured power steering as standard.

Engine: Front-mounted transverse four-cylinder with alloy head and twin ohc operating four valves per cylinder. Electronic fuel injection. Bore 80.6 mm, stroke 88.0 mm; capacity 1796 cc. Power 105 PS (77 kW) at 5500 rpm; torque 110 lb ft (153 Nm) at 4000 rpm. Compression 10.0-to-1. Catalyst: optional.

Transmission: Front-wheel drive; five-speed manual gearbox. Automatic, not available. Top gear speed at 1000 rpm: 22.7 mph (36.5 km/h).

Suspension: Front, independent, MacPherson struts with L-shaped strut-locating arms on double vertical bushes; anti-roll bar. Rear, semi-independent, trailing arms and torsion beam axle with coil springs.

Steering: Rack and pinion. Power assistance: standard. **Brakes:** Vented discs front, drums rear. ABS: optional. **Tyres:** 185/60 HR 14. **Fuel tank:** 12.1 Imp. gall (55 litres). **Unladen weight:** 2300 lb (1045 kg).

Dimensions: Length 158.9 in (4036 mm), width 66.3 in (1684 mm), height 53.2 in (1352 mm), wheelbase 99.4 in (2525 mm).

Performance Works: Maximum speed 116 mph (187 km/h); 0 to 62 mph (100 km/h) 10.5 sec. Fuel consumption at constant 75 mph (120 km/h): 37.2 mpg.

Features: This was initially the only one of the new Escort/Orion range to have power steering as standard. Leather seats, power-operated hood and alloy wheels all optional. **Summary:** Interior and map lights are built into the fixed roll bar, and the Cabriolet is structurally strong and very pleasant to drive. Neat tonneau cover can be fitted over the folded hood without a struggle, and complete hood raising or lowering takes only about a minute.

FORD (GB, D, E)   Escort LX 1.8 D

Identity: Just before the tremendous upheavals which took place in the (then) USSR during 1991, I was involved in organising and taking part in a seven-car economy run from Westminster Bridge to Red Square, Moscow. The diesel Escort was the car used, and it acquitted itself excellently.

Engine: Front-mounted transverse four-cylinder with cast-iron block and head; single ohc, eight valves. Bore 82.5 mm, stroke 82.0 mm; capacity 1753 cc. Power 60 PS (44 kW) at 4800 rpm; torque 80 lb ft (110 Nm) at 2500 rpm. Compression 21.5-to-1. Catalyst: not required.

Transmission: Front-wheel drive; five-speed manual gearbox. Automatic, not available. Top gear speed at 1000 rpm: 24.1 mph (38.8 km/h).

Suspension: Front, independent, MacPherson struts with L-shaped lower locating arms on double vertical bushes. Rear, trailing arms and torsion beam axle; coil springs.

Steering: Rack and pinion. Power assistance: not available. **Brakes:** Vented discs front, drums rear. ABS: optional. **Tyres:** 175/70 R 13-T. **Fuel tank:** 12.1 Imp. gall (55 litres). **Unladen weight:** 2216 lb (1005 kg).

Dimensions: Length 158.9 in (4036 mm), width 66.3 in (1684 mm), height 53.2 in (1350 mm), wheelbase 99.4 in (2524 mm).

Performance Works: Maximum speed 94 mph (151 km/h); 0 to 60 mph (97 km/h) 18.1 sec; 80 mph (130 km/h) 34.8 sec. Fuel consumption at constant 75 mph (120 km/h): 47.1 mpg.

Features: LX specification is quite generous, and includes glass sunroof, electric front windows and central locking with alarm. **Summary:** Lack of power steering—not available even as an option—is the chief criticism of the diesel Escort, but it provided very comfortable and extremely economical transport on our drive across Germany, Poland and Russia to Moscow, giving over 70 mpg. Picture shows one of the economy run cars at the start, with the oldest driver.

FORD   (GB, D, E)   Escort RS 2000

Identity: New at Motorfair 1991 was this performance version of the Escort with three-door body and the twin ohc 2-litre 16-valve engine featuring high turbulence for optimum efficiency. High engine mounts for smoothness and refinement. Louvred bonnet and distinctive rear wing are identity features.

Engine: Front-mounted transverse four-cylinder with alloy head and twin belt-driven ohc, working four valves per cylinder. Ford EEC IV fuel injection. Bore 86.0 mm, stroke 86.0 mm; capacity 1998 cc. Power 150 PS (112 kW) at 6000 rpm; torque 137 lb ft (190 Nm) at 4500 rpm. Compression 10.3-to-1. Catalyst: standard.

Transmission: Front-wheel drive; five-speed manual gearbox. Automatic, not available. Top gear speed at 1000 rpm: 20.1 mph (32.3 km/h).

Suspension: Front, independent, MacPherson struts with L-shaped lower locating arms on double vertical bushes; anti-roll bar. Rear, trailing arms and torsion beam axle; coil springs.

Steering: Rack and pinion. Power assistance: standard. **Brakes:** Vented discs front, solid discs rear. ABS: standard. **Tyres:** 195/50 VR 15. **Fuel tank:** 12.1 Imp. gall (55 litres). **Unladen weight:** 2445 lb (1110 kg).

Dimensions: Length 159.0 in (4040 mm), width 66.6 in (1692 mm), height 54.3 in (1378 mm), wheelbase 99.4 in (2525 mm).

Performance *Autocar & Motor* test: Maximum speed 131 mph (211 km/h); 0 to 60 mph (97 km/h) 8.3 sec; 80 mph (130 km/h) 13.7 sec. Fuel consumption at constant 75 mph (120 km/h): 35.8 mpg; overall test, 26.4 mpg.

Features: Recaro seats and special trim feature inside the RS 2000, and distinctive alloy wheels are standard; sports suspension is fitted. **Summary:** Full of zest, and most rewarding to drive, except for the lack of a cruising gear: fifth giving only 20.1 mph per 1000 rpm made the RS 2000 seem fussy at speed. The acceleration continues right through to 120 mph, however, reached in 40.7 sec from rest.

FORD (D, GB)   Escort RS Cosworth

Identity: Even as early as the original launch of the new Escort model, in September 1990, it was revealed that a high-performance version with Cosworth tuned engine and four-wheel drive would go on sale. This featured as the cover car on the 1991/92 edition, and was due to go on sale in limited numbers in the middle of 1992.

Engine: Front-mounted transverse four-cylinder with alloy head and twin ohc working four valves per cylinder. Turbocharger and electronic fuel injection. Bore 90.8 mm, stroke 77.0 mm; capacity 1993 cc. Power 240 PS (177 kW) at 6000 rpm; torque 217 lb ft (300 Nm) at 4000 rpm. Compression 8.0-to-1. Catalyst: standard.

Transmission: Four-wheel drive; five-speed manual gearbox. Automatic, not available. Top gear speed at 1000 rpm: 23.0 mph (37.0 km/h).

Suspension: Front, independent, MacPherson struts, anti-roll bar. Rear, independent, semi-trailing arms with coil springs.

Steering: Rack and pinion. Power assistance: standard. **Brakes:** Vented discs front, solid discs rear. ABS: standard. **Tyres:** 225/45–16. **Fuel tank:** 14.3 Imp. gall (65 litres). **Unladen weight:** 2712 lb (1230 kg).

Dimensions: Length 165.6 in (4205 mm), width 68.5 in (1740 mm), height 54.6 in (1387 mm), wheelbase 100.4 in (2550 mm).

Performance Works: Maximum speed 150 mph (241 km/h) ; 0 to 60 mph (97 km/h) 5.8 sec. Fuel consumption: no data.

Features: Aerodynamic aids, including high-level rear spoiler and distinctive paint finish, give a striking appearance to this special Escort. **Summary:** The main purpose of the Escort RS is to head Ford's rally effort, hence the name Ford Motorsport on the side, but a number of the very fast RS Cosworths are being sold to private buyers.

FORD　(B, D)

Identity: The new Ford XR3i with its Zeta 16-valve engine, being made at Bridgend in South Wales (although Escort models are no longer produced in GB) was previewed at Motorfair 1991; cars started reaching dealers at the end of February 1992. The same engine is offered in Escort and Orion, and both 105 and 130 PS versions are offered.

Engine: Front-mounted transverse four-cylinder with alloy head and twin belt-driven ohc working four valves per cylinder. EEC IV Module engine management system. Bore 80.6 mm, stroke 88.0 mm; capacity 1796 cc. Power 130 PS (96 kW) at 6250 rpm; torque 117 lb ft (162 Nm) at 4500 rpm. Compression 10.0-to-1. Catalyst: standard.

Transmission: Front-wheel drive; five-speed manual gearbox. Automatic, not available. Top gear speed at 1000 rpm: 20.1 mph (32.2 km/h).

Suspension: Front, independent, MacPherson struts, anti-roll bar. Rear, semi-independent, trailing arms and torsion beam axle; coil springs and anti-roll bar.

Steering: Rack and pinion. Power assistance: standard. **Brakes:** Vented discs front, solid discs rear. ABS: optional. **Tyres:** 185/60 VR 14. **Fuel tank:** 12.1 Imp. gall (55 litres). **Unladen weight:** 2400 lb (1090 kg).

Dimensions: Length 159.0 in (4040 mm), width 66.6 in (1692 mm), height 55.0 in (1397 mm), wheelbase 99.4 in (2525 mm).

Performance Works: Maximum speed 126 mph (202 km/h); 0 to 62 mph (100 km/h) 9.3 sec; 80 mph (130 km/h) 14.9 sec. Fuel consumption at constant 75 mph (120 km/h): 35.3 mpg.

Features: XR3i will have central locking and electrically heated windscreen as standard; options include air conditioning and ABS.
Summary: An important development for Ford, this new engine is scheduled for total production exceeding a million units a year. It is efficient and quiet, and meets the world's toughest exhaust emission regulations. Output at Bridgend is now running at 525,000 units a year.

FORD   (D, E, GB)   Fiesta 1.4 Ghia

Identity: Completely new Fiesta range was launched Amsterdam 1989, and on UK market April. Choice of six engines, and for the first time a five-door as well as a three-door. The range was topped off by Ghia specification with the 1.4-litre engine at launch, until the XR2i and Turbo RS became available later.

Engine: Front-mounted transverse four-cylinder with alloy head and single ohc operating inclined valves in hemi combustion chambers. Twin-choke carb. Bore 77.0 mm, stroke 74.0 mm; capacity 1392 cc. Power 75 PS (55 kW) at 5600 rpm; torque 80 lb ft (109 Nm) at 4000 rpm. Compression 9.5-to-1. Catalyst: optional.

Transmission: Front-wheel drive; five-speed manual gearbox. Automatic, optional extra. Top gear speed at 1000 rpm: 20.6 mph (33.1 km/h).

Suspension: Front, independent, MacPherson struts, anti-roll bar. Rear, independent, semi-trailing arms and coil springs.

Steering: Rack and pinion. Power assistance: not available. **Brakes:** Vented discs front, drums rear. ABS: optional. **Tyres:** 155/70 SR 13. **Fuel tank:** 9.2 Imp. gall (42 litres). **Unladen weight:** 1960 lb (890 kg).

Dimensions: Length 147.4 in (3743 mm), width 73.0 in (1854 mm), height 52.0 in (1320 mm), wheelbase 96.3 in (2446 mm).

Performance *Autocar & Motor* test: Maximum speed 98 mph (158 km/h); 0 to 60 mph (97 km/h) 13.4 sec; 80 mph (130 km/h) 27.2 sec. Fuel consumption at constant 75 mph (120 km/h): 42.2 mpg; overall test, 28.1 mpg.

Features: Ghia model gets good equipment for this size of car, but tailgate is self-locking with rather awkward electric release, and there is severe buffeting if the sunroof panel is taken out. **Summary:** Ford's new Fiesta jumped straight to the top of the sales league, and deserves its place as a very attractive small–medium size car.

FORD (E, GB)   Fiesta RS Turbo

Identity: At a brief but exciting launch in Northern Ireland, June 1990, Ford introduced what was proclaimed as the fastest Fiesta yet—a turbocharged version of the XR2i, with 133 PS output. Look for the louvres on the bonnet, and distinctive 'three-spoke' alloy wheels.

Engine: Front-mounted transverse four-cylinder with alloy head, belt-driven ohc, two valves per cylinder, and Garrett TO2 turbocharger. Bore 80.0 mm, stroke 79.5 mm; capacity 1596 cc. Power 133 PS (98 kW) at 5500 rpm; torque 132 lb ft (183 Nm) at 5500 rpm. Compression 8.2-to-1. Catalyst: not available.

Transmission: Front-wheel drive; five-speed manual gearbox. Automatic, not available. Top gear speed at 1000 rpm: 20.8 mph (33.5 km/h).

Suspension: Front, independent, MacPherson struts, anti-roll bar. Rear, semi-independent, trailing arms and torsion beam; coil springs, anti-roll bar.

Steering: Rack and pinion. Power assistance: not available. **Brakes:** Vented discs front, drums rear. ABS: optional. **Tyres:** 185/55 VR 14. **Fuel tank:** 9.2 Imp. gall (42 litres). **Unladen weight:** 2030 lb (920 kg).

Dimensions: Length 149.6 in (3801 mm), width 64.2 in (1630 mm), height 52.2 in (1326 mm), wheelbase 96.3 in (2446 mm).

Performance *Autocar & Motor* test: Maximum speed 129 mph (208 km/h); 0 to 60 mph (97 km/h) 7.9 sec; 80 mph (130 km/h) 12.7 sec. Fuel consumption at constant 75 mph (120 km/h): 34.0 mpg; overall test, 23.6 mpg.

Features: Special Recaro seats with dual-latch tracks are fitted for optimum location of front occupants. There are some other detail changes, such as the special small-diameter wheel and leather-trimmed gear knob. **Summary:** Ford have gone to the extreme in making the suspension ultra-firm, but the instant punch of the turbocharged engine gives wonderfully zippy motoring. A great fun car.

FORD   (E, GB)   **Fiesta XR2i**

Identity: Sporty three-door version of the Fiesta, with 1.6-litre injection engine, joined the range at Motorfair 1989. It has the 1.6 CVH (Compound Valve Hemi) engine, with advanced ignition system using no distributor.

Engine: Front-mounted transverse four-cylinder with ignition triggered directly from the flywheel, and electronic fuel injection. Alloy head, single ohc, and eight valves. Bore 80.0 mm, stroke 79.5 mm; capacity 1596 cc. Power 110 PS (81 kW) at 6000 rpm; torque 100 lb ft (138 Nm) at 2800 rpm. Compression 9.8-to-1. Catalyst: optional.

Transmission: Front-wheel drive; five-speed manual gearbox. Automatic, not available. Top gear speed at 1000 rpm: 20.3 mph (32.7 km/h).

Suspension: Front, independent, MacPherson struts with L-shaped locating arms mounted on double vertical bushes; anti-roll bar. Rear, semi-independent, trailing arms and torsion beam axle; coil springs.

Steering: Rack and pinion. Power assistance: not available. **Brakes:** Vented discs front, drums rear. ABS: optional (mechanical). **Tyres:** 185/60 HR 13. **Fuel tank:** 9.2 Imp. gall (42 litres). **Unladen weight:** 1962 lb (890 kg).

Dimensions: Length 149.6 in (3801 mm), width 64.2 in (1630 mm), height 52.2 in (1326 mm), wheelbase 96.3 in (2446 mm).

Performance *Autocar & Motor* test: Maximum speed 118 mph (190 km/h); 0 to 60 mph (97 km/h) 8.9 sec; 80 mph (130 km/h) 15.9 sec. Fuel consumption at constant 75 mph (120 km/h): 38.2 mpg; overall test, 28.4 mpg.

Features: Special bumpers incorporate an air dam at the front and house fog and driving lamps. A thin blue line runs along the top of the bumpers and continues along the body sides. **Summary:** Trying the XR2i on the bumpy roads of Northern Ireland, I again thought the suspension a little harsh, but it's a very sporty car with excellent handling and a superb range of performance.

FORD   (GB, B, D)   Orion 1.8i Ghia Si

Identity: As before, the new Orion is essentially the saloon version of the Ford Escort, though the model is aimed higher up-market, and there are no Popular versions. From February 1992, Orion became available also with the Zeta twin cam engine for LX and Ghia, and in more powerful 130 PS form for Ghia Si, the new top Orion.

Engine: Front-mounted transverse four-cylinder with alloy head and twin ohc operating four valves per cylinder. Ford EEC-IV fuel injection. Bore 80.6 mm, stroke 88.0 mm; capacity 1796 cc. Power 130 PS (96 kW) at 6250 rpm; torque 117 lb ft (162 Nm) at 6250 rpm. Compression 10.0-to-1. Catalyst: standard.

Transmission: Front-wheel drive; five-speed manual gearbox. Automatic, optional extra. Top gear speed at 1000 rpm: 20.1 mph (32.2 km/h).

Suspension: Front, independent, MacPherson struts with L-shaped strut-locating arms on double vertical bushes; anti-roll bar. Rear, semi-independent, trailing arms and torsion beam axle with coil springs.

Steering: Rack and pinion. Power assistance: standard. **Brakes:** Vented discs front, drums rear. ABS: optional. **Tyres:** 185/60 VR 14. **Fuel tank:** 12.1 Imp. gall (55 litres). **Unladen weight:** 2300 lb (1045 kg).

Dimensions: Length 166.5 in (4229 mm), width 66.3 in (1684 mm), height 53.0 in (1345 mm), wheelbase 99.4 in (2525 mm).

Performance Works: Maximum speed 126 mph (202 km/h); 0 to 62 mph (100 km/h) 9.4 sec. Fuel consumption at constant 75 mph (120 km/h): 35.3 mpg.

Features: Ghia specification is quite good, but even at this level, the Orion does not get anti-lock brakes as standard. **Summary:** As part of the improvements introduced with the Zeta engine, power assisted steering became standard, making the car much lighter to drive and bringing improved response, turning the Orion into a pleasant car. It offers more refinement, especially inside, than its predecessor.

FORD (GB, D)   Scorpio 2.9i 24V Cosworth

Identity: Last new model announcement of 1990 came just before Christmas: a more powerful version of the Scorpio with Cosworth engine, tuned to give 34 per cent more power but also to meet the world's toughest emission regulations. Look for the special wheels and tiny 24V badge on boot.

Engine: Front-mounted longitudinal V6-cylinder with cast-iron block, special Cosworth alloy heads, and twin ohc each bank. Ford injection and distributorless ignition. Bore 93.0 mm, stroke 72.0 mm; capacity 2933 cc. Power 195 PS (143 kW) at 5750 rpm; torque 199 lb ft (275 Nm) at 4500 rpm. Compression 9.7-to-1. Catalyst: standard.

Transmission: Rear-wheel drive; four-speed automatic, standard. Top gear speed at 1000 rpm: 25.5 mph (41.0 km/h).

Suspension: Front, independent, MacPherson struts, lower track control arms and rear-mounted anti-roll bar. Rear, independent, semi-trailing arms with coil springs and anti-roll bar.

Steering: Rack and pinion. Power assistance: standard. **Brakes:** Vented discs front and rear. ABS: standard. **Tyres:** 205/50 ZR 16. **Fuel tank:** 15.4 Imp. gall (70 litres). **Unladen weight:** 3053 lb (1385 kg).

Dimensions: Length 183.8 in (4669 mm), width 69.5 in (1766 mm), height 57.2 in (1453 mm), wheelbase 108.8 in (2765 mm).

Performance *Autocar & Motor* test: Maximum speed 136 mph (219 km/h); 0 to 60 mph (97 km/h) 8.5 sec; 80 mph (130 km/h) 14.1 sec. Fuel consumption at constant 75 mph (120 km/h): 28.0 mpg; overall test, 21.0 mpg.

Features: Special wheels are fitted, and top equipment includes CD player, electric seat adjustment front and rear, and fuel computer. **Summary:** Production started in February 1991, and the 24V went on sale in March. One of these provided very fast, comfortable and safe travel for my journey to the Frankfurt Show in 1991.

FORD (D)   Scorpio 4 × 4 2.9i

Identity: Slight increase in engine capacity for the new V6 engine launched October 1986 was achieved by lengthening the stroke; but engine also developed for more power, and catalyst-equipped version available for some markets including UK.

Engine: Front-mounted longitudinal 60 deg V6-cylinder with cast iron block and heads. Camshaft in block, and pushrod ohv. Bosch L-Jetronic fuel injection. Bore 93.0 mm, stroke 72.0 mm; capacity 2933 cc. Power 150 PS (110 kW) at 5700 rpm; torque 171 lb ft (233 Nm) at 3000 rpm. Compression 9.5-to-1. Catalyst: optional.

Transmission: Four-wheel drive; five-speed manual gearbox. No automatic option for 4 × 4. Top gear speed at 1000 rpm: 23.9 mph (38.4 km/h).

Suspension: Front, independent, MacPherson struts, lower track control arms and rear-mounted anti-roll bar. Coil springs and twin-tube telescopic dampers. Rear, independent, semi-trailing arms; coil springs and twin-tube telescopic dampers; anti-roll bar (larger dia. on 4 × 4).

Steering: Rack and pinion. Power assistance: standard, varying ratio.
Brakes: Vented discs front, solid rear. ABS: standard. **Tyres:** 205/60 VR 15. **Fuel tank:** 15.4 Imp. gall (70 litres). **Unladen weight:** 3053 lb (1385 kg).

Dimensions: Length 183.8 in (4669 mm), width 69.5 in (1766 mm), height 57.2 in (1453 mm), wheelbase 108.8 in (2765 mm).

Performance *Autocar & Motor* test: Maximum speed 125 mph (201 km/h); 0 to 60 mph (97 km/h) 9.4 sec; 80 mph (130 km/h) 16.8 sec. Fuel consumption at constant 75 mph (120 km/h): 27.9 mpg; overall test, 19.2 mpg.

Features: Permanent four-wheel drive, with torque distributed 34 per cent front, 66 rear. **Summary:** Most impressive car, combining superb handling with admirable capability as a car for severe winter weather, plus restricted off-road use.

FORD (B)   Sierra Sapphire RS Cosworth 4 × 4

Identity: The unlimited series production Cosworth appeared January 1988, using the Sierra Sapphire saloon body, with turbocharged 2-litre 16-valve engine by Cosworth Racing. Rear wing and special wheels identify this very fast version of the Sierra. Revised four-wheel drive version with more power, January 1990.

Engine: Front-mounted longitudinal four-cylinder with alloy head and twin belt-driven ohc operating four valves per cyl. Garrett TO3B turbocharger with air-air intercooler. Bore 90.8 mm, stroke 77.0 mm; capacity 1993 cc. Power 220 PS (162 kW) at 6250 rpm; torque 210 lb ft (290 Nm) at 3500 rpm. Compression 8.0-to-1. Catalyst: standard.

Transmission: Four-wheel drive; five-speed manual gearbox. Automatic, not available. Top gear speed at 1000 rpm: 22.8 mph (36.7 km/h).

Suspension: Front, independent, MacPherson struts, twin-tube gas-filled dampers; anti-roll bar. Rear, independent, semi-trailing arms and coil springs; gas-filled telescopic dampers, anti-roll bar.

Steering: Rack and pinion. Power assistance: standard, varying ratio. **Brakes:** Vented discs front, solid discs rear. ABS: standard. **Tyres:** Dunlop D40 205/50 VR 15. **Fuel tank:** 13.2 Imp. gall (60 litres). **Unladen weight:** 2869 lb (1300 kg).

Dimensions: Length 176.9 in (4494 mm), width 66.9 in (1698 mm), height 54.2 in (1376 mm), wheelbase 102.7 in (2608 mm).

Performance *Autocar & Motor* test: Maximum speed 144 mph (232 km/h); 0 to 60 mph (97 km/h) 6.6 sec; 80 mph (130 km/h) 10.9 sec. Fuel consumption at constant 75 mph (120 km/h): 30.4 mpg; overall test, 21.6 mpg.

Features: Equipment includes such items as electric front windows, central locking, and glass sunroof. **Summary:** Fantastic performance on dry roads, and the handling was made much safer by the 1990 introduction of four-wheel drive. A very refined, swift, long journey car, but it can also be docile as well; a handy shopping car!

FORD (USA)   Thunderbird SC

Identity: Substantially revised for 1989, with new front, wheelbase 9 in longer, and all-independent suspension. All interior dimensions are larger than before; inlets in the bumper identify 1992 model. SC stands for Super Coupé, which brings a supercharger with intercooler.

Engine: Front-mounted longitudinal V6-cylinder with alloy heads and central chain-driven camshaft. Supercharger and intercooler. Bore 96.5 mm, stroke 86.4 mm; capacity 3791 cc. Power 210 bhp (SAE) (140 kW) at 4000 rpm; torque 315 lb ft (435 Nm) at 2600 rpm. Compression 9.0-to-1. Catalyst: standard.

Transmission: Rear-wheel drive; five-speed manual gearbox. Automatic, four-speed, optional. Top gear speed at 1000 rpm: 36.2 mph (58.2 km/h).

Suspension: Front, independent, wishbones and struts; coil springs and gas-filled telescopic dampers, anti-roll bar. Rear, independent, lower H-arm and upper arms; coil springs and gas-filled telescopic dampers; anti-roll bar.

Steering: Rack and pinion. Power assistance: standard. **Brakes:** Solid discs front and rear. ABS: standard. **Tyres:** P225/60 VR 16. **Fuel tank:** 17.5 Imp. gall (80 litres). **Unladen weight:** 3542 lb (1607 kg).

Dimensions: Length 198.7 in (5047 mm), width 72.7 in (1847 mm), height 52.7 in (1339 mm), wheelbase 113.0 in (2870 mm).

Performance (est): Maximum speed 125 mph (201 km/h). Fuel consumption overall (est) 20.0 mpg.

Features: 'Handling' suspension has automatic ride control. Sports seats. Options include digital CD player and moon roof. **Summary:** A more exciting Thunderbird package, still with the sleek looks of the predecessor, but now bigger and with more power. The T-bird, as it is sometimes known, is also available in standard and LX form, automatic and without blower.

GINETTA   (GB)   **G33 V8 Roadster**

Identity: High-performance lightweight convertible with body in glass-reinforced polyester resin on galvanised steel chassis. Power unit is a Rover V8 3.9-litre giving 200 bhp, and staggering performance figures include 0 to 80 mph (not 60 mph) in 7.2 sec.

Engine: Front-mounted longitudinal V8-cylinder with alloy block and heads, and electronic fuel injection. Bore 94.0 mm, stroke 71.1 mm; capacity 3947 cc. Power 203 PS (149 kW) at 5280 rpm; torque 220 lb ft (304 Nm) at 3500 rpm. Compression 10.5-to-1. Catalyst: optional.

Transmission: Rear-wheel drive; five-speed manual gearbox. Automatic, not available. Top gear speed at 1000 rpm: 27.0 mph (43.5 km/h).

Suspension: Front, independent, wishbones and coil springs; anti-roll bar. Rear, independent, lower wishbones, longitudinal links and fixed-length drive shafts; coil springs and anti-roll bar.

Steering: Rack and pinion. Power assistance: not available. **Brakes:** Vented discs front, solid discs rear. ABS: not available. **Tyres:** 195/50 ZR 15. **Fuel tank:** 12.0 Imp. gall (55 litres). **Unladen weight:** 1500 lb (680 kg).

Dimensions: Length 139.6 in (3547 mm), width 57.8 in (1469 mm), height 39.9 in (1013 mm), wheelbase 85.0 in (2160 mm).

Performance Works: Maximum speed 145 mph (233 km/h); 0 to 60 mph (97 km/h) 5.0 sec; 80 mph (130 km/h) 7.2 sec. Fuel consumption at constant 75 mph (120 km/h): 35.0 mpg.

Features: Interior trim is in leather, with pile carpet floors and traditional instrument layout. Pop-up headlamps in one-piece nose section. **Summary:** An exciting sports car from the well-established Ginetta company of Scunthorpe, suitable for use on road or track. Chassis is a multi-tubular backbone type, and the body has two doors and detachable hood.

HONDA (J, USA)   Accord Aerodeck 2.2i

Identity: One of the more surprising industry developments of 1991 was the decision to import a Japanese car that is built in America. This is the one: the Accord Aerodeck. The Accord enjoyed phenomenal success in the USA, outselling every other model, including America's own products.

Engine: Front-mounted transverse four-cylinder with alloy block and head; belt-driven single ohc working four valves per cylinder. Programmed fuel injection. Bore 85.0 mm, stroke 95.0 mm; capacity 2156 cc. Power 150 PS (110 kW) at 5900 rpm; torque 148 lb ft (205 Nm) at 5000 rpm. Compression 9.8-to-1. Catalyst: standard.

Transmission: Front-wheel drive; five-speed manual gearbox. Automatic, optional extra, four-speed. Top gear speed at 1000 rpm: 21.6 mph (34.7 km/h).

Suspension: Front, independent, wishbones and coil springs; anti-roll bar. Rear, independent, wishbones and progressive rate coil springs; anti-roll bar.

Steering: Rack and pinion. Power assistance: standard. **Brakes:** Vented discs front, solid discs rear. ABS: not available. **Tyres:** 195/60 R 15. **Fuel tank:** 14.3 Imp. gall (65 litres). **Unladen weight:** 3097 lb (1405 kg).

Dimensions: Length 185.0 in (4700 mm), width 66.7 in (1695 mm), height 55.1 in (1400 mm), wheelbase 107.1 in (2720 mm).

Performance Works: Maximum speed 128 mph (206 km/h); 0 to 60 mph (97 km/h) 8.9 sec. Fuel consumption at constant 75 mph (120 km/h): 30.1 mpg.

Features: Generous 64 cu ft of load space; rear seats divided 60/40, folding, and a tonneau cover conceals luggage, with an adjustable net to keep contents secure. **Summary:** The Aerodeck conversion of the Accord was engineered, designed and built in the United States. It is only 1.2 in longer than the saloon, and except for the lack of ABS it comes well equipped, including air conditioning as standard.

HONDA (J)   Civic 1.6 VTi

Identity: Attractive and shapely new small to medium car launched Motorfair 1991, with choice of three-door hatchback body or four-door saloon. At top of the range, both are offered with this VTEC engine, using Honda's ingenious system of varying valve timing for optimum efficiency.

Engine: Front-mounted transverse four-cylinder with alloy head, twin ohc, and 16 valves with timing altering according to engine speed. Bore 81.0 mm, stroke 77.4 mm; capacity 1595 cc. Power 160 PS (118 kW) at 7600 rpm; torque 108 lb ft (150 Nm) at 7000 rpm. Compression 10.2-to-1. Catalyst: standard.

Transmission: Front-wheel drive; five-speed manual gearbox. Automatic, not available with VTi. Top gear speed at 1000 rpm: 18.0 mph (29.0 km/h).

Suspension: Front, independent, wishbones and coil springs, anti-roll bar. Rear, independent, wishbones and coil springs; anti-roll bar.

Steering: Rack and pinion. Power assistance: standard. **Brakes:** Vented discs front, solid discs rear. ABS: standard. **Tyres:** 195/55 VR 15. **Fuel tank:** 9.9 Imp. gall (45 litres). **Unladen weight:** 2337 lb (1060 kg).

Dimensions: Length 173.4 in (4405 mm), width 66.7 in (1695 mm), height 54.1 in (1375 mm), wheelbase 103.1 in (2620 mm).

Performance *Autocar & Motor* test: Maximum speed 132 mph (212 km/h); 0 to 60 mph (97 km/h) 7.3 sec; 80 mph (130 km/h) 12.3 sec. Fuel consumption at constant 75 mph (120 km/h): 37.7 mpg; overall test, 26.9 mpg.

Features: Unusual and very effective two-piece rear hatch with top part opening upwards, lower part downwards. Generous equipment.
Summary: Very sporty and enjoyable little hatchback, with wonderfully responsive and free-revving engine. Precise handling, crisp controls and fun to drive, but rather fussy at speed because of the low overall gearing.

HONDA (GB, J)

Concerto 1.6i-16 SE

Identity: First launched at Tokyo 1988, and in Britain from Motorfair 1989, the Concerto became the first British-built volume model to have catalyst as standard, from August 1991. This top model loses a bit of its former power, down from 130 to 121 PS, but is still a brisk performer.

Engine: Front-mounted transverse four-cylinder with alloy head and block; twin ohc, 16 valves. Honda PGM-F1 fuel injection. Bore 75.0 mm, stroke 90.0 mm; capacity 1590 cc. Power 121 PS (89 kW) at 6800 rpm; torque 101 lb ft (140 Nm) at 5700 rpm. Compression 9.5-to-1. Catalyst: standard.

Transmission: Front-wheel drive; five-speed manual gearbox. Automatic, not available (1.6i SOHC only). Top gear speed at 1000 rpm: 18.2 mph (29.2 km/h).

Suspension: Front, independent, MacPherson struts, anti-roll bar. Rear, independent, wishbones and coil springs; anti-roll bar.

Steering: Rack and pinion. Power assistance: standard. **Brakes:** Vented discs front, solid discs rear. ABS: standard. **Tyres:** 185/60 R 14 82H. **Fuel tank:** 12.1 Imp. gall (55 litres). **Unladen weight:** 2440 lb (1105 kg).

Dimensions: Length 167.9 in (4265 mm), width 66.5 in (1690 mm), height 54.9 in (1395 mm), wheelbase 100.3 in (2550 mm).

Performance Works: Maximum speed 122 mph (196 km/h); 0 to 60 mph (97 km/h) 8.9 sec; 80 mph (130 km/h) 15.7 sec. Fuel consumption at constant 75 mph (120 km/h): 33.6 mpg.

Features: SE comes with top equipment: electric sunroof, all windows electric, heated door mirrors, alloy wheels and leather upholstery.
Summary: Compared with the *Autocar & Motor* test figures quoted in last year's edition for the non-cat. model, the claims for this less powerful version seem optimistic. It's still a very attractive car, however, for those seeking performance and luxury within compact dimensions.

HONDA (J)   Legend Coupé

Identity: All-new Legend was introduced at Geneva 1991, with more rounded body, and engine capacity increased to 3.2 litres and power now 205 PS. As before, the Legend is offered as saloon or in this attractive Coupé format. Both offer choice of manual or automatic.

Engine: Front-mounted longitudinal V6-cylinder with all-alloy construction and single ohc per bank, working four valves per cylinder. Distributorless ignition; varying intake system. Bore 90.0 mm, stroke 84.0 mm; capacity 3206 cc. Power 205 PS (153 kW) at 5500 rpm; torque 212 lb ft (293 Nm) at 4400 rpm. Compression 9.6-to-1. Catalyst: standard.

Transmission: Front-wheel drive; five-speed manual gearbox. Automatic, optional. Top gear speed at 1000 rpm: 34.6 mph (55.6 km/h).

Suspension: Front, independent, wishbones and coil springs with lateral arms; anti-roll bar. Rear, independent, wishbones and coil springs with lateral arms; anti-roll bar.

Steering: Rack and pinion. Power assistance: standard. **Brakes:** Vented discs front, solid discs rear. ABS: standard. **Tyres:** 205/65 ZR 15. **Fuel tank:** 15.0 Imp. gall (68 litres). **Unladen weight:** 3406 lb (1545 kg).

Dimensions: Length 192.3 in (4885 mm), width 71.3 in (1810 mm), height 53.9 in (1370 mm), wheelbase 114.6 in (2910 mm).

Performance *Autocar & Motor* test: Maximum speed 141 mph (227 km/h); 0 to 60 mph (97 km/h) 8.2 sec; 80 mph (130 km/h) 13.5 sec. Fuel consumption at constant 75 mph (120 km/h): 28.0 mpg; overall test, 19.1 mpg.

Features: Full equipment even includes an air bag on the driver's side, and there are heated front seats; doors have electric closing on Coupé. **Summary:** Major change from the previous Legend is that the engine is now installed longitudinally (previously transverse). Promising new car introducing a number of special features.

Identity: At a Honda test day in 1990, everyone wanted to drive the NSX. I had given up waiting and was unlocking my car to leave when suddenly a chance presented itself, and I enjoyed a magnificent drive in this superbly competent, fast, very safe, high-performance GT. It is every bit as good as it looks – or better.

Engine: Mid-mounted transverse V6-cylinder with twin ohc each bank working four valves per cylinder, and varying valve timing. Programmed electronic ignition with varying volume induction system. Bore 90.0 mm, stroke 78.0 mm; capacity 2977 cc. Power 273 PS (201 kW) at 7300 rpm; torque 205 lb ft (284 Nm) at 5400 rpm. Compression 10.2-to-1. Catalyst: two standard.

Transmission: Rear-wheel drive; five-speed manual gearbox. Automatic, optional extra. Top gear speed at 1000 rpm: 24.1 mph (38.8 km/h).

Suspension: Front, independent, aluminium wishbones and coil springs; anti-roll bar. Rear, independent, aluminium wishbones and coil springs; anti-roll bar.

Steering: Rack and pinion. Power assistance: standard with automatic transmission. **Brakes:** Vented discs front and rear. ABS: standard. **Tyres:** 205/50 ZR 15 (front); 225/50 ZR 16 (rear). **Fuel tank:** 15.4 Imp. gall (70 litres). **Unladen weight:** 3020 lb (1370 kg).

Dimensions: Length 173. 4 in (4405 mm), width 71.3 in (1810 mm), height 46.1 in (1170 mm), wheelbase 99.6 in (2530 mm).

Performance *Autocar & Motor* test: Maximum speed 159 mph (256 km/h); 0 to 60 mph (97 km/h) 5.8 sec; 80 mph (130 km/h) 8.9 sec. Fuel consumption at constant 75 mph (120 km/h): 30.7 mpg; overall test, 19.6 mpg.

Features: Space is rather limited, but there's a small boot at each end and snug seats give good lateral location. Power steering on automatic models is electrically operated. **Summary:** Certainly an important addition to the ranks of the top supercars, offering fantastic grip on corners and very vigorous acceleration. A short but memorable drive.

HONDA   (J)

Prelude 2.3i 4WS

Identity: Replacement for the Prelude was introduced in Europe at Brussels 1992, on British market from April. Completely new body, and Prelude introduces a new form of electronic four-wheel steering control (previously mechanical). 2.0-litre also available, but not with 4WS.

Engine: Front-mounted transverse four-cylinder with alloy head and die-cast fibre-refinforced block. Belt-driven twin ohc, 16 valves, and twin counter-rotating balance shafts. Bore 87.0 mm, stroke 95.0 mm; capacity 2259 cc. Power 160 PS (118 kW) at 5800 rpm; torque 154 lb ft (209 Nm) at 4500 rpm. Compression 9.8-to-1. Catalyst: standard.

Transmission: Front-wheel drive; five-speed manual gearbox. Automatic, optional extra, four-speed. Top gear speed at 1000 rpm: 21.3 mph (34.2 km/h).

Suspension: Front, independent, wishbones and coil springs; anti-roll bar. Rear, wishbones and coil springs with trailing arms; anti-roll bar.

Steering: Rack and pinion with electronically controlled electric rear wheel steering optional. Power assistance: standard. **Brakes:** Vented discs front, solid discs rear. ABS: standard. **Tyres:** 205/55R15 87V. **Fuel tank:** 13.2 Imp. gall (60 litres) **Unladen weight:** 2794 lb (1270 kg).

Dimensions: Length 174.8 in (4440 mm), width 69.5 in (1765 mm), height 50.8 in (1290 mm), wheelbase 100.4 in (2550 mm).

Performance Works: Maximum speed 134 mph (216 km/h); 0 to 62 mph (100 km/h) 7.7 sec; 80 mph (130 km/h) 12.5 sec. Fuel consumption at 75 mph (120 km/h): 32.8 mpg.

Features: Rear wheels steer in the same direction as the front ones above 18 mph, and in the opposite direction at lower speeds. **Summary:** Very pleasant and fast car to drive, but on test in Spain I felt that the amount of rear wheel steer above 18 mph had been reduced to the level where it did not contribute very much. The new 2.3-litre engine was the more impressive aspect of the latest Prelude 2.3.

HYUNDAI (K)

Lantra 1.6 Cdi

Identity: Launched in UK June 1991, Lantra is an important new model for the Korean company, bringing advanced engineering with high performance twin ohc engine and front-wheel drive, tidy and functional interior, and yet retaining the marque's tradition for good value.

Engine: Front-mounted transverse four-cylinder with alloy head and twin ohc working 16 valves; multi-point fuel injection. Bore 82.0 mm, stroke 75.0 mm; capacity 1596 cc. Power 112 PS (84 kW) at 6200 rpm; torque 103 lb ft (140 Nm) at 4500 rpm. Compression 9.2-to-1. Catalyst: standard.

Transmission: Front-wheel drive; five-speed manual gearbox. Automatic, optional extra, four-speed optional. Top gear speed at 1000 rpm: 18.9 mph (30.4 km/h).

Suspension: Front, independent, MacPherson struts, anti-roll bar. Rear, torsion beam axle on trailing arms; Panhard rod and integral anti-roll bar. Coil springs.

Steering: Rack and pinion. Power assistance: standard. **Brakes:** Solid discs front, drums rear. ABS: not available. **Tyres:** 185/60 HR 14. **Fuel tank:** 11.4 Imp. gall (52 litres). **Unladen weight:** 2588 lb (1174 kg).

Dimensions: Length 171.6 in (4358 mm), width 65.7 in (1675 mm), height 54.5 in (1385 mm), wheelbase 98.5 in (2500 mm).

Performance *Autocar & Motor* test: Maximum speed 110 mph (177 km/h); 0 to 60 mph (97 km/h) 10.9 sec; 80 mph (130 km/h) 20.1 sec. Fuel consumption at constant 75 mph (120 km/h): 36.2 mpg; overall test, 27.1 mpg.

Features: Roomy body with folding rear seat; generous equipment includes such features as tilt-adjust steering column and remote central locking. **Summary:** Acceleration to 80 mph in just over 20 seconds is very good for a 1.6, and the Lantra is also comfortable and handles acceptably well—helped by firmer damping since the car was first introduced in UK.

74

HYUNDAI (K) S Coupé GSi

Identity: Prototype of the S Coupé was a surprise release at Motorfair 1989, but it did not come to the UK market until Birmingham 1990. Suspension a little too soft, but otherwise it is an attractively styled, quite roomy family car.

Engine: Front-mounted transverse four-cylinder with alloy head on cast iron block. Single ohc and multi-point fuel injection. Bore 75.5 mm, stroke 82.0 mm; capacity 1468 cc. Power 84 PS (62 kW) at 5500 rpm; torque 89 lb ft (123 Nm) at 4000 rpm. Compression 9.4-to-1. Catalyst: standard.

Transmission: Front-wheel drive; five-speed manual gearbox. Automatic, optional extra. Top gear speed at 1000 rpm: 19.4 mph (31.2 km/h).

Suspension: Front, independent, MacPherson struts, anti-roll bar. Rear, independent, trailing arms and coil springs; anti-roll bar.

Steering: Rack and pinion. Power assistance: standard. **Brakes:** Vented discs front, drums rear. ABS: not available. **Tyres:** 185/60 HR 14. **Fuel tank:** 9.9 Imp. gall (45 litres). **Unladen weight:** 2094 lb (950 kg).

Dimensions: Length 165.8 in (4213 mm), width 64.0 in (1626 mm), height 52.3 in (1328 mm), wheelbase 93.8 in (2382 mm).

Performance *Autocar & Motor* test: Maximum speed 104 mph (167 km/h); 0 to 60 mph (97 km/h) 12.5 sec; 80 mph (130 km/h) 24.3 sec. Fuel consumption at constant 75 mph (120 km/h): 38.7 mpg; overall test, 30.8 mpg.

Features: Good equipment includes all the usual luxury items, such as electric windows and mirrors, but no sunroof. Cheaper LSi is also available. **Summary:** Sporty to look at, the S Coupé is also fun to handle. Better-damped suspension was fitted to later models, giving a tauter ride and better handling.

HYUNDAI (K)   Sonata 2.4i GLS

Identity: Entirely new model, launched Birmingham 1988, to replace the Stellar. Sonata is a front-drive car, and is offered with three engine sizes, two trim levels and manual or automatic transmission. Engines are 1.8, 2.0 and 2.4. Details follow for the 'big four'.

Engine: Front-mounted transverse four-cylinder with belt-driven single ohc and inclined valves; hydraulic tappets and alloy head. Electronic multi-point fuel injection. Bore 86.5 mm, stroke 100.0 mm; capacity 2351 cc. Power 110 PS (81 kW) at 4500 rpm; torque 140 lb ft (193 Nm) at 3500 rpm. Compression 8.6-to-1. Catalyst: not available.

Transmission: Front-wheel drive; five-speed manual gearbox. Automatic, four-speed optional, with electronic control. Top gear speed at 1000 rpm: 26.7 mph (43 km/h).

Suspension: Front, independent, MacPherson struts, anti-roll bar. Rear, torsion beam axle with trailing arms and Panhard rod; coil springs; anti-roll bar.

Steering: Rack and pinion. Power assistance: standard. **Brakes:** Solid discs front, drums rear. ABS: not available. **Tyres:** 185/70 SR 14. **Fuel tank:** 13.2 Imp. gall (60 litres). **Unladen weight:** 2684 lb (1217 kg).

Dimensions: Length 184.2 in (4680 mm), width 68.9 in (1750 mm), height 55.4 in (1408 mm), wheelbase 104.3 in (2650 mm).

Performance *Autocar & Motor* test: Maximum speed 112 mph (180 km/h); 0 to 60 mph (97 km/h) 12.3 sec; 80 mph (130 km/h) 22.4 sec. Fuel consumption at constant 75 mph (120 km/h): 29.4 mpg; overall test, 22.7 mpg.

Features: High specification including electric windows and mirrors; among options are cruise control, air conditioning and power sunroof.
Summary: Hyundai moved up the market some way with this new model, aiming at the executive buyer, hoping to tempt him or her with a well-furnished and equipped car at a highly competitive price. On UK market from May 1989.

Identity: A major move up-market for Isuzu came at the end of March 1992 with launch of a completely new Trooper range featuring a more rounded body shape and V6 3.2-litre petrol engine to replace the 2.6 four-cylinder. Also available with turbocharged 3.1-litre four-cyl. diesel.

Engine: Front-mounted longitudinal V-6 cylinder with all-alloy construction and single ohc per bank working four valves per cylinder. Multi-point fuel injection. Bore 93.4 mm, stroke 77.0 mm; capacity 3165 cc. Power 176 PS (130 kW) at 5200 rpm; torque 192 lb ft (265 Nm) at 3750 rpm. Compression 9.3-to-1. Catalyst: standard.

Transmission: Rear-wheel drive plus selectable front drive; five-speed manual gearbox. Automatic, optional extra, four-speed. Freewheeling front hubs. Top gear speed at 1000 rpm: 20.7 mph (33.4 km/h).

Suspension: Front, independent, wishbones and torsion bars; gas-filled dampers. Rear, live axle on four-link location, with coil springs.

Steering: Recirculating ball. Power assistance: standard. **Brakes:** Vented discs front, and rear. ABS: standard. **Tyres:** 245/70 R 16. **Fuel tank:** 18.7 Imp. gall (85 litres). **Unladen weight:** 3957 lb (1795 kg).

Dimensions: Length (swb), 162.0 in (4115 mm); lwb, 178.9 (4545 mm); width 68.7 in (1745 mm), height 72.2 in (1835 mm), wheelbase swb, 91.7 in (2330 mm); lwb, 108.6 (2760 mm).

Performance Works: Maximum speed 106 mph (171 km/h) 0 to 62 mph (100 km/h) 11.5 sec. Fuel consumption at 75 mph (120 km/h): 19.3 mpg.

Features: Improved interior for better passenger comfort. Rear seats are divided 60/40, and there are two asymmetric side-hinged rear doors.
Summary: Short-wheelbase version seats four, and lwb five; third row of seats optionally available. Lwb models went on the market in UK in April 1992; swb availability July.

JAGUAR (GB)   XJ6 3.2

Identity: Since introduction, the 2.9-litre had been the disappointing model of the new Jaguar XJ6 and Sovereign ranges, and for Birmingham 1990 it was replaced by a new and much better 24-valve engine with 3.2-litre capacity. Other changes included a sports suspension option.

Engine: Front-mounted longitudinal six-cylinder with head and block of alloy, and twin ohc working four valves per cylinder. Lucas fuel injection and ignition. Bore 91.0 mm, stroke 83.0 mm; capacity 3239 cc. Power 203 PS (149 kW) at 5250 rpm; torque 220 lb ft (304 Nm) at 4000 rpm. Compression 9.75-to-1. Catalyst: standard.

Transmission: Rear-wheel drive; five-speed manual gearbox. Automatic, optional extra. Top gear speed at 1000 rpm: 26.6 mph (42.8 km/h).

Suspension: Front, independent, unequal length wishbones giving anti-dive effect, coil springs; anti-roll bar. Rear, independent, wishbones using drive shafts as upper links, with anti-squat, anti-lift geometry; concentric coil springs and dampers.

Steering: Rack and pinion. Power assistance: standard. **Brakes:** Vented discs front, solid discs rear. ABS: standard. **Tyres:** 225/65 VR 15. **Fuel tank:** 19.0 Imp. gall (86.4 litres). **Unladen weight:** 3969 lb (1800 kg).

Dimensions: Length 196.4 in (4988 mm), width 71.3 in (1811 mm), height 54.3 in (1380 mm), wheelbase 113.0 in (2870 mm).

Performance *Autocar & Motor* test: Maximum speed 135 mph (217 km/h); 0 to 60 mph (97 km/h) 8.3 sec; 80 mph (130 km/h) 13.5 sec. Fuel consumption at constant 75 mph (120 km/h): 29.1 mpg; overall test, 19.9 mpg.

Features: Among the many changes introduced for the 1991 model were a better audio system with CD option, and new wheels and tyres.
Summary: With its extra power and torque, this bigger engine is a much more acceptable alternative to the 4-litre, which continues. I tried a car with the sports handling pack but, although the extra tautness was appreciated, felt that it spoilt the superb ride of the standard model.

JAGUAR (GB)   Sovereign 4.0

Identity: One of the important new models of 1989 was the Jaguar in revised form with a host of minor improvements, headed by increase of capacity of the six-cylinder 24-valve engine to 4.0-litre, giving better response and quieter cruising. The 4-litre version is identified by the plinth badges at rear; 3.2 has free-standing letters.

Engine: Front-mounted longitudinal six-cylinder with twin overhead camshafts and 24 valves. Lucas electronic fuel injection. Bore 91.0 mm, stroke 102.0 mm; capacity 3980 cc. Power 235 PS (175 kW) at 4750 rpm; torque 285 lb ft (387 Nm) at 3750 rpm. Compression 9.5-to-1. Catalyst: standard.

Transmission: Rear-wheel drive; four-speed automatic, standard. Five-speed manual is no-cost option. Top gear speed at 1000 rpm: 29.2 mph (47.0 km/h).

Suspension: Front, independent, wishbones with anti-dive provision; coil springs and anti-roll bar. Rear, independent, wishbones with drive shafts acting as upper links; anti-squat and anti-lift provisions; coil springs concentric with dampers.

Steering: Rack and pinion. Power assistance: standard. **Brakes:** Vented discs front, solid discs rear. ABS: standard. **Tyres:** 220/65 VR 390 TD. **Fuel tank:** 19.5 Imp. gall (89 litres). **Weight:** 3969 lb (1800 kg).

Dimensions: Length 196.4 in (4988 mm), width 71.3 in (1811 mm), height 53.5 in (1358 mm), wheelbase 113.0 in (2870 mm).

Performance *Autocar & Motor* test: Maximum speed 140 mph (225 km/h); 0 to 60 mph (97 km/h) 8.3 sec; 80 mph (130 km/h) 13.5 sec. Fuel consumption at constant 75 mph (120 km/h): 30.4 mpg; overall, 18.5 mpg.

Features: Not quite as extravagantly equipped as the Daimler, but such items as electric sunroof and heated front seats can be specified.
Summary: One of the most improved cars of 1989 and considering how good the Sovereign was before, that's really saying something! Superb driver's car, yet also providing top quality and wonderful comfort.

JAGUAR (GB)   XJ220

Identity: Star of Birmingham 1988, the XJ220 made its spectacular first appearance as a mid-engined V12 prototype. It was finally revealed in production form as a turbocharged V6 at Tokyo 1991, and is currently being built at the rate of two cars a week. First owners have now taken delivery. Only 350 cars to be built.

Engine: Mid-mounted longitudinal V6-cylinder with alloy block and heads, twin ohc per bank; 48 valves. Zytek electronic fuel injection and twin water-cooled turbochargers. Bore 94.0 mm, stroke 84.0 mm; capacity 3498 cc. Power 549 PS (404 kW) at 7000 rpm; torque 475 lb ft (642 Nm) at 4500 rpm. Compression 8.3-to-1. Catalyst: standard.

Transmission: Rear-wheel drive; five-speed manual gearbox. Automatic, not available. Top gear speed at 1000 rpm: 28.7 mph (46.2 km/h).

Suspension: Front, independent, wishbones and coil springs, anti-roll bar. Rear, independent, wishbones and coil springs with concentric dampers, mounted transversely; anti-roll bar.

Steering: Rack and pinion. Power assistance: not available. **Brakes:** Vented discs front and rear. ABS: not available. **Tyres:** 255/45 ZR 17 (front); 345/35 ZR 18 (rear). **Fuel tank:** 20.0 Imp. gall (91 litres). **Unladen weight:** 3448 lb (1560 kg).

Dimensions: Length 194.0 in (4930 mm), width 79.4 in (2017 mm), height 45.0 in (1150 mm), wheelbase 104.0 in (2640 mm).

Performance Works: Maximum speed 200 mph (322 km/h); 0 to 60 mph (97 km/h) 4.0 sec; 100 mph (161 km/h) 8.0 sec. Fuel consumption at constant 75 mph (120 km/h): no data.

Features: Many standard features including air conditioning, electric windows, central locking and advanced Alpine audio system. **Summary:** Jaguar say they have carried out extensive high-speed testing on the XJ220, and although no precise maximum is quoted (just 'over 200 mph') it is claimed to be the world's fastest standard production car.

JAGUAR (GB)   XJR-S 6.0

Identity: High-performance version of the XJ-S V12 with engine enlarged to 6 litres and power increased to 333 PS. It is identified by styling embellishments and wing on boot and was shown in revised form at Frankfurt 1991. Grille and headlamps surround now finished in matt black, and mirrors in body colour.

Engine: Front-mounted longitudinal V12-cylinder with alloy block and heads. Single ohc each bank working two valves per cylinder. Zytek engine management system. Bore 90.0 mm, stroke 78.5 mm; capacity 5993 cc. Power 337 PS (248 kW) at 5250 rpm; torque 365 lb ft (504 Nm) at 3650 rpm. Compression 11.0-to-1. Catalyst: standard.

Transmission: Rear-wheel drive. Automatic, three-speed, standard. No manual option. Top gear speed at 1000 rpm: 26.1 mph (42.0 km/h).

Suspension: Front, independent, wishbones and coil springs with Bilstein gas-filled dampers; anti-roll bar. Rear, independent, lower wishbones and radius arms, with fixed length drive shafts acting as upper links; coil springs and Bilstein dampers.

Steering: Rack and pinion. Power assistance: standard. **Brakes:** Vented discs front, solid discs rear. ABS: standard. **Tyres:** 225/50 ZR 16, front; 245/55 ZR 16, rear. **Fuel tank:** 19.6 Imp. gall (89 litres). **Unladen weight:** 4023 lb (1825 kg).

Dimensions: Length 189.7 in (4820 mm), width 70.6 in (1793 mm), height 49.2 in (1250 mm), wheelbase 102.0 in (2591 mm).

Performance Works: Maximum speed 158 mph (254 km/h); 0 to 60 mph (97 km/h) 6.5 sec; 80 mph (130 km/h) 10.4 sec. Fuel consumption at 75 mph (120 km/h): 20.2 mpg.

Features: Superb equipment runs to luxuries such as electric seats with memory, air-conditioning and trip computer; top audio with compact disc. **Summary:** In latest form the XJR-S has an even more sumptuous interior with natural grain leather, and the improved engine gives much more torque for effortless swift performance.

JAGUAR (GB)   XJS V12 Convertible

Identity: In May 1991, Jaguar updated the XJS range. Although £50m was claimed to have been spent, the visible changes were minimal, differences being most evident in this rear view showing the revised tail lamp treatment. Jaguar themselves didn't seem proud of it, and ran a very low-key launch. Convertible 4.0 was added at Geneva 1992.

Engine: Front-mounted longitudinal V12-cylinder with alloy construction and single ohc each bank; 24 valves. Lucas electronic fuel injection. Bore 90.0 mm, stroke 70.0 mm; capacity 5345 cc. Power 280 PS (209 kW) at 5550 rpm; torque 306 lb ft (415 Nm) at 2800 rpm. Compression 11.5-to-1. Catalyst: standard.

Transmission: Rear-wheel drive. Automatic, three-speed, standard. Top gear speed at 1000 rpm: 26.1 mph (42.0 km/h).

Suspension: Front, independent, wishbones with anti-dive geometry; coil springs, anti-roll bar. Rear, independent, lower transverse wishbones, drive shafts serve as upper links with radius arms; coil springs and anti-roll bar.

Steering: Rack and pinion. Power assistance: standard. **Brakes:** Vented discs front, solid discs rear. ABS: standard. **Tyres:** 235/60 VR 15. **Fuel tank:** 18.0 Imp. gall (82 litres). **Unladen weight** 4233 lb (1920 kg).

Dimensions: Length 187.6 in (4764 mm), width 74.1 in (1883 mm), height 49.4 in (1254 mm), wheelbase 102.0 in (2591 mm).

Performance Works: Maximum speed 143 mph (230 km/h); 0 to 60 mph (97 km/h) 8.1 sec. Fuel consumption at constant 75 mph (120 km/h): 21.9 mpg.

Features: Improved audio unit, new headlamps and electric adjustment and heating for seats, with lumbar support. **Summary:** All that money spent, and still no more attractive frontal appearance! But it does at last have anti-lock brakes. Build quality is claimed to be better, but otherwise the 1991 changes have not been very significant.

KIA   (K)   Pride 1.3 LX

Identity: Not until Pride was launched at Motorfair 1991 had I realised what a big concern Kia is in Korea, where it built over half a million vehicles in 1990. The Pride is derived from the now-discontinued Mazda 121, and is offered as 1.1 L or this 1.3 LX version.

Engine: Front-mounted transverse four-cylinder with alloy head and single ohc; eight valves. Two-stage downdraught carb. Bore 71.0 mm, stroke 83.6 mm; capacity 1324 cc. Power 61 PS (45 kW) at 5500 rpm; torque 87 lb ft (120 Nm) at 3500 rpm. Compression 9.7-to-1. Catalyst: standard.

Transmission: Front-wheel drive; five-speed manual gearbox. Automatic, not available. Top gear speed at 1000 rpm: 23.5 mph (37.8 km/h).

Suspension: Front, independent, MacPherson struts, anti-roll bar. Rear, torsion beam axle with struts and coil springs.

Steering: Rack and pinion. Power assistance: not available. **Brakes:** Solid discs front, drums rear. ABS: not available. **Tyres:** 165/70 SR 12. **Fuel tank:** 8.4 Imp. gall (38 litres). **Unladen weight** 2794 lb (1270 kg).

Dimensions: Length 140.4 in (3565 mm), width 63.2 in (1605 mm), height 57.5 in (1460 mm), wheelbase 90.4 in (2295 mm).

Performance *Autocar & Motor* test: Maximum speed 92 mph (148 km/h); 0 to 60 mph (97 km/h) 12.8 sec; 80 mph (130 km/h) 28.3 sec. Fuel consumption at constant 75 mph (120 km/h): 38.7 mpg; overall test, 33.0 mpg.

Features: Choice of three or five doors for 1.3, which comes with five-speed gearbox, rev counter and remote tailgate release. 1.1 is four-speed only. **Summary:** When I tried the Kia in August, I was impressed by the smoothness of the engine, lightness of controls and ease of driving. Top speed is reached in fourth, and fifth gives pleasantly quiet and unfussed cruising.

LADA (SU)

Samara 1.5 GL

Identity: At Birmingham 1988 the Lada Samara three-door was supplemented by five-door versions and by a larger engine with 1500 c.c. capacity. The Lada gets better, but as it moves towards western standards so the prices move up, and it's no longer quite as good value as it used to be.

Engine: Front-mounted transverse four-cylinder with alloy head and belt-driven ohc. Downdraught twin-choke carb. Bore 82.0 mm, stroke 71.0 mm; capacity 1499 cc. Power 76 PS (56 kW) at 5600 rpm; torque 78 lb ft (108 Nm) at 3600 rpm. Compression 9.9-to-1. Catalyst: not available.

Transmission: Front-wheel drive; five-speed manual gearbox. Automatic, not available. Top gear speed at 1000 rpm: 21.0 mph (33.7 km/h).

Suspension: Front, independent, MacPherson struts. Rear, independent, trailing arms and coil springs, telescopic dampers.

Steering: Rack and pinion. Power assistance: not available. **Brakes:** Solid discs front, drums rear. ABS: not available. **Tyres:** 165/70 SR 13. **Fuel tank:** 9.5 Imp. gall (43 litres). **Unladen weight:** 1984 lb (900 kg).

Dimensions: Length 157.7 in (4006 mm), width 63.7 in (1620 mm), height 52.5 in (1335 mm), wheelbase 96.8 in (2460 mm).

Performance Works: Maximum speed 98 mph (158 km/h); 0 to 60 mph (97 km/h) 12.0 sec. Fuel consumption at constant 75 mph (120 km/h): 36.7 mpg.

Features: GL version gets better interior trim in tweed-style polyester, by Autotrim of Huddersfield. Stereo radio cassette standard. **Summary:** Compared with the 1300, which continues, the 1500 gives noticeably better performance, but it's still a rather basic car to drive. Side stripe and vented wheel trims identify the 1.5.

LANCIA (I)   Dedra 2000 Turbo

Identity: One of the last model announcements to be made in 1990 was the addition of a turbocharged version to the Dedra range, available as here with front-wheel drive, or as the Dedra Integrale, having four-wheel drive. The Integrale is no longer available. Engine features continuous modulation of turbo boost throughout the engine speed range.

Engine: Front-mounted transverse four-cylinder with alloy head and twin ohc; eight valves. Weber IAW fuel injection and Garrett 60/48 turbocharger with air–heat exchanger. Bore 84.0 mm, stroke 90.0 mm; capacity 1995 cc. Power 165 PS (121 kW) at 5500 rpm; torque 199 lb ft (275 Nm) at 3000 rpm. Compression 7.5-to-1. Catalyst: not available.

Transmission: Front-wheel drive; five-speed manual gearbox. Automatic, not available. Top gear speed at 1000 rpm: 22.8 mph (36.7 km/h).

Suspension: Front, independent, MacPherson struts; anti-roll bar. Rear, independent, semi-trailing arms and coil springs with gas-filled dampers separate from coil springs; anti-roll bar.

Steering: Rack and pinion. Power assistance: standard. **Brakes:** Vented discs front, solid discs rear. ABS: optional. **Tyres:** 195/50 R 15V. **Fuel tank:** 13.9 Imp. gall (63 litres). **Unladen weight:** 2712 lb (1230 kg).

Dimensions: Length 171.0 in (4343 mm), width 66.9 in (1700 mm), height 56.3 in (1430 mm), wheelbase 100.0 in (2540 mm).

Performance *Autocar & Motor* test: Maximum speed 132 mph (212 km/h); 0 to 60 mph (97 km/h) 7.4 sec; 80 mph (130 km/h) 12.5 sec. Fuel consumption at constant 75 mph (120 km/h): 30.7 mpg; overall test, 22.1 mpg.

Features: Viscodrive anti-wheelspin system reduces torque-steer effects. Spoiler on boot lid. Performance Pack optional, bringing leather trim, electric seat adjustment, and automatic suspension control. **Summary:** In standard form, Dedra is a sporty car with crisp handling. This turbocharged version gives useful extra performance, with special control of turbo boost to spread the extra power and avoid 'peakiness'.

LANCIA (I)   Thema 2.0i.e. 16V

Identity: New zest came to the Thema range in mid-1989 with introduction of new lead-free burning 16-valve engines, available as turbo and as this injection version. As well as giving more power, the engines were developed for high torque at low revs; and ZF automatic became available.

Engine: Front-mounted transverse four-cylinder with alloy head and belt-driven twin ohc working 16 valves. Bosch LE 3.1 Jetronic injection. Bore 84.0 mm, stroke 90.0 mm; capacity 1995 cc. Power 150 PS (108 kW) at 6000 rpm; torque 136 lb ft (188 Nm) at 4000 rpm. Compression 9.9-to-1. Catalyst: not available.

Transmission: Front-wheel drive; five-speed manual gearbox. Automatic, optional extra. Top gear speed at 1000 rpm: 21.4 mph (34.4 km/h).

Suspension: Front, independent, MacPherson struts, anti-roll bar. Rear, independent, struts with twin transverse links; anti-roll bar.

Steering: Rack and pinion. Power assistance: standard. **Brakes:** Vented discs front, solid discs rear. ABS: special option. **Tyres:** 195/60 R 14H. **Fuel tank:** 15.4 Imp. gall (70 litres). **Unladen weight:** 2755 lb (1250 kg).

Dimensions: Length 180.7 in (4590 mm), width 69.0 in (1752 mm), height 56.4 in (1433 mm), wheelbase 104.7 in (2660 mm).

Performance *Autocar & Motor* test: Maximum speed 124 mph (199 km/h); 0 to 60 mph (97 km/h) 8.8 sec; 80 mph (130 km/h) 15.2 sec. Fuel consumption at constant 75 mph (120 km/h): 34.4 mpg; overall test, 24.4 mpg.

Features: Reduced noise levels, better brakes, and more use of zinc coated steel in the body were among features of the new Thema. Good equipment including central locking, but sunroof only on SE model. **Summary:** Substantially improved car with better performance and a lot more refinement. Although not on the standard options list, anti-lock brakes can be obtained to special order, also air conditioning and leather.

Identity: Announced at the end of 1989 was a new automatic Lancia Y10, selectronic (always with a small 's'), featuring the Ford-Fiat CVT transmission, which uses steel segment belts under compression, and pulleys of varying diameter, but with electronic control.

Engine: Front-mounted transverse four-cylinder with alloy head and belt-driven single ohc. Bosch Monojetronic fuel injection. Bore 70.0 mm, stroke 72.0 mm; capacity 1108 cc. Power 57 PS (41 kW) at 5500 rpm; torque 64 lb ft (88 Nm) at 3000 rpm. Compression 9.6-to-1. Catalyst: not available.

Transmission: Front-wheel drive. Automatic, standard, continuously variable, with segment steel belts, electromagnetic powder clutch; electronic control. Top gear speed at 1000 rpm: 24.5 mph (39.5 km/h), highest value on light load.

Suspension: Front, independent, MacPherson struts, anti-roll bar. Rear, semi-independent, centre-pivoted dead beam axle on semi-trailing arms with coil springs.

Steering: Rack and pinion. Power assistance: not available. **Brakes:** Solid discs front, drums rear. ABS: not available. **Tyres:** 135 SR 13. **Fuel tank:** 10.1 Imp. gall (46 litres). **Unladen weight:** 1786 lb (810 kg).

Dimensions: Length 133.5 in (3392 mm), width 59.3 in (1507 mm), height 49.0 in (1245 mm), wheelbase 85.0 in (2159 mm).

Performance Works: Maximum speed 93 mph (150 km/h); 0 to 62mph (100 km/h) 17.5 sec. Fuel consumption at constant 75 mph (120 km/h): 46.3 mpg.

Features: Simple selector control with P-R-N-D-L positions (L giving more effective engine braking for steep hill descents); and the electric clutch means that the engine is disengaged when idling. **Summary:** Lancia claim that the Y10 selectronic brings a new blend of liveliness with economy and smoothness. It came on to the UK market from April 1990.

LAND ROVER (GB) Defender 110 Tdi

Identity: Following introduction of the new and much-praised direct injection diesel engine for the Discovery in 1989, the same engine was adopted for the Land Rover One Ten at Birmingham 1990. At the same time, the Defender name was introduced.

Engine: Front-mounted longitudinal four-cylinder with alloy head and single ohc; eight valves. Direct fuel injection and Garrett T25 turbocharger. Bore 90.5 mm, stroke 97.0 mm; capacity 2495 cc. Power 108 PS (80 kW) at 3800 rpm; torque 188 lb ft (260 Nm) at 1800 rpm. Compression 19.5-to-1. Catalyst: not available.

Transmission: Four-wheel drive; five-speed manual gearbox. Automatic, not available. Permanent four-wheel drive, with low-ratio transfer gearbox. Selectable centre differential lock. Top gear speed at 1000 rpm: 21.7 mph (34.9 km/h).

Suspension: Front, live axle on radius arms with Panhard rod and long travel coil springs. Rear, live axle on radius arms with upper A-frame and long travel coil springs.

Steering: Worm and roller. Power assistance: optional. **Brakes:** Solid discs front, drums rear. ABS: not available. **Tyres:** 7.50-16. **Fuel tank:** 17.5 Imp. gall (79.5 litres). **Unladen weight:** 4257 lb (1931 kg).

Dimensions: Length 175.0 in (4445 mm), width 70.5 in (1790 mm), height 80.1 in (2035 mm), wheelbase 110.0 in (2795 mm).

Performance Works: Maximum speed 84 mph (135 km/h); 0 to 60 mph (97 km/h) 17.4 sec. Fuel consumption at constant 75 mph (120 km/h): 19.0 mpg.

Features: Elaborate paintwork of the Defender name three times across the door doesn't seem appropriate for an off-road vehicle. Interior still looks crude and unnecessarily basic in relation to the Discovery. **Summary:** The direct injection diesel seemed notably harsher and more noisy in the new Defender than remembered from the Discovery, but it offers all-round improvements on the previous indirect injection engine.

LAND ROVER (GB)   Discovery V8i

Identity: A removals journey to south-east France was in prospect, and a Discovery with the five-door body, newly introduced at Birmingham 1990, filled the role admirably. Keeping the speed down to 80 mph helps to contain the fuel consumption, which is much better now with the fuel injection engine.

Engine: Front-mounted longitudinal V8-cylinder with alloy block and heads, and electronic fuel injection. Bore 89.0 mm, stroke 71.0 mm; capacity 3528 cc. Power 166 PS (122 kW) at 4750 rpm; torque 212 lb ft (293 Nm) at 2600 rpm. Compression 9.4-to-1. Catalyst: optional.

Transmission: Four-wheel drive; five-speed manual gearbox. Automatic, not available. Permanent four-wheel drive, with low-ratio transfer gearbox. Top gear speed at 1000 rpm: 25.1 mph (40.4 km/h).

Suspension: Front, live axle on radius arms with Panhard rod and long travel coil springs. Rear, live axle on radius arms with upper A-frame and long travel coil springs.

Steering: Recirculating ball. Power assistance: standard. **Brakes:** Vented discs front, solid discs rear. ABS: not available. **Tyres:** 205 R 16. **Fuel tank:** 19.5 Imp. gall (88 litres). **Unladen weight:** 4150 lb (1882 kg).

Dimensions: Length 178.0 in (4521 mm), width 70.6 in (1793 mm), height 75.6 in (1919 mm), wheelbase 110.0 in (2540 mm).

Performance _Autocar & Motor_ test: Maximum speed 105 mph (169 km/h); 0 to 60 mph (97 km/h) 11.7 sec; 80 mph (130 km/h) 21.8 sec. Fuel consumption at constant 75 mph (120 km/h): 19.0 mpg; overall test, 16.5 mpg.

Features: Choice of three- or five-door body. Attractive interior for this kind of vehicle: practical layout, good controls. Two sunroofs. **Summary:** Steering is the disappointing aspect of the Discovery; I found it very vague when trying to steer a tidy course between a lorry and the crash barrier. In other respects, however, it's comfortable as well as rugged, and performs well enough if the gears are used freely.

LAND ROVER (GB) Range Rover Turbo D

Identity: All was set for a major advance on the Range Rover in autumn 1991, with introduction of air suspension; but the launch was postponed as the company decided more development work was needed. Instead, a package of detail improvements was announced.

Engine: Front-mounted longitudinal four-cylinder with anodised alloy head and pushrod ohv. Bosch indirect fuel injection. Bore 92.0 mm, stroke 94.0 mm; capacity 2500 cc. Power 121 PS (89 kW) at 4200 rpm; torque 209 lb ft (284 Nm) at 1950 rpm. Compression 22.5-to-1. Catalyst: not required.

Transmission: Four-wheel drive; five-speed manual gearbox with low-ratio transfer gearbox; automatically locking centre differential. Automatic, not available with diesel. Top gear speed at 1000 rpm: 25.5 mph (41.0 km/h).

Suspension: Front, live axle on radius arms with Panhard rod and coil springs; anti-roll bar. Rear, live axle on radius arms with upper A-bracket; coil springs and self-levelling Boge strut. Anti-roll bar.

Steering: Worm and roller. Power assistance: standard. **Brakes:** Vented discs front, solid discs rear. ABS: optional. **Tyres:** 205 R 16 XM + S. **Fuel tank:** 18.0 Imp. gall (82 litres). **Unladen weight:** 4455 lb (2020 kg).

Dimensions: Length 175.0 in (4447 mm), width 72.0 in (1813 mm), height 71.0 in (1792 mm), wheelbase 100.0 in (2540 mm).

Performance Works: Maximum speed 95 mph (153 km/h); 0 to 60 mph (97 km/h) 15.8 sec; 80 mph (130 km/h) 31.2 sec. Fuel consumption at constant 75 mph (120 km/h): 24.1 mpg; overall test, 25.8 mpg.

Features: Luxury Vogue trim is also available for the Turbo D. Improved sound insulation and electric de-icing for door locks were among the gains for 1992 models. **Summary:** Diesel power helps to take the sting out of the heavy running costs of this kind of vehicle, and with the larger 2½-litre Italian VM unit, the Range Rover is responsive and cruises well. It also has power to spare for towing a big caravan.

LINCOLN (USA)   Continental

Identity: New body shape with more elegant styling instead of the former 'ruler design' was launched in 1988; and 1989 brought 3.8-litre V6 engine with multiple port fuel injection. Better automatic transmission with higher change points was among many improvements at the same time, and new electronic control was introduced 1991.

Engine: Front-mounted transverse V6-cylinder with pushrod ohv and roller tappets. Multi-port fuel injection and turbocharger with intercooler. Bore 96.7 mm, stroke 86.1 mm; capacity 3801 cc. Power 155 PS (114 kW) at 4000 rpm; torque 220 lb ft (304 Nm) at 2600 rpm. Compression 8.2-to-1. Catalyst: standard (dual).

Transmission: Front-wheel drive; four-speed automatic, standard. Top gear speed at 1000 rpm: 32.6 mph (52.4 km/h).

Suspension: Front, independent, MacPherson struts with nitrogen springs and computer controlled damping; anti-roll bar. Rear, independent, MacPherson struts with nitrogen springs and computer controlled damping, ride height and roll restriction.

Steering: Rack and pinion. Power assistance: standard. **Brakes:** Solid discs front and rear. ABS: standard. **Tyres:** P205/70 R 15. **Fuel tank:** 18.6 Imp. gall (85 litres). **Unladen weight:** 3663 lb (1661 kg).

Dimensions: Length 205.1 in (5210 mm), width 72.3 in (1847 mm), height 55.6 in (1412 mm), wheelbase 109.0 in (2769 mm).

Performance (est): Maximum speed 115 mph (185 km/h). Fuel consumption overall (est), 17.0 mpg.

Features: New instrument panel was introduced for 1989, with digital instrumentation. Electric seat adjustment with memory is optional. **Summary:** Very spacious and comfortable executive car, and the air and nitrogen suspension system gives a luxuriously level ride.

LOTUS (GB)

Elan SE

Identity: GM ownership of Lotus transformed the company's fortunes and made possible the long-postponed development of this exciting little two-seater sports car, launched Motorfair 1989. It was not properly in producton until early 1991. Body is glass fibre, on a steel backbone chassis.

Engine: Front-mounted transverse four-cylinder with alloy head and twin ohc working four valves per cylinder. Electronic fuel injection and water-cooled turbocharger. Bore 80.0 mm, stroke 79.0 mm; capacity 1588 cc. Power 165 PS (123 kW) at 6600 rpm; torque 145 lb ft (200 Nm) at 4200 rpm. Compression 8.2-to-1. Catalyst: not available.

Transmission: Front-wheel drive; five-speed manual gearbox. Automatic, not available. Top gear speed at 1000 rpm: 20.9 mph (33.6 km/h).

Suspension: Front, independent, wishbones and coil springs; anti-roll bar. Rear, independent, upper links and wide-based lower wishbones; coil springs and anti-roll bar.

Steering: Rack and pinion. Power assistance: not available. **Brakes:** Vented discs front, solid discs rear. ABS: not available. **Tyres:** 205/50 ZR 15. **Fuel tank:** 10.2 Imp. gall. (46.4 litres). **Unladen weight:** 2249 lb (1020 kg).

Dimensions: Length 149.7 in (3803 mm), width 68.3 in (1734 mm), height 48.4 in (1230 mm), wheelbase 88.6 in (2250 mm).

Performance *Autocar & Motor* test: Maximum speed 136 mph (219 km/h); 0 to 60 mph (97 km/h) 6.5 sec; 80 mph (130 km/h) 10.9 sec. Fuel consumption at constant 75 mph (120 km/h): 31.8 mpg; overall test, 20.1 mpg.

Features: Snug-looking interior with well-bolstered side seats and sporty flavour to the design and layout. Easy action folding hood. **Summary:** A chance to drive the Elan finally came in summer 1991, when I was enthralled by the handling. Extremely lively and responsive, and build quality of my test car was first rate.

LOTUS (GB)   Esprit Turbo SE

Identity: New version of mid-engined Esprit, launched Motorfair 1987 with choice of non-turbo or turbo 16-valve engine. Glass panel across rear behind back window identifies Turbo model. Many improvements, including more attractive interior with better seats and instruments.

Engine: Mid-mounted longitudinal four-cylinder with alloy head and block; twin ohc operating four valves per cyl.; two twin-choke Dellorto carbs and Garrett T3 turbocharger. Bore 95.3 mm, stroke 76.2 mm; capacity 2174 cc. Power 212 PS (160 kW) at 6000 rpm; torque 220 lb ft (298 Nm) at 4250 rpm. Compression 8.0-to-1. Catalyst: standard.

Transmission: Rear-wheel drive; five-speed manual gearbox. Automatic, not available. Top gear speed at 1000 rpm: 23.7 mph (38.1 km/h).

Suspension: Front, independent, wishbones and coil springs with coaxial dampers; anti-roll bar. Rear, independent, transverse links with box section trailing arms; coil springs and coaxial telescopic dampers.

Steering: Rack and pinion. Power assistance: not available. **Brakes:** Vented discs front, solid discs rear. ABS: standard. **Tyres:** 195/60 VR 15 (front), 235/60 VR 15 (rear). **Fuel tank:** 17.3 Imp. gall (78.6 litres). **Unladen weight:** 2795 lb (1268 kg).

Dimensions: Length 170.5 in (4331 mm), width 73.2 in (1859 mm), height 44.8 in (1138 mm), wheelbase 96.8 in (2459 mm).

Performance *Autocar & Motor* test: Maximum speed 159 mph (256 km/h); 0 to 60 mph (97 km/h) 4.9 sec; 80 mph (130 km/h) 8.2 sec. Fuel consumption at 75 mph (120 km/h): 29.9 mpg; overall test, 23.5 mpg.

Features: Knock resistant bumpers in body colour; tilt/remove glass roof panel. SE is special equipment model. **Summary:** Well-planned redesign of this exciting mid-engined two-seater GT, introduced sensible improvements while retaining the outstanding handling. Body in composite material with some Kevlar reinforcement, and bolted to backbone chassis.

MAZDA (J)

121 GLX

Identity: No one can say that the new Mazda 121, launched February 1991 in UK, does not look distinctively different; and the rounded body shape is also very practical, offering generous roominess and rear headroom in a small car. Available with automatic transmission only.

Engine: Front-mounted transverse four-cylinder with alloy head and single ohc working four valves per cylinder. Electronic single point fuel injection. Bore 71.0 mm, stroke 83.6 mm; capacity 1324 cc. Power 73 PS (54 kW) at 6000 rpm; torque 78 lb ft (108 Nm) at 370 rpm. Compression 9.4-to-1. Catalyst: standard.

Transmission: Front-wheel drive. Automatic, four-speed standard. Top gear speed at 1000 rpm: 24.5 mph (39.5 km/h).

Suspension: Front, independent, MacPherson struts. Rear, semi-independent, trailing arms and torsion beam; anti-roll bar.

Steering: Rack and pinion. Power assistance: not available. **Brakes:** Solid discs front, drums rear. ABS: not available. **Tyres:** 165/70 R 13. **Fuel tank:** 9.5 Imp. gall (43 litres). **Unladen weight:** 1841 lb (835 kg).

Dimensions: Length 149.6 in (3800 mm), width 65.1 in (655 mm), height 57.8 in (1470 mm), wheelbase 94.1 in (2390 mm).

Performance *Autocar & Motor* test: Maximum speed 88 mph (142 km/h); 0 to 60 mph (97 km/h) 15.3 sec; 80 mph (130 km/h) 39.0 sec. Fuel consumption at constant 75 mph (120 km/h): 39.8 mpg; overall test, 30.7 mpg.

Features: Rear seat centrally divided and folding. Standard equipment includes central locking and electric front windows, but no sunroof. **Summary:** Automatic transmission has an unusual control system, with change-down and freewheel when selector is moved back, or change down with engine braking on pressing a button in the side of the selector. Pleasant small car, easy to drive but nowhere near as fast as the makers originally claimed.

MAZDA (J)

MX-3 V6

Identity: My agent in Japan rang excitedly to say that a Mazda was to have its world première at Geneva 1991, and he wanted pictures and full report. It seemed strange to report back to Japan on a Japanese car, but this is the one, the stylish 2 + 2, which caused all the excitement.

Engine: Front-mounted transverse V6-cylinder with alloy block and heads in 60 deg. V format. Twin overhead camshafts working four valves per cylinder. Bore 75.0 mm, stroke 69.6 mm; capacity 1845 cc. Power 134 PS (100 kW) at 6800 rpm: torque 118 lb ft (160 Nm) at 5300 rpm. Compression 9.2-to-1. Catalyst: standard.

Transmission: Front-wheel drive; five-speed manual gearbox. Automatic, not available. Top gear speed at 1000 rpm: 18.8 mph (30.1 km/h).

Suspension: Front, independent, MacPherson struts, anti-roll bar. Rear, independent, struts with lower trapezoidal links; anti-roll bar.

Steering: Rack and pinion. Power assistance: standard. **Brakes:** Vented discs front, solid discs rear. ABS: standard. **Tyres:** 205/55 VR 15. **Fuel tank:** 11.0 Imp. gall (50 litres). **Unladen weight:** 2500 lb (1135 kg).

Dimensions: Length 166.1 in (4220 mm), width 66.7 in (1695 mm), height 51.6 in (1310 mm), wheelbase 96.7 in (2455 mm).

Performance *Autocar & Motor* test: Maximum speed 124 mph (200 km/h); 0 to 60 mph (97 km/h) 8.9 sec; 80 mph (130 km/h) 15.4 sec. Fuel consumption at constant 75 mph (120 km/h): 32.1 mpg; overall test, 25.0 mpg.

Features: Very restricted rear accommodation, but good as a snug two-seater. Reasonable equipment includes a steel panel sunroof with electric action. **Summary:** Compact and sporty to drive, with good road behaviour to go with the brisk performance. As well as the 1.8 V6 version, there's a four-cylinder 1.6, identified by its lack of spoilers and single tail pipe.

MAZDA   (J, GB)   MX-5 BBR Turbo

Identity: In conjunction with Brodie Brittain Racing (hence the BBR initials), this turbocharged version of the very successful little MX-5 sports car was developed for the UK market, and announced towards the end of 1990. Power is increased to 150 PS, giving sizzling acceleration.

Engine: Front-mounted longitudinal four-cylinder with alloy head and twin ohc working four valves per cylinder. Garrett T25 turbocharger with integral waste gate and water cooling. Bore 78.0 mm, stroke 84.0 mm; capacity 1598 cc. Power 150 PS (110 kW) at 6500 rpm; torque 154 lb ft (213 Nm) at 5500 rpm. Compression 9.4-to-1. Catalyst: standard.

Transmission: Rear-wheel drive; five-speed manual gearbox. Automatic, not available. Top gear speed at 1000 rpm: 18.8 mph (30.3 km/h).

Suspension: Front, independent, wishbones and coil springs; anti-roll bar. Rear, independent, wishbones and coil springs; anti-roll bar.

Steering: Rack and pinion. Power assistance: standard. **Brakes:** Vented discs front, solid discs rear. ABS: not available. **Tyres:** D40 M2 6.5 VR 15. **Fuel tank:** 10.0 Imp. gall (46 litres). **Unladen weight:** 2170 lb (985 kg).

Dimensions: Length 156.5 in (3975 mm), width 65.9 in (1675 mm), height 48.4 in (1230 mm), wheelbase 89.2 in (2265 mm).

Performance *Autocar & Motor* test: Maximum speed 122 mph (196 km/h); 0 to 60 mph (97 km/h) 7.8 sec; 80 mph (130 km/h) 13.5 sec. Fuel consumption: overall test, 24.1 mpg.

Features: Extensive modifications include a modified sump with oil return from the turbocharger and reprogramming of electronic settings for injection and ignition. **Summary:** In standard form, the MX-5 is quite a nippy little sports car. Turbocharging moves it into a different class altogether, increasing the appeal, while retaining the charm of this little two-seater.

MAZDA (J)   MX-6 2.5i V6

Identity: Following the launch of the striking MX-3 at Geneva, Mazda developed the theme for Frankfurt 1991 with release of the MX-6 four-seater coupé, which went on sale in Britain early 1992. As with the MX-3, there is a choice of two engines, but they are different: a 2-litre four-cylinder and this V6.

Engine: Front-mounted transverse V6-cylinder with alloy block and heads in 60 deg. V. Twin overhead camshafts working four valves per cylinder. Bore 84.5 mm, stroke 74.2 mm; capacity 2497 cc. Power 165 PS (121 kW) at 5600 rpm; torque 163 lb ft (225 Nm) at 4800 rpm. Compression 9.2-to-1. Catalyst: standard.

Transmission: Front-wheel drive; five-speed manual gearbox. Automatic, optional extra, electronic four-speed. Top gear speed at 1000 rpm: 18.8 mph (30.1 km/h).

Suspension: Front, independent, MacPherson struts; anti-roll bar. Rear, independent, struts with lower trapezoidal links; anti-roll bar.

Steering: Rack and pinion. Power assistance: standard. **Brakes:** Vented discs front, solid discs rear. ABS: standard. **Tyres:** 205/55 R 15 87V. **Fuel tank:** 13.2 Imp. gall (60 litres). **Unladen weight:** 2610 lb (1220 kg).

Dimensions: Length 181.6 in (4615 mm), width 68.9 in (1750 mm), height 51.6 in (1310 mm), wheelbase 102.8 in (2610 mm).

Performance Works: Maximum speed 136 mph (219 km/h); 0 to 60 mph (97 km/h) 8.2 sec. Fuel consumption: no data available.

Features: Like the MX-3, the MX-5 has narrow headlamps, blended neatly into the frontal styling, and fog lamps are set into the bumper. Distinctive alloy wheels. **Summary:** An aerofoil wing on the back identifies the 2.5i version, and the suspension features fluid-filled bushes claimed to give ride comfort with driving stability. This is another new Mazda which I hope to catch up with in 1992.

MERCEDES-BENZ (D)

190E 1.8

Identity: Bottom model of the Mercedes range used to be the carburettor 190, but in June 1990 the 1.8-litre version was launched, with fuel injection. It probably represents best value of the entire range, and although thin on equipment it is a very pleasing car, with traditional Mercedes qualities.

Engine: Front-mounted longitudinal four-cylinder with alloy head and single ohc; eight valves. Bosch electronic fuel injection. Bore 89.0 mm, stroke 72.2 mm; capacity 1797 cc. Power 110 PS (81 kW) at 5500 rpm; torque 111 lb ft (153 Nm) at 3700 rpm. Compression 9.1-to-1. Catalyst: standard.

Transmission: Rear-wheel drive; five-speed manual gearbox. Automatic, optional extra, four-speed. Top gear speed at 1000 rpm: 23.9 mph (38.5 km/h).

Suspension: Front, independent, MacPherson struts, anti-roll bar. Rear, independent, five-link location; coil springs and anti-roll bar.

Steering: Recirculating ball. Power assistance: standard. **Brakes:** Solid discs front and rear. ABS: optional. **Tyres:** 185/65 HR 15. **Fuel tank:** 12.1 Imp. gall (55 litres). **Unladen weight:** 2557 lb (1160 kg).

Dimensions: Length 175.1 in (4448 mm), width 66.5 in (1690 mm), height 54.7 in (1390 mm), wheelbase 104.9 in (2665 mm).

Performance *Autocar & Motor* test (auto): Maximum speed 118 mph (190 km/h); 0 to 60 mph (97 km/h) 12.3 sec; 80 mph (130 km/h) 21.6 sec. Fuel consumption at constant 75 mph (120 km/h): 30.4 mpg; overall test, 26.1 mpg.

Features: No audio unit is provided as standard, but the 190E does get central locking and electric action for the passenger-door mirror. **Summary:** A very good automatic transmission, with excellent selector, is optional and was fitted for the test quoted above. My test car had the manual five-speed gearbox, with delightful change, and apart from the rather leisurely acceleration, it is enjoyable and safe to drive.

MERCEDES-BENZ (D)

190E 2.5-16V

Identity: At the same time as the 190 range was revised in 1988, Mercedes increased the power of the 16-valve performance model by extending the stroke and raising capacity to 2½-litre. Already a very fast car, it gains a lot more torque for better low-speed response.

Engine: Front-mounted longitudinal four-cylinder with alloy head and twin chain-driven ohc operating four valves per cyl. Bosch K-Jetronic fuel injection. Bore 95.5 mm, stroke 87.3 mm; capacity 2498 cc. Power 200 PS (147 kW) at 6200 rpm; torque 176 lb ft (242 Nm) at 4500 rpm. Compression 9.7-to-1. Catalyst: standard.

Transmission: Rear-wheel drive; five-speed manual gearbox. Automatic, four-speed, optional. Top gear speed at 1000 rpm: 23.5 mph (37.8 km/h).

Suspension: Front, independent, MacPherson struts, anti-roll bar. Rear, independent, five-link system with anti-dive, anti-squat control; coil springs, anti-roll bar.

Steering: Recirculating ball. Power assistance: standard. **Brakes:** Vented discs front, solid discs rear. ABS: standard. **Tyres:** 205/55 ZR 15 TL. **Fuel tank:** 15.4 Imp. gall (70 litres). **Unladen weight:** 2866 lb (1300 kg).

Dimensions: Length 174.4 in (4430 mm), width 67.2 in (1706 mm), height 53.5 in (1361 mm), wheelbase 104.9 in (2665 mm).

Performance *Autocar & Motor* test: Maximum speed 142 mph (229 km/h); 0 to 62 mph (100 km/h) 7.2 sec; 80 mph (130 km/h) 11.8 sec. Fuel consumption at constant 75 mph (120 km/h): 32.8 mpg; overall test, 22.0 mpg.

Features: Many refinements to make this quick version of the 190 very enjoyable. Snug sports seats give good location. **Summary:** Close ratio gearchange with offset first, and upper four gears in H layout, takes a little familiarisation; but it is certainly a most exciting car and one that gobbles up long journeys in fine style.

MERCEDES-BENZ (D) 300CE-24 Convertible

Identity: Frankfurt 1991 brought an interesting addition to the W124 range in the form of this elegant convertible. It has the same safety feature as the SL models: a roll-over bar which springs up automatically when the computer detects that a major accident is about to occur.

Engine: Front-mounted longitudinal six-cylinder with alloy head and twin ohc working four valves per cylinder. Bosch KE 5 fuel injection. Bore 88.5 mm, stroke 80.2 mm; capacity 2960 cc. Power 220 PS (162 kW) at 6400 rpm; torque 197 lb ft (265 Nm) at 4600 rpm. Compression 10.0-to-1. Catalyst: standard.

Transmission: Rear-wheel drive; five-speed manual gearbox. Automatic, optional extra, four- or five-speed to choice. Top gear speed at 1000 rpm: 23.0 mph (37.1 km/h).

Suspension: Front, independent, MacPherson struts, anti-roll bar. Rear, independent, five-link location; coil springs and anti-roll bar.

Steering: Recirculating ball. Power assistance: standard. **Brakes:** Vented discs front, solid discs rear. ABS: standard. **Tyres:** 195/65 ZR 15. **Fuel tank:** 15.4 Imp. gall (70 litres). **Unladen weight:** 3770 lb (1710 kg).

Dimensions: Length 183.2 in (4655 mm), width 68.5 in (1740 mm), height 55.2 in (1740 mm), wheelbase 106.9 in (2715 mm).

Performance Works: Maximum speed 143 mph (230 km/h); 0 to 62 mph (100 km/h) 8.7 sec; 80 mph (130 km/h) 13.4 sec. Fuel consumption at constant 75 mph (120 km/h): 26.7 mpg.

Features: Hood folding is easy, but power operation comes only as an extra cost option; rear window is of safety glass, with heating. **Summary:** According to the Press department in Stuttgart, 'Even the delicate hands of a woman can open and close the top with ease.' Supplies of this fine convertible are expected to be severely limited, with demand far outstripping supply.

MERCEDES-BENZ (D)　　　　　300GD

Identity: Always very competent, if rather basic in its performance on the road, the Geländewagen – commonly known as the G-wagon – was vastly improved in 1990. In September the importers arranged a spectacular mountain test of the new version in Scotland. Sidelamps recessed in the bumper identify the later model, which has permanent four-wheel drive.

Engine: Front-mounted longitudinal six-cylinder with cast iron head and block, and single ohc; indirect fuel injection, no turbo. Bore 87.0 mm, stroke 84.0 mm; capacity 2,996 cc. Power 113 PS (83 kW) at 4600 rpm; torque 141 lb ft (195 Nm) at 2700 rpm. Compression 22.0-to-1. Catalyst: not available.

Transmission: Four-wheel drive; five-speed manual gearbox. Automatic, optional extra. Four-wheel drive is permanently engaged, with low ratio transfer gearbox. Top gear speed at 1000 rpm: 18.8 mph (30.3 km/h).

Suspension: Front, live axle on trailing arms with Panhard rod; coil springs. Rear, live axle on trailing arms with Panhard rod; coil springs, anti-roll bar.

Steering: Recirculating ball. Power assistance: standard. **Brakes:** Solid discs front, drums rear. ABS: standard. **Tyres:** 205 R 16. **Fuel tank:** 20.1 Imp. gall (95 litres). **Unladen weight:** 4905 lb (2225 kg).

Dimensions: Length (long wheelbase) 173.0 in (4395 mm), (swb): 155.3 in (3945 mm), width 66.9 in (1700 mm), height 77.8 in (1975 mm), wheelbase 112.2 in (2850 mm).

Performance *Autocar & Motor* test: Maximum speed 84 mph (135 km/h); 0 to 60 mph (97 km/h) 25.4 sec. Fuel consumption at constant 75 mph (120 km/h): 17.7 mpg; overall test, 17.1 mpg.

Features: Differential locks (front, centre and rear) have electric switch control on facia. Much better interior trim and layout, derived from the W123 car range. **Summary:** Still the same rather angular body, but very impressive cross-country ability, helped by the huge ground clearance.

MERCEDES-BENZ (D)

300SL-24 5-Speed automatic

Identity: In the 1990 edition we covered the fabulously fast 500SL with 32-valve engine. This is the later arrival: the six-cylinder version of this lovely sports car with the unusual feature of a five-speed automatic transmission.

Engine: Front-mounted longitudinal six-cylinder with alloy head and block and twin ohc working four valves per cylinder. Bosch KE5 CIS fuel injection. Bore 89.0 mm, stroke 80.0 mm; capacity 2960 cc. Power 231 PS (170 kW) at 6300 rpm; torque 200 lb ft (277 Nm) at 4600 rpm. Compression 10.0-to-1. Catalyst: standard.

Transmission: Rear-wheel drive; five-speed automatic, standard. Top gear speed at 1000 rpm: 28.9 mph (46.5 km/h).

Suspension: Front, independent, MacPherson struts, anti-roll bar. Rear, independent, five-link location with coil springs and anti-roll bar. Anti-squat and anti-dive control.

Steering: Recirculating ball. Power assistance: standard. **Brakes:** Vented discs front, solid discs rear. ABS: standard. **Tyres:** 225/55 ZR 16. **Fuel tank:** 17.6 Imp. gall (80 litres). **Unladen weight:** 3725 lb (1690 kg).

Dimensions: Length 175.9 in (4470 mm), width 71.3 in (1812 mm), height 51.2 in (1303 mm), wheelbase 99.0 in (2515 mm).

Performance *Autocar & Motor* test: Maximum speed 134 mph (216 km/h); 0 to 60 mph (97 km/h) 8.6 sec; 80 mph (130 km/h) 14.1 sec. Fuel consumption at constant 75 mph (120 km/h): 26.6 mpg; overall test, 19.2 mpg.

Features: Five-speed transmission selector has only four positions, no first gear hold, and is moved sideways for fifth, which is marked OD (overdrive). **Summary:** Most of the superb furnishings and safety features are the same as for the 500SL, though leather upholstery is an option on the six-cylinder. Automatic transmission has the usual Mercedes mode control switch offering E (Economy) or S (Sport).

MERCEDES-BENZ (D)   500E

Identity: It came as something of a surprise to hear at the Paris Show 1990 that the Porsche factory at Zuffenhausen was to build a Mercedes – but that is what is happening with the very special 5-litre V8 500 model. It is produced by craftsmen for enthusiasts, at the rate of only 12 a day.

Engine: Front-mounted longitudinal V8-cylinder with alloy block and heads, and twin ohc each bank, working four valves per cylinder. Bosch LH Jetronic fuel injection. Bore 96.5 mm, stroke 85.0 mm; capacity 4973 cc. Power 326 PS (240 kW) at 5700 rpm; torque 347 lb ft (480 Nm) at 3900 rpm. Compression 10.0-to-1. Catalyst: standard.

Transmission: Rear-wheel drive; five-speed automatic, standard. Top gear speed at 1000 rpm: 26.6 mph (42.8 km/h).

Suspension: Front, independent, MacPherson struts with anti-dive control; anti-roll bar. Rear, independent, five-link system with anti-dive, anti-squat control; self-levelling, coil springs and anti-roll bar.

Steering: Recirculating ball. Power assistance: standard. **Brakes:** Vented discs front and rear. ABS: standard. **Tyres:** 225/55 ZR 16. **Fuel tank:** 19.8 Imp. gall (90 litres). **Unladen weight:** 3748 lb (1700 kg).

Dimensions: Length 187.0 in (4750 mm), width 70.7 in (1796 mm), height 55.4 in (1408 mm), wheelbase 110.2 in (2800 mm).

Performance *Autocar & Motor* test: Maximum speed 156 mph (251 km/h); 0 to 60 mph (97 km/h) 6.3 sec; 80 mph (130 km/h) 10.0 sec. Fuel consumption at constant 75 mph (120 km/h): 23.0 mpg; overall test, 16.5 mpg.

Features: Elaborate standard equipment provides such items as air conditioning and electric seat adjustment, and a new 'world first' is that all the electronic systems constantly communicate with each other.
Summary: A car for the very discerning buyer. A lot of attention has been paid to roadholding, including moving the battery to the boot for optimum weight balance; the Mercedes wheelspin control system is standard.

MERCEDES-BENZ (D)

Identity: A completely new luxury model from Mercedes-Benz, the S-Class was introduced Geneva 1991, with shapely aerodynamic body and many special features. Four engines are offered: six-cylinder 3.2-litre, this V8, larger V8 of 5-litre capacity, and the superb V12 described on the next page.

Engine: Front-mounted longitudinal V8-cylinder with alloy block and heads; twin ohc each bank, working four valves per cylinder. Bosch LH Jetronic fuel injection. Bore 92.0 mm, stroke 78.9 mm; capacity 4196 cc. Power 286 PS (210 kW) at 5700 rpm; torque 302 lb ft (410 Nm) at 3900 rpm. Compression 10.0-to-1. Catalyst: standard.

Transmission: Rear-wheel drive; four-speed automatic, standard. Top gear speed at 1000 rpm: 27.7 mph (44.6 km/h).

Suspension: Front, independent, wishbones and coil springs, anti-roll bar. Rear, independent, five-link location; coil springs and anti-roll bar.

Steering: Recirculating ball. Power assistance: standard. **Brakes:** Vented discs front and rear. ABS: standard. **Tyres:** 235/60 ZR 16. **Fuel tank:** 22.0 Imp. gall (100 litres). **Unladen weight:** 4387 lb (1990 kg).

Dimensions: Length 201.2 in (5113 mm), width 74.2 in (1886 mm), height 58.9 in (1497 mm), wheelbase 119.6 in (3040 mm).

Performance *Autocar & Motor* test: Maximum speed 144 mph (232 km/h); 0 to 60 mph (97 km/h) 8.4 sec; 80 mph (130 km/h) 13.6 sec. Fuel consumption at constant 75 mph (120 km/h): 23.2 mpg; overall test, 14.6 mpg.

Features: Self-tensioning seat belts and a driver's air-bag restraint system are among the standard safety features; passenger air bag optional. **Summary:** Wonderfully relaxing and confident car to drive, with its supple ride and well-balanced handling, but I did feel the steering could usefully be a little more direct. Magnificent comfort and refinement.

MERCEDES-BENZ (D)   600SEL

Identity: Only badging and the discreet V12 emblem, on the side to the rear of each back door, identify the top model of the S-Class range. It has a magnificent V12 engine of 6-litre capacity, much more impressive than BMW's V12, and it's coupled to a far superior automatic.

Engine: Front-mounted longitudinal V12-cylinder with alloy block and heads; twin ohc per bank, working four valves per cylinder. Bosch 2 LH Jetronic fuel injection. Bore 89.0 mm, stroke 80.2 mm; capacity 5987 cc. Power 408 PS (300 kW) at 5200 rpm; torque 420 lb ft (580 Nm) at 3800 rpm. Compression 10.0-to-1. Catalyst: standard.

Transmission: Rear-wheel drive; four-speed automatic, standard. Top gear speed at 1000 rpm: 29.5 mph (47.5 km/h).

Suspension: Front, independent, wishbones and coil springs, anti-roll bar. Rear, independent, five-link location; coil springs and anti-roll bar.

Steering: Recirculating ball. Power assistance: standard. **Brakes:** Vented discs front and rear. ABS: standard. **Tyres:** 235/60 ZR 16. **Fuel tank:** 22.0 Imp. gall (100 litres). **Unladen weight:** 4805 lb (2180 kg).

Dimensions: Length 205.2 in (5213 mm), width 74.2 in (1886 mm), height 58.7 in (1492 mm), wheelbase 123.6 in (3140 mm).

Performance *Autocar & Motor* test: Maximum speed 159 mph (256 km/h); 0 to 60 mph (97 km/h) 6.7 sec; 80 mph (130 km/h) 10.3 sec. Fuel consumption at constant 75 mph (120 km/h): 20.6 mpg; overall test, 15.5 mpg.

Features: Fabulous range of standard equipment, including such details as electric adjustment for steering column; there are a few options, including rear climate control and adjustment of the front passenger seat from the rear. **Summary:** As with all the S-Class range, the SEL is the long-wheelbase version, and standard wheelbase is available as the SE. The strongest rival yet to a Rolls-Royce, and one which beats it on many counts.

MERCURY (USA) Grand Marquis

Identity: Rebodied for 1992, the Grand Marquis appears also in the Ford range as the Crown Victoria. Described as, 'For many Americans, the only kind of car they've known: full-size six-seater roominess, big boot, V8 power, boulevard ride.'

Engine: Front-mounted longitudinal V8-cylinder with overhead camshaft on each bank, and sequential multi-port electronic fuel injection. Bore 90.2 mm, stroke 90.0 mm; capacity 4601 cc. Power 213 PS (157 kW) at 4600 rpm; torque 265 lb ft (366 Nm) at 3400 rpm. Compression 9.0-to-1. Catalyst: standard.

Transmission: Rear-wheel drive; four-speed automatic, standard. Top gear speed at 1000 rpm: 21.6 mph (34.8 km/h).

Suspension: Front, independent, wishbones and coil springs; anti-roll bar. Rear, live axle with four-link location; coil springs and anti-roll bar.

Steering: Recirculating ball. Power assistance: standard. **Brakes:** Solid discs front and rear. ABS: optional. **Tyres:** P215/70 R 15. **Fuel tank:** 16.7 Imp. gall (76 litres). **Unladen weight:** 3767 lb (1709 kg).

Dimensions: Length 212.4 in (5395 mm), width 77.8 in (1976 mm), height 56.9 in (1445 mm), wheelbase 114.4 in (2906 mm).

Performance Works: Maximum speed 108 mph (174 km/h); 0 to 62 mph (100 km/h) 9.5 sec. Fuel consumption overall (est): 22 mpg.

Features: Standard equipment includes air conditioning, and a wide range of options is offered, including choice of tyres and final drive ratio.
Summary: Described as having a sleek look for the 1990s, the Grand Marquis is better on drag coefficient than its predecessor—down from 0.45 to a reasonable (by American standards) 0.36. Rear air suspension is optional.

MITSUBISHI   (J)   Colt 1600 GLXi

Identity: Successor for the popular little Colt hatchback was launched Brussels 1992, with more rounded body distinguished by its protective side flash and elongated oval lamp units. 1300 12-valve engine continues, but the former 1500 GLX graduates to this model with 1.6-litre engine and 16 valves.

Engine: Front-mounted transverse four-cylinder with alloy block and head and single ohc; 16 valves. ECI-MULTI fuel injection. Bore 81.0 mm, stroke 77.5 mm; capacity 1597 cc. Power 113 PS (83 kW) at 6000 rpm; torque 99 lb ft (137 Nm) at 5000 rpm. Compression 10.5-to-1. Catalyst: standard.

Transmission: Front-wheel drive; five-speed manual gearbox. Automatic, optional extra, four-speed. Top gear speed at 1000 rpm: 21.3 mph (34.3 km/h).

Suspension: Front, independent, MacPherson struts, anti-roll bar. Rear, independent, multi-link layout with coil springs and anti-roll bar.

Steering: Rack and pinion. Power assistance: optional. **Brakes:** Vented discs front, drums rear. ABS: optional. **Tyres:** 175/70 R 13 82 H. **Fuel tank:** 11.0 Imp. gall (50 litres). **Unladen weight:** 2080 lb (945 kg).

Dimensions: Length 155.7 in (3955 mm), width 66.5 in (1690 mm), height 53.7 in (1365 mm), wheelbase 96.1 in (2440 mm).

Performance Works: Maximum speed 118 mph (190 km/h); 0 to 62 mph (100 km/h) 9.8 sec; 80 mph (130 km/h) 14.9 sec. Fuel consumption at constant 75 mph (120 km/h): 39.2 mpg.

Features: Night reversing aid helps distance judgement by a light spot seen in the mirror, which goes out of sight when the back of the car is 50 cm from an obstruction. Good equipment, and sunroof now offered.
Summary: Attractive small three-door hatchback with roomy interior and great attention paid to safety. It offers much more load space than the previous model, as well as extra performance and comfort. This version is also built with four-wheel drive, though not offered in the UK.

MITSUBISHI (J) Colt 1800 GTi

Identity: Top model of the new Colt range, launched Brussels 1992, is this GTi model with new engine, essentially an enlarged version of the 1.6 (same bore but longer stroke) and with twin overhead camshafts. It gives 4 PS more than the 136 peak of the former Colt GTi.

Engine: Front-mounted transverse four-cylinder with alloy block and head, and twin ohc; 16 valves. ECI-MULTI fuel injection. Bore 81.0 mm, stroke 89.0 mm; capacity 1834 cc. Power 140 PS (103 kW) at 6500 rpm; torque 121 lb ft (167 Nm) at 5500 rpm. Compression 10.5-to-1. Catalyst: standard.

Transmission: Front-wheel drive; five-speed manual gearbox. Automatic, not available. Top gear speed at 1000 rpm: 20.1 mph (32.3 km/h).

Suspension: Front, independent, MacPherson struts, anti-roll bar. Rear, independent, multi-link layout with coil springs and anti-roll bar.

Steering: Rack and pinion. Power assistance: optional. **Brakes:** Vented discs front, solid discs rear. ABS: optional. **Tyres:** 185/60 R 14 85 V. **Fuel tank:** 11.0 Imp. gall (50 litres). **Unladen weight:** 2193 lb (995 kg).

Dimensions: Length 155.7 in (3955 mm), width 66.5 in (1690 mm), height 53.3 in (1355 mm), wheelbase 96.1 in (2440 mm).

Performance Works: Maximum speed 130 mph (210 km/h); 0 to 62 mph (100 km/h) 7.6 sec; 80 mph (130 km/h) 12.2 sec. Fuel consumption at constant 75 mph (120 km/h): 37.7 mpg.

Features: Exact specification details were still awaited when we went to press, but power steering and ABS may well be made standard for UK. **Summary:** With its better shape and a little more power, the new GTi is claimed to be 5 mph faster than the previous one. Its main appeal is unchanged: a compact, well-designed hatchback, fun to drive, with very high performance.

MITSUBISHI (J)   Galant Coupé Dynamic Four

Identity: Following the successful launch of four-wheel drive and four-wheel steering on the Galant saloon in May 1989, the same specification was extended to the attractively styled Galant Coupé, Geneva 1990. Four-wheel drive is permanently engaged. One of these cars was my superb transport to the Geneva Show in 1992.

Engine: Front-mounted transverse four-cylinder with alloy head and twin ohc working four valves per cylinder. Electronic multi-point fuel injection. Bore 85.0 mm, stroke 88.0 mm; capacity 1997 cc. Power 150 PS (110 kW) at 6750 rpm; torque 129 lb ft (178 Nm) at 5500 rpm. Compression 9.8-to-1. Catalyst: standard.

Transmission: Four-wheel drive; five-speed manual gearbox. Automatic, optional extra. Top gear speed at 1000 rpm: 19.5 mph (31.4 km/h).

Suspension: Front, independent, MacPherson struts, anti-roll bar. Rear, independent, wishbones with trailing arms and concentric coil springs; anti-roll bar.

Steering: Rack and pinion. Power assistance: standard. **Brakes:** Vented discs front, solid discs rear. ABS: standard. **Tyres:** 195/60 R 15 87V. **Fuel tank:** 13.7 Imp. gall (62 litres). **Unladen weight:** 2954 lb (1340 kg).

Dimensions: Length 180.0 in (4570 mm), width 66.7 in (1695 mm), height 55.5 in (1410 mm), wheelbase 102.4 in (2600 mm).

Performance *Autocar & Motor* test (saloon): Maximum speed 118 mph (190 km/h); 0 to 60 mph (97 km/h) 9.4 sec; 80 mph (130 km/h) 16.7 sec. Fuel consumption at constant 75 mph (120 km/h): 31.7 mpg; overall test, 21.4 mpg.

Features: Rear wheels turn always in the same direction as the front ones, returning to straight ahead below 31 mph. Full equipment.
Summary: A very capable and reassuring car to drive. One drawback is that the air conditioning and electronic suspension control options are not available for the Dynamic Four.

MITSUBISHI (J)

Lancer 1800 GLXi 4WD Liftback

Identity: The model which rejoices in one of the longest names of any car was launched Motorfair 1989, and continues alongside the new Colt models which were launched at Brussels 1992. Although engine size is the same, the Lancer has the single ohc version with eight valves.

Engine: Front-mounted transverse four-cylinder with alloy head and belt-driven ohc; eight valves. Electronic fuel injection. Bore 80.6 mm, stroke 86.0 mm; capacity 1755 cc. Power 95 PS (71 kW) at 5500 rpm; torque 104 lb ft (141 Nm) at 4000 rpm. Compression 9.5-to-1. Catalyst: standard.

Transmission: Four-wheel drive; five-speed manual gearbox. Automatic, not available. Top gear speed at 1000 rpm: 19.8 mph (31.9 km/h).

Suspension: Front, independent, MacPherson struts, anti-roll bar. Rear, live axle with five-link location and coil springs; anti-roll bar.

Steering: Rack and pinion. Power assistance: standard. **Brakes:** Vented discs front, drums rear. ABS: not available. **Tyres:** 175/70 HR 13. **Fuel tank:** 11.0 Imp. gall (50 litres). **Unladen weight:** 2500 lb (1134 kg).

Dimensions: Length 166.7 in (4235 mm), width 65.7 in (1670 mm), height 56.1 in (1425 mm), wheelbase 96.7 in (2455 mm).

Performance *Autocar & Motor* test: Maximum speed 103 mph (166 km/h); 0 to 60 mph (97 km/h) 11.7 sec; 80 mph (130 km/h) 23.4 sec. Fuel consumption at constant 75 mph (120 km/h): 30.4 mpg; overall test, 24.6 mpg.

Features: Viscous couplings are used for the centre and rear differentials; four-wheel drive is permanently engaged. Generous equipment, and no options are offered. **Summary:** Four-wheel drive contributes to the stability and handling of the Lancer in this version, but in combination with the catalyst it takes away the power advantage over the 1.5. At Birmingham 1990, the twin-cam 16-valve engine became available, but with front drive only.

MITSUBISHI (J) Shogun Turbo D five-door

Identity: Good though the old Shogun was, the new model launched at the beginning of May 1991 was even better. Choice of three- or five-door body, and either this turbo diesel engine, or the 3-litre V6 with single ohc and roller rocker arms. The diesel has counter-rotating balance shafts for smoothness.

Engine: Front-mounted longitudinal four-cylinder with single ohc; turbocharger and intercooler. Bore 91.1 mm, stroke 95.0 mm; capacity 2477 cc. Power 99 PS (73 kW) at 4200 rpm; torque 177 lb ft (245 Nm) at 2000 rpm. Compression 21.0-to-1. Catalyst: not required.

Transmission: Rear-wheel drive plus selectable front drive; five-speed manual gearbox. Automatic, not available; option for V6. Top gear speed at 1000 rpm: 19.3 mph (31.1 km/h).

Suspension: Front, independent, wishbones and torsion bars; anti-roll bar. Rear, live axle with three-link location, and progressive taper coil springs; anti-roll bar.

Steering: Recirculating ball. Power assistance: standard. **Brakes:** Vented discs front, solid discs rear. ABS: optional. **Tyres:** 265/70 R 15. **Fuel tank:** 20.4 Imp. gall (93 litres). **Unladen weight:** 4288 lb (1945 kg).

Dimensions: Length 186.0 in (4725 mm), width 70.3 in (1785 mm), height 73.6 in (1870 mm), wheelbase 107.3 in (2725 mm).

Performance Works: Maximum speed 88 mph (142 km/h). No acceleration data available for new model; previous Turbo D, 0 to 60 mph (97 km/h) 18.8 sec. Fuel consumption at constant 75 mph (120 km/h): 19.5 mpg.

Features: A single lever beside the gear lever gives selection of four-wheel drive, then locks the centre differential, and finally engages the low-ratio transfer gearbox. **Summary:** Shogun has a huge payload of 2650 kg (5842 lb), and by exploiting this to the maximum last year I won the Caravan Club's Economy Run, which was based on an efficiency formula, relating fuel used to weight moved. Nothing came anywhere near the Shogun's figure.

MITSUBISHI (J)   Sigma

Identity: Moving upmarket into the luxury saloon class, Mitsubishi launched the Sigma at Paris 1990; on the British market from spring 1991. It introduces a number of new features, including Mitsubishi's Traction Control system and Trace control, adjusting traction and cornering forces in relation to available grip.

Engine: Front-mounted transverse V6-cylinder with alloy block and heads; twin ohc working 24 valves, electronic fuel injection, and varying induction control. Bore 91.1 mm, stroke 76.0 mm; capacity 2972 cc. Power 205 PS (151 kW) at 6000 rpm; torque 195 lb ft (270 Nm) at 3000 rpm. Compression 10.0-to-1. Catalyst: standard.

Transmission: Front-wheel drive; five-speed manual gearbox. Automatic, optional extra. Top gear speed at 1000 rpm: 24.0 mph (38.6 km/h).

Suspension: Front, independent, MacPherson struts, anti-roll bar. Computer control. Rear, independent, multi-link location, with coil springs and anti-roll bar. Computer control.

Steering: Rack and pinion. Power assistance: standard. **Brakes:** Vented discs front and rear. ABS: standard. **Tyres:** 205/65 R 15. **Fuel tank:** 15.8 Imp. gall (72 litres). **Unladen weight:** 3252 lb (1475 kg).

Dimensions: Length 187.0 in (4750 mm), width 69.9 in (1775 mm), height 56.5 in (1435 mm), wheelbase 107.1 in (2720 mm).

Performance *Autocar & Motor* test: Maximum speed 128 mph (206 km/h); 0 to 60 mph (97 km/h) 9.3 sec; 80 mph (130 km/h) 15.3 sec. Fuel consumption at constant 75 mph (120 km/h): 28.5 mpg; overall test, 18.3 mpg.

Features: Every conceivable item of luxury equipment is included plus many not so easily imagined, such as the four-wheel steering, advanced suspension control and anti-skid systems. **Summary:** Experienced on snowy roads in Switzerland, it gave traction and cornering grip that I would not have believed possible in such conditions with only front-wheel drive.

MITSUBISHI   (J)   Space Runner 1800-16V GLXi

Identity: This successor to the 1982 Space Wagon was launched Frankfurt 1991, and on British market from the beginning of October. A sliding door is fitted on the nearside only, plus front doors and top-hinged rear tailgate. High body allows easy access and a spacious interior.

Engine: Front-mounted transverse four-cylinder with alloy head and single ohc working four valves per cylinder. ECI-Multi fuel injection. Bore 81.0 mm, stroke 89.0 mm; capacity 1834 cc. Power 122 PS (90 kW) at 6000 rpm; torque 119 lb ft (164 Nm) at 4500 rpm. Compression 10.0-to-1. Catalyst: standard.

Transmission: Front-wheel drive; five-speed manual gearbox. Automatic, optional extra, four-speed. Top gear speed at 1000 rpm: 20.3 mph (32.7 km/h).

Suspension: Front, independent, MacPherson struts, anti-roll bar. Rear, independent, semi-trailing arms, coil springs; anti-roll bar.

Steering: Rack and pinion. Power assistance: standard. **Brakes:** Vented discs front, drums rear. ABS: not available. **Tyres:** 185/70 HR 14. **Fuel tank:** 12.1 Imp. gall (55 litres). **Unladen weight:** 2612 lb (1185 kg).

Dimensions: Length 168.9 in (4290 mm), width 66.7 in (1695 mm), height 64.0 in (1625 mm), wheelbase 99.2 in (2520 mm).

Performance *Autocar & Motor* test: Maximum speed 113 mph (182 km/h); 0 to 60 mph (97 km/h) 10.6 sec; 80 mph (130 km/h) 19.8 sec. Fuel consumption at constant 75 mph (120 km/h): 32.5 mpg; overall test, 27.2 mpg.

Features: Versatile seating arrangement allows the back seat to be folded forward for extra load space, or it can easily be taken out. **Summary:** Easy to drive, helped by the commanding view. Clever interior styling and design make the Runner a very suitable alternative to the conventional concept of a large estate car, particularly suitable for big families.

MITSUBISHI (J) Space Wagon 1800-16V GLXi

Identity: Although similar in appearance to the Space Runner, and using much the same running gear, the Space Wagon is cleverly designed to appeal to a different market, the need of which is for maximum seating capacity. It deserves the space for a separate entry.

Engine: Front-mounted transverse four-cylinder with alloy head and single ohc working four valves per cylinder. ECI-Multi fuel injection. Bore 81.0 mm, stroke 89.0 mm; capacity 1834 cc. Power 122 PS (90 kW) at 6000 rpm; torque 119 lb ft (164 Nm) at 4500 rpm. Compression 10.0-to-1. Catalyst: standard.

Transmission: Front-wheel drive; five-speed manual gearbox. Automatic, optional extra, four-speed. Top gear speed at 1000 rpm: 20.3 mph (32.7 km/h).

Suspension: Front, independent, MacPherson struts, anti-roll bar. Rear, independent, semi-trailing arms, coil springs; anti-roll bar. Load-dependent dampers.

Steering: Rack and pinion. Power assistance: standard. **Brakes:** Vented discs front, drums rear. ABS: not available. **Tyres:** 185/70 HR 14. **Fuel tank:** 13.2 Imp. gall (60 litres). **Unladen weight:** 2745 lb (1245 kg).

Dimensions: Length 177.8 in (4515 mm), width 66.7 in (1695 mm), height 62.2 in (1580 mm), wheelbase 107.1 in (2720 mm).

Performance Works: Maximum speed 113 mph (182 km/h); 0 to 62 mph (100 km/h) 11.6 sec. Fuel consumption at constant 75 mph (120 km/h): 32.5 mpg.

Features: In place of the sliding door of the Runner, the Wagon has four front-hinged doors, and internal seating is in three rows, to seat up to seven. **Summary:** Very similar to the Runner to drive, the Wagon benefits from its slightly longer wheelbase and load-responsive suspension, but feels a larger vehicle on the road. Clever design, with second and third rows of seats arranged to form a bed for camping if required.

MORGAN (GB)   Plus 8

Identity: Last year I included the Plus 4 16V, launched May 1988, using the Rover M16 engine. Then Charles Morgan wrote, saying: 'Why don't you feature the Plus 8? It's our best seller, and more exciting.' So here it is. Power unit is the Rover engine, in Range Rover 3.9-litre form.

Engine: Front-mounted longitudinal V8-cylinder with alloy block and heads; pushrod ohv with hydraulic tappets. Lucas electronic fuel injection. Bore 94.0 mm, stroke 71.1 mm; capacity 3946 cc. Power 190 PS (140 kW) at 4750 rpm; torque 235 lb ft (325 Nm) at 2600 rpm. Compression 9.4-to-1. Catalyst: standard.

Transmission: Rear-wheel drive; five-speed manual gearbox. Automatic, not available. Top gear speed at 1000 rpm: 27.6 mph (44.4 km/h).

Suspension: Front, independent, sliding pillars and coil springs. Rear, live axle on leaf springs.

Steering: Rack and pinion. Power assistance: not available. **Brakes:** Solid discs front, drums rear. ABS: not available. **Tyres:** 205/60 VR 15. **Fuel tank:** 12.0 Imp gall (55 litres). **Unladen weight:** 2060 lb (934 kg).

Dimensions: Length 156.0 in (3962 mm), width 63.0 in (1600 mm), height 48.0 in (1219 mm), wheelbase 98.0 in (2489 mm).

Performance _Autocar & Motor_ test: Maximum speed 121 mph (195 km/h); 0 to 60 mph (97 km/h) 6.1 sec; 80 mph (130 km/h) 10.6 sec. Fuel consumption at constant 75 mph (120 km/h): no data; overall test, 20.1 mpg.

Features: Very basic equipment, but there are hood and tonneau covers, and the V8 has stylish alloy wheels. **Summary:** Morgan was one of the few companies to manage an increase in production during 1991, which perhaps means you only have to wait six years now to take delivery, instead of seven! Totally impractical, but great fun—when it's in contact with the road.

Identity: This new range of saloon and hatchback models was launched Birmingham 1990, to succeed the Bluebird. Front-wheel drive and choice of 1.6- or 2.0-litre engines, both with 16 valves. Best value is at the lower end of the range. Choice of L, LS, GS, GSX and even ZX trim.

Engine: Front-mounted transverse four-cylinder with alloy head and twin ohc working four valves per cylinder. Twin-choke carb. Bore 76.0 mm, stroke 88.0 mm; capacity 1597 cc. Power 95 PS (70 kW) at 6000 rpm; torque 99 lb ft (137 Nm) at 4000 rpm. Compression 9.8-to-1. Catalyst: optional.

Transmission: Front-wheel drive; five-speed manual gearbox. Automatic, optional extra on 2-litre only. Top gear speed at 1000 rpm: 22.7 mph (36.6 km/h).

Suspension: Front, independent, MacPherson struts with multi-link location; anti-roll bar. Rear, independent, struts with parallel links; anti-roll bar.

Steering: Rack and pinion. Power assistance: standard. **Brakes:** Vented discs front, solid discs rear. ABS: not available. **Tyres:** 165 R 13. **Fuel tank:** 13.2 Imp. gall (60 litres). **Unladen weight:** 2375 lb (1077 kg).

Dimensions: Length 173.2 in (4400 mm), width 66.9 in (1700 mm), height 54.7 in (1390 mm), wheelbase 100.4 in (2550 mm).

Performance *Autocar & Motor* test: Maximum speed 111 mph (179 km/h); 0 to 60 mph (97 km/h) 12.4 sec; 80 mph (130 km/h) 22.1 sec. Fuel consumption at constant 75 mph (120 km/h): 42.2 mpg; overall test, 29.2 mpg.

Features: Neat finish and quite generous equipment, even at the LS level, includes such items as sunroof and tilt-adjustable steering column.
Summary: Perhaps it's because the Primera does everything unobtrusively well that it seems somewhat lacking in character; even with the 16-valve engine, performance is unremarkable. The engine is extremely smooth, and all controls are precise, making it an easy car to drive.

NISSAN   (J)   Primera 2.0 SLX Estate

Identity: Although the Primera saloon is the mainstay of production at the Nissan plant in Sunderland, the estate car is imported fully made-up from Japan. There are six versions, with 1.6- or 2.0-litre engine, two trim levels, and manual or automatic transmission.

Engine: Front-mounted transverse four-cylinder with all-alloy construction and twin ohc working four valves per cylinder. Single point fuel injection. Bore 86.0 mm, stroke 86.0 mm; capacity 1998 cc. Power 116 PS (85 kW) at 6000 rpm; torque 122 lb ft (169 Nm) at 4000 rpm. Compression 9.5-to-1. Catalyst: standard.

Transmission: Front-wheel drive; five-speed manual gearbox. Automatic, optional extra, four-speed. Top gear speed at 1000 rpm: 20.8 mph (33.5 km/h).

Suspension: Front, independent, MacPherson struts, anti-roll bar. Rear, torsion beam axle on trailing arms with Panhard rod; coil springs.

Steering: Rack and pinion. Power assistance: standard. **Brakes:** Vented discs front, solid discs rear. ABS: not available. **Tyres:** 195/65 R 14. **Fuel tank:** 13.2 Imp. gall (60 litres). **Unladen weight:** 2678 lb (1215 kg).

Dimensions: Length 175.6 in (4460 mm), width 66.7 in (1694 mm), height 57.9 in (1470 mm), wheelbase 100.4 in (2550 mm).

Performance *Autocar & Motor* test (saloon): Maximum speed 121 mph (195 km/h); 0 to 60 mph (97 km/h) 8.9 sec; 80 mph (130 km/h) 15.5 sec. Fuel consumption at constant 75 mph (120 km/h): 34.9 mpg; overall test, 26.0 mpg.

Features: Tailgate opens wide and high to facilitate loading; rear seats divide 60/40 and fold. Luggage tonneau cover provided. **Summary:** Roof rails are fitted, and the Primera Estate comes with central locking and electric action for door mirrors and windows; SLX also gets an electric sunroof. The estate is longer and taller than the saloon.

117

NISSAN (J)   Sunny 100 NX 1.6 Coupé

Identity: Replacement Sunny range introduced February 1991 offers 1.4 LS with three, four or five doors, 1.6 GS four- or five-door, and this attractive little coupé, the 100 NX. There are deep scoops for the headlamps; otherwise it's pleasantly styled.

Engine: Front-mounted transverse four-cylinder with alloy block and twin ohc working four valves per cylinder; single point fuel injection. Bore 76.0 mm, stroke 88.0 mm; capacity 1597 cc. Power 95 PS (70 kW) at 6000 rpm; torque 97 lb ft (134 Nm) at 4000 rpm. Compression 9.8-to-1. Catalyst: standard.

Transmission: Front-wheel drive; five-speed manual gearbox. Automatic, optional extra. Top gear speed at 1000 rpm: 21.1 mph (33.9 km/h).

Suspension: Front, independent, MacPherson struts. Rear, independent, parallel links.

Steering: Rack and pinion. Power assistance: standard. **Brakes:** Vented discs front, drums rear. ABS: not available. **Tyres:** 155 SR 13. **Fuel tank:** 11.0 Imp. gall (50 litres). **Unladen weight:** 2072 lb (940 kg).

Dimensions: Length 162.8 in (4135 mm), width 65.7 in (1670 mm), height 51.6 in (1310 mm), wheelbase 95.7 in (2430 mm).

Performance *Autocar & Motor* test: Maximum speed 114 mph (183 km/h); 0 to 60 mph (97 km/h) 10.1 sec; 80 mph (130 km/h) 18.8 sec. Fuel consumption at constant 75 mph (120 km/h): 40.9 mpg; overall test, 27.2 mpg.

Features: Sporty appearance inside, with wrap-round seats and good instrumentation. T-bar roof with removable panels as illustrated is an option. **Summary:** The unhappy dispute between the European HQ and the British importer put rather a damper on the launch. The new Sunny appeared clearly over-priced, taking away the attraction, with the Coupé priced over £15,000 with UK taxes. A year later, in February 1992, it was at a more realistic price of £12,290.

NISSAN (J)   200 SX

Identity: Replacement for the Silvia Turbo 1.8ZX, the 200 SX was launched Birmingham 1988; on market early 1989 as a stylish 2 + 2 sports coupé, again with 1.8 turbo engine. Bumpers are colour keyed, and there are deeply recessed side and indicator lamps, with pop-up headlamps.

Engine: Front-mounted longitudinal four-cylinder with twin ohc operating four valves per cylinder. Electronic injection/ignition and turbocharger. Bore 83.0 mm, stroke 83.6 mm; capacity 1809 cc. Power 171 PS (126 kW) at 6400 rpm; torque 165 lb ft (228 Nm) at 4000 rpm. Compression 8.5-to-1. Catalyst: not available.

Transmission: Rear-wheel drive; five-speed manual gearbox. Automatic, four-speed optional. Top gear speed at 1000 rpm: 23.6 mph (37.9 km/h).

Suspension: Front, independent, MacPherson struts, anti-roll bar. Rear, independent, multi-link location; coil springs, anti-roll bar.

Steering: Rack and pinion. Power assistance: standard. **Brakes:** Vented discs front, solid discs rear, servo-assisted. ABS: standard. **Tyres:** 195/60 VR 15. **Fuel tank:** 13.2 Imp. gall (60 litres). **Unladen weight:** 2623 lb (1190 kg).

Dimensions: Length 178.5 in (4535 mm), width 66.5 in (1690 mm), height 50.8 in (1290 mm), wheelbase 97.4 in (2475 mm).

Performance *Autocar & Motor* test: Maximum speed 140 mph (225 km/h); 0 to 60 mph (97 km/h) 7.2 sec; 80 mph (130 km/h) 11.9 sec. Fuel consumption at constant 75 mph (120 km/h): 34.9; overall test, 19.3 mpg.

Features: Boomerang-shaped rear spoiler and generally smooth shape contribute to 0.30 CD factor. Full instrumentation and equipment. **Summary:** A most exciting GT to drive, with vigorous performance and very pleasing handling and controls. It was relaunched with reduced price in January 1992.

OLDSMOBILE (USA)   **Bravada**

Identity: Described as 'another new Oldsmobile thrust into a fresh area of the marketplace', the Bravada was added to the range for 1991, featuring a V6 engine and permanent four-wheel drive. It is not very inspiring to look at, but promises roominess and ruggedness.

Engine: Front-mounted longitudinal V6-cylinder with central camshaft and pushrod overhead valves; hydraulic tappets. Electronic fuel injection. Bore 101.6 mm, stroke 88.4 mm; capacity 4300 cc. Power 162 PS (119 kW) at 4000 rpm; torque 230 lb ft (318 Nm) at 2800 rpm. Compression 9.3-to-1. Catalyst: standard.

Transmission: Four-wheel drive; four-speed automatic, standard. Electronically controlled torque converter lock-up. Top gear speed at 1000 rpm: 34.2 mph (55.0 km/h).

Suspension: Front, independent, wishbones and torsion bars; anti-roll bar. Rear, live axle on semi-elliptic leaf springs.

Steering: Recirculating ball. Power assistance: standard. **Brakes:** Solid discs front, drums rear. ABS: standard. **Tyres:** P235/75 R 15. **Fuel tank:** 16.7 Imp. gall (76 litres). **Unladen weight:** 3720 lb (1687 kg).

Dimensions: Length 178.9 in (4544 mm), width 65.2 in (1656 mm), height 65.6 in (1666 mm), wheelbase 107.0 in (2717 mm).

Performance (est): Maximum speed 105 mph (169 km/h); 0 to 60 mph (97 km/h) 12.0 sec. Fuel consumption overall (est): 20 mpg.

Features: Four-wheel drive is permanently engaged, using a centre viscous coupling. Bucket seats are fitted, with leather trim optional.
Summary: This is a fairly late entry into a market already well supplied with a big choice of Japanese and British off-road vehicles. A more original design might have been expected from the vast Oldsmobile resources.

PEUGEOT (F)   106 1.1 XT

Identity: When trying the new 106 range in France, I was well pleased by them all, but particularly taken with the quietness and eagerness of the 1.1, in relation to its engine size. Launched Frankfurt 1991, and shown at Motorfair; on sale in UK from November 1991, initially only three-door.

Engine: Front-mounted transverse four-cylinder with alloy block and head, single ohc; eight valves. Solex carb. Bore 72.0 mm, stroke 69.0 mm; capacity 1124 cc. Power 60 PS (44 kW) at 5800 rpm; torque 66 lb ft (90 Nm) at 3200 rpm. Compression 9.4-to-1. Catalyst: optional.

Transmission: Front-wheel drive; five-speed manual gearbox. Automatic, not available. Top gear speed at 1000 rpm: 20.2 mph (32.5 km/h).

Suspension: Front, independent, MacPherson struts, anti-roll bar. Rear, independent, trailing arms and transverse torsion bars.

Steering: Rack and pinion. Power assistance: not available. **Brakes:** Solid discs front, drums rear. ABS: not available. **Tyres:** 145/70 TR 13. **Fuel tank:** 9.9 Imp. gall (45 litres). **Unladen weight:** 1740 lb (790 kg).

Dimensions: Length 140.3 in (3564 mm), width 62.5 in (1590 mm), height 53.8 in (1369 mm), wheelbase 93.8 in (2385 mm).

Performance *Autocar & Motor* test: Maximum speed 97 mph (156 km/h); 0 to 60 mph (97 km/h) 13.8 sec; 80 mph (130 km/h) 27.9 sec. Fuel consumption at constant 75 mph (120 km/h): 47.9 mpg; overall test, 32.1 mpg.

Features: Remote central locking featured on my test car, but it turned out to be an extra; standard equipment is fairly basic. **Summary:** Lively and pleasant car to drive, and proved very acceptable for a long journey in the UK, after the launch. Seats are comfortable, but ride not as good as in the larger 205 model.

PEUGEOT   (F)   **106 XSi**

Identity: Top of the new 106 range is the sporty XSi, still only with 1360 cc, but in more highly tuned form than the XT version. It is available with or without catalyst, giving 95 or 100 PS respectively. Special alloy wheels and wheel-arch fairings identify the XSi.

Engine: Front-mounted transverse four-cylinder with alloy head; single ohc working eight valves. Bosch Motronic fuel injection/ignition system. Bore 75.0 mm, stroke 77.0 mm; capacity 1360 cc. Power 95 PS (69 kW) at 6600 rpm; torque 88 lb ft (122 Nm) at 4200 rpm. Compression 9.6-to-1. Catalyst: optional.

Transmission: Front-wheel drive; five-speed manual gearbox. Automatic, not available. Top gear speed at 1000 rpm: 17.7 mph (28.5 km/h).

Suspension: Front, independent, MacPherson struts, anti-roll bar. Rear, independent, trailing arms and transverse torsion bars.

Steering: Rack and pinion. Power assistance: not available. **Brakes:** Vented discs front, drums rear. ABS: optional. **Tyres:** 175/60 R 14. **Fuel tank:** 9.9 Imp. gall (45 litres). **Unladen weight:** 1896 lb (860 kg).

Dimensions: Length 140.3 in (3564 mm), width 63.3 in (1607 mm), height 53.5 in (1360 mm), wheelbase 93.8 in (2385 mm).

Performance Works: Maximum speed 118 mph (190 km/h); 0 to 62 mph (100 km/h) 9.6 sec. Fuel consumption at constant 75 mph (120 km/h): 38.7 mpg.

Features: Body-coloured front skirt houses twin long-range lamps; spoiler at rear. More generous equipment includes central locking and electric windows, but sunroof is an extra. **Summary:** Very sporty little car to drive, with excellent handling and a delightfully taut feel, but it is geared for performance only, and becomes very fussy on a motorway.

PEUGEOT (F)   205 CTI Cabriolet

Identity: For the first five years since its 1986 introduction, the charming little 205 CTI was not available with the 1.9-litre engine. The CTI 1.9 was finally introduced late 1991 to offset the power loss of standard fitting of an exhaust catalyst. Electric hood action was introduced Geneva 1990.

Engine: Front-mounted transverse four-cylinder with alloy block and head; wet cylinder liners. Belt-driven ohc; eight valves. Single point fuel injection. Bore 83.0 mm, stroke 88.0 mm; capacity 1905 cc. Power 105 PS (77 kW) at 6000 rpm; torque 103 lb ft (142 Nm) at 4000 rpm. Compression 8.4-to-1. Catalyst: standard.

Transmission: Front-wheel drive; five-speed manual gearbox. Automatic, not available. Top gear speed at 1000 rpm: 18.7 mph (30.1 km/h).

Suspension: Front, independent, MacPherson struts, anti-roll bar. Rear, independent, trailing arms and transverse torsion bars; anti-roll bar.

Steering: Rack and pinion. Power assistance: optional. **Brakes:** Vented discs front, drums rear. ABS: not available. **Tyres:** 185/60 HR 14. **Fuel tank:** 11.0 Imp. gall (50 litres). **Unladen weight:** 2060 lb (935 kg).

Dimensions: Length 145.9 in (3705 mm), width 62.6 in (1589 mm), height 54.3 in (1381 mm), wheelbase 95.3 in (2420 mm).

Performance Works: Maximum speed 115 mph (185 km/h); 0 to 62 mph (100 km/h) 10.6 sec. Fuel consumption at constant 75 mph (120 km/h): 32.1 mpg.

Features: Electric hood action is standard; electric front windows and central locking come as a combined option. **Summary:** Some of the sparkle seems to have gone from the CTI as a result of the catalyst: it's now slower, and uses more fuel. It will also no doubt be even more expensive to insure on account of the larger engine size, despite the loss of performance.

PEUGEOT (F)   205 D Turbo

Identity: Having a Peugeot 205 GRD in the family, I have often wondered what it would be like if the turbocharged version of the 1.8-litre diesel could be squeezed in. Then, at Paris 1990, this very concept was added to the range, though without intercooler. On the British market early 1991.

Engine: Front-mounted transverse four-cylinder with alloy head and belt-driven ohc. Bosch or Lucas fuel injection, and KKK-K14 turbocharger. Bore 80.0 mm, stroke 88.0 mm; capacity 1769 cc. Power 78 PS (57.5 kW) at 4300 rpm; torque 114 lb ft (157 Nm) at 2100 rpm. Compression 22.0-to-1. Catalyst: not required.

Transmission: Front-wheel drive; five-speed manual gearbox. Automatic, not available. Top gear speed at 1000 rpm: 24.5 mph (39.4 km/h).

Suspension: Front, independent, MacPherson struts, anti-roll bar. Rear, independent, trailing arms and transverse torsion bars.

Steering: Rack and pinion. Power assistance: optional. **Brakes:** Solid discs front, drums rear. ABS: not available. **Tyres:** 165/65 R 14. **Fuel tank:** 11.0 Imp. gall (50 litres). **Unladen weight:** 2030 lb (920 kg).

Dimensions: Length 145.9 in (3706 mm), width 61.9 in (1572 mm), height 53.9 in (1369 mm), wheelbase 95.3 in (2421 mm).

Performance *Autocar & Motor* test: Maximum speed 103 mph (166 km/h); 0 to 60 mph (97 km/h) 12.3 sec; 80 mph (130 km/h) 24.0 sec. Fuel consumption at constant 75 mph (120 km/h): 40.9 mpg; overall test, 34.4 mpg.

Features: GTI-type skirt is fitted at the front, housing two long-range spot lamps. The name on the boot shows '205 D' in grey, and 'Turbo' in red. **Summary:** Improved instrumentation for this more sporty version of the popular 205 diesel includes a rev counter, and seats are upholstered in two-tone velour. The D Turbo should prove an ideal long-distance commuting car.

PEUGEOT (F)

Identity: During 1986 the power of the 1-6-litre GTI engine was increased to 115 PS, and then a new high performance version with 1.9-litre injection engine was launched Birmingham 1986, in production December—a superb little flyer! Supplementing the 205 GTI 1.6, it came on to the British market from beginning of 1987.

Engine: Front-mounted transverse four-cylinder with alloy head and block; wet cylinder liners. Belt-driven ohc. Bosch L-Jetronic fuel injection. Bore 83.0 mm, stroke 88.0 mm; capacity 1905 cc. Power 130 PS (96 kW) at 6000 rpm; torque 119 lb ft (165 Nm) at 4750 rpm. Compression 9.6-to-1. Catalyst: optional.

Transmission: Front-wheel drive; five-speed manual gearbox. No automatic transmission option. Top gear speed at 1000 rpm: 20.9 mph (33.6 km/h).

Suspension: Front, independent, MacPherson struts; anti-roll bar. Rear, independent, trailing arms and transverse torsion bars; anti-roll bar.

Steering: Rack and pinion. Power assistance: not available. **Brakes:** Vented discs front, solid rear. ABS: optional. **Tyres:** 185/55 VR 15. **Fuel tank:** 11.0 Imp. gall (50 litres). **Unladen weight:** 1929 lb (875 kg).

Dimensions: Length 145.9 in (3706 mm), width 61.9 in (1572 mm), height 53.3 in (1354 mm), wheelbase 95.3 in (2421 mm).

Performance *Autocar & Motor* test: Maximum speed 120 mph (193 km/h); 0 to 60 mph (97 km/h) 7.8 sec; 80 mph (130 km/h) 13.7 sec. Fuel consumption at constant 75 mph (120 km/h): 36.7 mpg. Overall test, 28.1 mpg.

Features: Luxury interior, including leather-trimmed wheel, and seats with velour facings and leather side cushions. Sunroof optional.
Summary: Delightful car to drive with its very responsive and smooth engine bringing new boost of power to the already quick GTI. Contender for the title of 'most desirable hot hatchback'.

PEUGEOT (F)

309 GTI

Identity: One of the criticisms of Peugeot's superbly responsive and fast 309 GTI was answered at Motorfair 1989 when the tailgate was continued down between the tail lamps, making loading up easier. The spoiler, previously at the base of the rear window, became a separate wing at the back.

Engine: Front-mounted transverse four-cylinder with alloy block and head. Single ohc and Bosch LE2 fuel injection. Bore 83.0 mm, stroke 88.0 mm; capacity 1905 cc. Power 130 PS (96 kW) at 6000 rpm; torque 119 lb ft (165 Nm) at 4750 rpm. Compression 9.6-to-1. Catalyst: optional.

Transmission: Front-wheel drive; five-speed manual gearbox. Automatic, not available. Top gear speed at 1000 rpm: 20.9 mph (33.6 km/h).

Suspension: Front, independent, MacPherson struts, anti-roll bar. Rear, independent, trailing arms and transverse torsion bars, anti-roll bar.

Steering: Rack and pinion. Power assistance: standard. **Brakes:** Vented discs front, solid discs rear. ABS: not available. **Tyres:** 185/55 HR 15. **Fuel tank:** 12.1 Imp. gall (55 litres). **Unladen weight:** 2050 lb (930 kg).

Dimensions: Length 159.4 in (4051 mm), width 64.0 in (1628 mm), height 54.3 in (1380 mm), wheelbase 97.2 in (2469 mm).

Performance *Autocar & Motor* test: Maximum speed 119 mph (191 km/h); 0 to 60 mph (97 km/h) 8.7 sec; 80 mph (130 km/h) 15.6 sec. Fuel consumption at constant 75 mph (120 km/h): 36.2 mpg; overall test, 28.2 mpg.

Features: Improved specification for 1990 brought in electric windows and central locking as standard, previously options. Sliding glass sunroof is also provided. **Summary:** Very attractive car offering a good combination of speed, handling and comfort. Tends to get a bit busy on a motorway journey, but great fun on twisting roads, with the inevitable penalty of rather firm ride.

PEUGEOT (GB, F)

Identity: Impressive four-wheel drive versions were added to the 405 range in March 1989, and the GL × 4 is essentially a 'working' car, rather than a prestige model, to give very competent road behaviour and the traction to keep going in all conditions.

Engine: Front-mounted transverse four-cylinder with alloy block and head. Single ohc carburettor. Bore 83.0 mm, stroke 88.0 mm; capacity 1905 cc. Power 110 PS (81 kW) at 6000 rpm; torque 119 lb ft (165 Nm) at 3000 rpm. Compression 9.3-to-1. Catalyst: not available.

Transmission: Four-wheel drive; five-speed manual gearbox. Automatic, not available. Lockable centre and rear diffs. Top gear speed at 1000 rpm: 22.0 mph (35.4 km/h).

Suspension: Front, independent, MacPherson struts, anti-roll bar. Rear, independent, trailing arms and electrically pressurised gas springs with hydrauulic self-levelling; anti-roll bar.

Steering: Rack and pinion. Power assistance: standard. **Brakes:** Vented discs front, solid discs rear. ABS: optional. **Tyres:** 185/65 R 14T. **Fuel tank:** 15.4 Imp. gall (70 litres). **Unladen weight:** 2557 lb (1160 kg).

Dimensions: Length 173.5 in (4408 mm), width 67.5 in (1714 mm), height 55.1 (1400 mm), wheelbase 105.0 in (2667 mm).

Performance *Autocar & Motor* test: Maximum speed 115 mph (185 km/h); 0 to 60 mph (97 km/h) 10.9 sec; 80 mph (130 km/h) 20.3 sec. Fuel consumption at constant 75 mph (120 km/h): 34.5 mpg; overall test, 24.4 mpg.

Features: Equipment is the same as for the front-drive GL and includes remote control central locking and electric glass sunroof. **Summary:** Four-wheel drive plus the oleo-pneumatic rear suspension with self-levelling achieves a tremendous improvement to the handling of the already good 405, and makes this a most attractive and competent car.

Identity: In July 1988 I ran an extended economy test for Lucas on a Peugeot 405 GTDT equipped with their new Epic fuel pump, and travelled 1,118 miles on a tankful, at 73.4 mpg. Later, the same car lapped Millbrook test track at 113 mph—highly impressive for a 1.8-litre diesel.

Engine: Front-mounted transverse four-cylinder with cast iron block and alloy head; belt-driven single ohc. KKK or Garrett Turbocharger, with inter-cooler. Bore 80.0 mm, stroke 88.0 mm; capacity 1769 cc. Power 92 PS (67 kW) at 4300 rpm; torque 132 lb ft (183 Nm) at 2200 rpm. Compression 22.0-to-1. Catalyst: not required.

Transmission: Front-wheel drive; five-speed manual gearbox. Automatic, not available. Top gear speed at 1000 rpm: 25.3 mph (40.7 km/h).

Suspension: Front, independent, MacPherson struts, anti-roll bar. Rear, independent, trailing arms, transverse torsion bars; anti-roll bar.

Steering: Rack and pinion. Power assistance: standard. **Brakes:** Vented discs front, drums rear. ABS: optional. **Tyres:** 185/66 HR 14. **Fuel tank:** 15.4 Imp. gall (70 litres). **Unladen weight:** 2680 lb (1215 kg).

Dimensions: Length 173.5 in (4408 mm), width 66.6 in (1694 mm), height 55.4 in (1406 mm), wheelbase 105.1 in (2669 mm).

Performance *Autocar & Motor* test: Maximum speed 108 mph (174 km/h); 0 to 62 mph (100 km/h) 12.2 sec; 80 mph (130 km/h) 23.5 sec. Fuel consumption at constant 75 mph (120 km/h): 45.6 mpg; overall test, 31.3 mpg.

Features: This is the top diesel of the 405 range, and it is well-equipped to the same level as the GTX. **Summary:** On that extended test run, the 405 GTDT proved very comfortable during long hours at the wheel, and the turbocharged diesel engine copes manfully with this big saloon.

PEUGEOT (F, GB)

405 Mi16 4 × 4

Identity: As well as the GL version, the 405 is also available with four-wheel drive in Mi16 form, and with this 16-valve 160 bhp engine, the performance and handling are outstandingly good. Badge in red at rear of boot identifies the 4 × 4 version, and it differs from the GL in having a viscous coupling and Torsen rear diff.

Engine: Front-mounted transverse four-cylinder with alloy block and head. Twin ohc working four valves per cylinder; Bosch Motronic fuel injection. Bore 83.0 mm, stroke 88.0 mm; capacity 1905 cc. Power 160 PS (116 kW) at 6500 rpm; torque 133 lb ft (183 Nm) at 5000 rpm. Compression 10.4-to-1. Catalyst: optional.

Transmission: Four-wheel drive; five-speed manual gearbox. Automatic, not available. Self-blocking viscous differential control. Top gear speed at 1000 rpm: 20.0 mph (32.2 km/h).

Suspension: Front, independent, MacPherson struts, anti-roll bar. Rear, independent, trailing arms and electrically pressurised gas springs with hydraulic self-levelling; anti-roll bar.

Steering: Rack and pinion. Power assistance: standard. **Brakes:** Vented discs front, solid discs rear. ABS: standard. **Tyres:** 195/55 R 15V. **Fuel tank:** 15.4 Imp. gall (70 litres). **Unladen weight:** 2734 lb (1240 kg).

Dimensions: Length 173.5 in (4408 mm), width 67.6 in (1716 mm), height 55.1 in (1400 mm), wheelbase 105.0 in (2667 mm).

Performance *Autocar & Motor* test: Maximum speed 127 mph (204 km/h); 0 to 60 mph (97 km/h) 9.5 sec; 80 mph (130 km/h) 16.5 sec. Fuel consumption at constant 75 mph (120 km/h): 33.2 mpg; overall test, 26.0 mpg.

Features: Equipment is the same as for the front-drive Mi16, and is very comprehensive; air conditioning and leather seats with heating are about the only options to be considered. **Summary:** An outstandingly safe car with magnificent handling, and still very fast although of course the extra weight and resistance take away some of the Mi16 sparkle.

PEUGEOT (F)   605 SRi 2.0

Identity: France's new big car—in addition to the Citroen XM—to fight back against Jaguar, BMW, Mercedes, is the 605, launched Frankfurt 1989, and on British market from May 1990. In this form as the SRi, it is aimed firmly at the executive fleet market. It bears family resemblance to the 405, but is sufficiently different not to be confused with it.

Engine: Front-mounted transverse four-cylinder with alloy head and single ohc. Bosch LE2 fuel injection. Bore 86.0 mm, stroke 86.0 mm; capacity 1998 cc. Power 94 PS (68 kW) at 5600 rpm; torque 175 lb ft (242 Nm) at 4800 rpm. Compression 8.8-to-1. Catalyst: standard.

Transmission: Front-wheel drive; five-speed manual gearbox. Automatic, not available. Top gear speed at 1000 rpm: 20.3 mph (32.7 km/h).

Suspension: Front, independent, MacPherson struts, anti-roll bar. Rear, independent, wishbones and coil springs; anti-roll bar.

Steering: Rack and pinion. Power assistance: standard. **Brakes:** Vented discs front, solid discs rear. ABS: optional. **Tyres:** 195/65 R 15H. **Fuel tank:** 17.6 Imp. gall (80 litres). **Unladen weight:** 2920 lb (1325 kg).

Dimensions: Length 185.9 in (4723 mm), width 70.8 in (1799 mm), height 55.8 in (1417 mm), wheelbase 110.2 in (2800 mm).

Performance *Autocar & Motor* test: Maximum speed 121 mph (195 km/h); 0 to 60 mph (97 km/h) 11.8 sec; 80 mph (130 km/h) 20.2 sec. Fuel consumption at constant 75 mph (120 km/h): 32.1 mpg; overall test, 24.7 mpg.

Features: SRi is the sporting model of the 605 range and has intermediate level equipment with such features as outside temperature gauge, and seats with height adjustment. **Summary:** Smooth, rapid transport with generous five-seater space, and good handling. The optional four-speed automatic transmission is also outstandingly good.

PEUGEOT (F) 605 SVE 24

Identity: Luxury model of the new 605 range is the SVE24, with 24-valve V6 engine, giving really vigorous performance. There is also an intermediate V6 with 12 valves, offered in the SV and SVE automatic. The standard 3-litre goes well, but as the SVE24 with the multi-valve heads it's very quick indeed.

Engine: Front-mounted transverse V6-cylinder with alloy heads and block; single ohc per bank, working four valves per cylinder. Fenix 4 fuel injection. Bore 93.0 mm, stroke 73.0 mm; capacity 2975 cc. Power 147 PS (106 kW) at 6000 rpm; torque 260 lb ft (360 Nm) at 4800 rpm. Compression 9.5-to-1. Catalyst: standard.

Transmission: Front-wheel drive; five-speed manual gearbox. Automatic, optional. Top gear speed at 1000 rpm: 22.9 mph (36.9 km/h).

Suspension: Front, independent, MacPherson struts with automatic damper control; anti-roll bar. Rear, independent, wishbones and coil springs with automatic damper control; anti-roll bar.

Steering: Rack and pinion. Power assistance: standard. **Brakes:** Vented discs front, solid discs rear. ABS: standard. **Tyres:** 205/55 R 16V. **Fuel tank:** 17.6 Imp. gall (80 litres). **Unladen weight:** 3220 lb (1460 kg).

Dimensions: Length 185.9 in (4723 mm), width 70.8 in (1799 mm), height 55.5 in (1411 mm), wheelbase 110.2 in (2800 mm).

Performance *Autocar & Motor* test: Maximum speed 142 mph (228 km/h); 0 to 60 mph (97 km/h) 7.9 sec; 80 mph (130 km/h) 13.6 sec. Fuel consumption at constant 75 mph (120 km/h): 27.7 mpg; overall test, 20.4 mpg.

Features: Luxurious trim and equipment in this top version of the 605, includes leather upholstery and electric sunroof. **Summary:** With the 24-valve engine, the 605 gives really vigorous response and is a strong contender for the senior executive market. On the launch in Egypt I was most impressed by the 605's comfort and stability when cruising at 120 mph.

PONTIAC (USA) SSEi

Identity: Both the Bonneville and the Grand Am model ranges are new for 1992, and the SSEi is the top version of the Bonneville line. This is the thirty-fifth year there has been a Bonneville in the Pontiac range. The SSEi has a supercharged V6 engine developing 205 PS.

Engine: Front-mounted transverse V6-cylinder with sequential port fuel injection, counter-rotating balance shaft, and belt-driven Roots-type supercharger. Bore 96.5 mm, stroke 86.4 mm; capacity 3800 cc. Power 205 PS (151 kW) at 4400 rpm; torque 260 lb ft (360 Nm) at 2800 rpm. Compression 8.5-to-1. Catalyst: standard.

Transmission: Front-wheel drive; four-speed automatic, standard. Top gear speed at 1000 rpm: 35.1 mph (56.5 km/h).

Suspension: Front, independent, MacPherson struts, anti-roll bar. Rear, semi-independent, torsion beam and coil springs; anti-roll bar.

Steering: Rack and pinion. Power assistance: standard. **Brakes:** Vented discs front, drums rear. ABS: standard. **Tyres:** P225/60 ZR 16. **Fuel tank:** 15.0 Imp. gall (68 litres). **Unladen weight:** 3607 lb (1636 kg).

Dimensions: Length 200.6 in (5095 mm), width 73.6 in (1869 mm), height 55.5 in (1410 mm), wheelbase 110.8 in (2814 mm).

Performance Works: Maximum speed 115 mph (185 km/h); 0 to 60 mph (97 km/h) 8.7 sec. Fuel consumption overall (est). 24.0 mpg.

Features: All Bonnevilles have driver's side air-bag restraint system, and the SSEi has one on the passenger side as well. Many standard features, and only four options are listed. **Summary:** A number of new ideas are incorporated in the SSEi, including head-up display instruments, traction control system, and radio controls on the steering wheel. These are all familiar enough in Europe, but novelties in the American market.

Identity: Dealers were shocked by the Porsche decision not to attend Motorfair 1991, and on re-think a small stand tucked away at the back was taken. One of the new cars for 1992 was the Cabriolet Turbo Look, which means what it says: looks like the turbo, with the wide wheel arches, but isn't!

Engine: Rear-mounted longitudinal flat six-cylinder with alloy block and heads; single ohc each bank; 12 valves. Bosch Motronic injection and ignition system. Bore 100.0 mm, stroke 76.4 mm; capacity 3600 cc. Power 250 PS (184 kW) at 6100 rpm; torque 224 lb ft (310 Nm) at 4800 rpm. Compression 11.3-to-1. Catalyst: standard.

Transmission: Rear-wheel drive; five-speed manual gearbox. Automatic, optional extra, four-speed. Top gear speed at 1000 rpm: 24.2 mph (38.9 km/h).

Suspension: Front, independent, MacPherson struts, anti-roll bar. Rear, independent, semi-trailing arms and coil springs; anti-roll bar.

Steering: Rack and pinion. Power assistance: standard. **Brakes:** Vented discs front and rear. ABS: standard. **Tyres:** Front, 205/50 ZR 17; rear, 255/40 ZR 17. **Fuel tank:** 17.0 Imp. gall (77 litres). **Unladen weight:** 3130 lb (1420 kg).

Dimensions: Length 167.3 in (4250 mm), width 69.8 in (1715 mm), height 51.5 in (1310 mm), wheelbase 89.4 in (2272 mm).

Performance *Autocar & Motor* test (RS Coupé): Maximum speed 161 mph (259 km/h); 0 to 60 mph (97 km/h) 4.9 sec; 80 mph (130 km/h) 7.9 sec. Fuel consumption at constant 75 mph (120 km/h): 29.1 mpg; overall test, 19.3 mpg.

Features: Hood action is electric, though there is a conventional soft tonneau cover; rear spoiler extends electrically at speed. **Summary:** Performance figures quoted are those for the RS Coupé version of the Carrera, which is slightly quicker than the Cabriolet would be able to manage, but they give an idea of the staggering acceleration.

PORSCHE (D) 928 GTS

Identity: The 928 becomes still more powerful with the introduction of the 5.4-litre version at Frankfurt 1991, on British market from May. Identity features are the new 17 in. 'cup design' wheels and wider rear end styling, and there are more aerodynamically shaped door mirrors.

Engine: Front-mounted longitudinal V8-cylinder with all-alloy construction. Chain and toothed belt drive to twin ohc each bank, working four valves per cylinder. Bosch LH Jetronic fuel injection. Bore 100.0 mm, stroke 85.9 mm; capacity 5396 cc. Power 340 PS (250 kW) at 5700 rpm; torque 362 lb ft (500 Nm) at 5700 rpm. Compression 10.4-to-1. Catalyst: standard.

Transmission: Rear-wheel drive; five-speed manual gearbox in rear transaxle. Automatic, optional extra, four-speed. Top gear speed at 1000 rpm: 26.7 mph (42.9 km/h).

Suspension: Front, independent, wishbones and coil springs, anti-roll bar. Rear, independent, semi-trailing arms and upper transverse links; coil springs with self-levelling provision; anti-roll bar.

Steering: Rack and pinion. Power assistance: standard. **Brakes:** Vented discs front and rear. ABS: standard. **Tyres:** Front, 225/45 ZR 17; rear, 255/40 ZR 17. **Fuel tank:** 19.0 Imp. gall (86 litres). **Unladen weight:** 3570 lb (1620 kg).

Dimensions: Length 177.9 in (4520 mm), width 72.8 in (1836 mm), height 50.5 in (1282 mm), wheelbase 98.4 in (2500 mm).

Performance Works: Maximum speed 171 mph (275 km/h); 0 to 62 mph (100 km/h) 5.7 sec. Fuel consumption at constant 75 mph (120 km/h): 23.7 mpg.

Features: Electronically controlled differential lock-up and tyre-pressure monitoring system are standard features. **Summary:** Top speed is given as 'over 171 mph', which might well be achieved with this bigger engine, although power is up only 10 PS from the 330 developed by the previous 5-litre unit at 6200 rpm. Still one of the world's fastest cars.

Identity: The 968 is a replacement for the 944, launched Frankfurt 1991 and on British market from April 1992, with the biggest four-cylinder engine of recent time. It is offered as Coupé or Cabriolet, and has 928-style lie-back headlamps.

Engine: Front-mounted longitudinal four-cylinder with alloy block and head; two counter-rotating balance shafts. Twin ohc; 16 valves, with varying camshaft timing. Bosch Motronics. Bore 104.0 mm, stroke 88.0 mm; capacity 2990 cc. Power 240 PS (176 kW) at 6200 rpm; torque 221 lb ft (305 Nm) at 4100 rpm. Compression 11.0-to-1. Catalyst: standard.

Transmission: Rear-wheel drive; six-speed manual gearbox in transaxle at rear. Automatic, optional extra, four-speed. Top gear speed at 1000 rpm: 24.9 mph (40.0 km/h).

Suspension: Front, independent, MacPherson struts; anti-roll bar. Rear, independent, semi-trailing arms and transverse torsion bars; anti-roll bar.

Steering: Rack and pinion. Power assistance: standard. **Brakes:** Vented discs front and rear. ABS: standard. **Tyres:** Front, 205/55 ZR 16; rear, 225/50 ZR 16. **Fuel tank:** 16.3 Imp. gall (74 litres). **Unladen weight:** 3020 lb (1370 kg).

Dimensions: Length 170.0 in (4320 mm), width 68.3 in (1735 mm), height 50.2 in (1275 mm), wheelbase 94.5 in (2400 mm).

Performance Works: Maximum speed 156 mph (251 km/h); 0 to 62 mph (100 km/h) 6.5 sec. Fuel consumption at constant 75 mph (120 km/h): 32.1 mpg.

Features: Auxiliary driving and fog lamps are built into the front nose section, which is of deformable polyurethane; sport suspension package and 17 in wheels optional. **Summary:** It remains to be seen whether adoption of such a big engine with only four cylinders will prove wise. Optional automatic transmission is Porsche's over-rated Tiptronic system, which just seems an elaborate way of overcoming the weakness of a poor selector layout.

PROTON (MAL)   1.5 SE Triple Valve

Identity: The first new model to be launched in 1991 was Proton's new range with triple-valve engines, released at one minute past midnight on 31 December. I think most people may have been thinking of something else, or singing, at that time, but the new Proton is worth singing about!

Engine: Front-mounted transverse four-cylinder with alloy head and belt-driven single ohc working three valves per cylinder. Single choke carb. Bore 75.5 mm, stroke 82 mm; capacity 1468 cc. Power 87 PS (64 kW) at 6000 rpm; torque 87 lb ft (120 Nm) at 4000 rpm. Compression 9.5-to-1. Catalyst: not available.

Transmission: Front-wheel drive; five-speed manual gearbox. Automatic, optional extra. Top gear speed at 1000 rpm: 20.0 mph (32.2 km/h).

Suspension: Front, independent, MacPherson struts, anti-roll bar. Rear, independent, trailing arms and coil springs; anti-roll bar.

Steering: Rack and pinion. Power assistance: standard. **Brakes:** Solid discs front, drums rear. ABS: not available. **Tyres:** 155 SR 13. **Fuel tank:** 10.0 Imp. gall (45.5 litres). **Unladen weight:** 2172 lb (985 kg).

Dimensions: Length 169.7 in (4311 mm), width 64.8 in (1645 mm), height 53.5 in (1360 mm), wheelbase 93.7 in (2380 mm).

Performance *Autocar & Motor* test: Maximum speed 98 mph (158 km/h); 0 to 60 mph (97 km/h) 12.4 sec. Fuel consumption at constant 75 mph (120 km/h): 32.8 mpg; overall test, 28.5 mpg.

Features: Many detail improvements were introduced at the same time as the 12-valve engines, including new centre console and better seats. **Summary:** Assessed before the launch, in 1990, the new 12-valve Protons appeared substantially improved, and effectively even better value for money, especially with power steering on the 1.5. The 1.3 is also available, but does not get power steering.

RENAULT (F)   19 1.7 16v

Identity: Renault first unveiled the 19 with more powerful 16-valve engine at Geneva 1990, but it did not come on to the British market until February 1991. At Paris 1990, five-door and saloon versions with the 16-valve engine were added to the previous three-door 16v.

Engine: Front-mounted transverse four-cylinder with alloy head and twin ohc operating four valves per cylinder. Electronic multi-point fuel injection. Bore 82.0 mm, stroke 83.5 mm; capacity 1764 cc. Power 140 PS (103 kW) at 6500 rpm; torque 116 lb ft (161 Nm) at 4250 rpm. Compression 10.0-to-1. Catalyst: not available.

Transmission: Front-wheel drive; five-speed manual gearbox. Automatic, not available. Top gear speed at 1000 rpm: 20.3 mph (31.4 km/h).

Suspension: Front, independent, MacPherson struts; anti-roll bar. Rear, independent, trailing arms with four transverse torsion bars; anti-roll bar.

Steering: Rack and pinion. Power assistance: standard. **Brakes:** Vented discs front, solid discs rear. ABS: optional. **Tyres:** 195/50 R 15 V. **Fuel tank:** 12.1 Imp. gall (55 litres). **Unladen weight:** 2315 lb (1050 kg).

Dimensions: Length 167.7 in (4260 mm), width 66.5 in (1689 mm), height 55.9 in (1420 mm), wheelbase 100.4 in (2550 mm).

Performance *Autocar & Motor* test: Maximum speed 128 mph (206 km/h); 0 to 60 mph (97 km/h) 9.5 sec; 80 mph (130 km/h) 15.9 sec. Fuel consumption at constant 75 mph (120 km/h): 38.2 mpg; overall test, 28.2 mpg.

Features: Double headlamps, a front bumper with soft spoiler beneath and separate wing spoiler on the boot are features of the 16v. **Summary:** With its top speed of over 130 mph and impressive acceleration continuing right through the range, to cover a standing km in under 30 sec, this 16-valve version of the 19 is a very fast car indeed.

RENAULT (F)   19 16v Cabriolet

Identity: Having no roll-over bar, the Renault 19 is a true convertible, but the manufacturer prefers to call it the Cabriolet. It was first shown at Barcelona 1991, and on British market from January 1992, and is available as 16-valve 1764 cc (16v badge on boot), or 1721 cc eight-valve.

Engine: Front-mounted transverse four-cylinder with alloy head and twin ohc working four valves per cylinder. Electronic multi-point fuel injection. Bore 82.0 mm, stroke 83.5 mm; capacity 1764 cc. Power 137 PS (100 kW) at 6500 rpm; torque 119 lb ft (165 Nm) at 4250 rpm. Compression 10.0-to-1. Catalyst: standard.

Transmission: Front-wheel drive; five-speed manual gearbox. Automatic, optional extra, four-speed (eight-valve only). Top gear speed at 1000 rpm: 20.3 mph (31.4 km/h).

Suspension: Front, independent, MacPherson struts, anti-roll bar. Rear, independent, trailing arms with four transverse torsion bars; anti-roll bar.

Steering: Rack and pinion. Power assistance: standard. **Brakes:** Vented discs front, solid discs rear. ABS: optional. **Tyres:** 195/50 R 15V. **Fuel tank:** 12.1 Imp. gall (55 litres). **Unladen weight:** 2601 lb (1180 kg).

Dimensions: Length 167.7 in (4260 mm), width 66.5 in (1689 mm), height 55.9 in (1420 mm), wheelbase 100.4 in (2550 mm).

Performance Works: Maximum speed 130 mph (209 km/h); 0 to 62 mph (100 km/h) 9.4 sec; 80 mph (130 km/h) 16.0 sec. Fuel consumption at constant 75 mph (120 km/h): 35.7 mpg.

Features: Neat hood-folding arrangement into a well with hinged rigid cover, but electric action not available. Generous equipment. **Summary:** A lot of fun to drive, as I discovered in Spain during the winter, but the body is rather lacking in rigidity, with considerable scuttle shake. Alloy wheels are standard (optional for eight-valve), and the 16v can have leather upholstery.

RENAULT (F) 19 Turbo DX

Identity: At the same time as the Cabriolet versions of the 19 were launched in Britain—January 1992—Renault added a most impressive 1.9-litre turbo diesel to the range. With claimed top speed of 114 mph, it is among the fastest diesels on the market, as well as being exceptionally refined.

Engine: Front-mounted transverse four-cylinder with alloy head and single ohc; eight valves. Garrett T2 turbocharger. Bore 80.0 mm, stroke 93.0 mm; capacity 1870 cc. Power 93 PS (68 kW) at 4250 rpm; torque 127 lb ft (175 Nm) at 2250 rpm. Compression 20.5-to-1. Catalyst: not required.

Transmission: Front-wheel drive; five-speed manual gearbox. Automatic, not available. Top gear speed at 1000 rpm: 26.8 mph (43.1 km/h).

Suspension: Front, independent, MacPherson struts, anti-roll bar. Rear, independent, trailing arms with four transverse torsion bars; anti-roll bar.

Steering: Rack and pinion. Power assistance: standard. **Brakes:** Solid discs front, drums rear. ABS: not available. **Tyres:** 175/70 R 13T. **Fuel tank:** 12.1 Imp. gall (55 litres). **Unladen weight:** 2337 lb (1060 kg).

Dimensions: Length 163.5 in (4155 mm), width 66.7 in (1694 mm), height 55.7 in (1416 mm), wheelbase 100.2 in (2545 mm).

Performance Works: Maximum speed 114 mph (183 km/h); 0 to 62 mph (100 km/h) 11.3 sec; 80 mph (130 km/h) 21.1 sec. Fuel consumption at constant 75 mph (120 km/h): 46.3 mpg.

Features: Unusually well-equipped for a diesel, the 19 Turbo DX comes with electric sunroof, electric front windows and remote locking. **Summary:** A little jerky and difficult to drive smoothly in town traffic, but very responsive and quiet at speed. Outstanding for a diesel is the acceleration, which is well sustained at the upper speeds, as shown by the 0–80 mph time.

Identity: Following launch of the 19 16V, the same 137 PS engine became available for the little Clio hatchback model from Motorfair 1991. It offers impressive performance, well ahead of the 5 GT Turbo. Bumpers in body colour, with front fog lamps underneath, and small spoiler above roof are identifying features.

Engine: Front-mounted transverse four-cylinder with alloy head and twin ohc working four valves per cylinder; Renault multi-point fuel injection. Bore 82.0 mm, stroke 83.5 mm; capacity 1764 cc. Power 137 PS (101 kW) at 6500 rpm; torque 114 lb ft (158 Nm) at 4250 rpm. Compression 10.0-to-1. Catalyst: standard.

Transmission: Front-wheel drive; five-speed manual gearbox. Automatic, not available. Top gear speed at 1000 rpm: 19.5 mph (31.4 km/h).

Suspension: Front, independent, MacPherson struts, anti-roll bar. Rear, independent, trailing arms and four transverse torsion bars; anti-roll bar.

Steering: Rack and pinion. Power assistance: standard. **Brakes:** Vented discs front, solid discs rear. ABS: optional. **Tyres:** 185/55 R 15V. **Fuel tank:** 11.0 Imp. gall (50 litres). **Unladen weight:** 2160 lb (980 kg).

Dimensions: Length 146.0 in (3709 mm), width 63.9 in (1625 mm), height 54.9 in (1395 mm), wheelbase 97.3 in (2472 mm).

Performance *Autocar & Motor* test: Maximum speed 126 mph (203 km/h); 0 to 60 mph (97 km/h) 8.6 sec; 80 mph (130 km/h) 14.6 sec. Fuel consumption at constant 75 mph (120 km/h): 36.7 mpg; overall test, 26.0 mpg.

Features: Good equipment includes manual sunroof, remote central locking, and divided folding rear seats. Eight-year anti-corrosion warranty. **Summary:** Attractive combination of vigorous performance with reasonable comfort and very good handling; the Clio 16v is intended to take the place of the very fast little 5 GT Turbo.

RENAULT (F)   Espace V6

Identity: It was quite a surprise to learn that the Espace—one of the most successful of the multi-seat all-purpose vehicles—was to be revised in May 1991, but one reason for this was to launch the new 2.9-litre V6 version. Appearance is also altered, with more aerodynamic frontal shape.

Engine: Front-mounted longitudinal V6-cylinder with alloy block and heads; single ohc each bank, 12 valves. Bendix-Siemens multi-point fuel injection. Bore 91.0 mm, stroke 73.0 mm; capacity 2849 cc. Power 150 PS (110 kW) at 5400 rpm; torque 163 lb ft (225 Nm) at 2500 rpm. Compression 9.5-to-1. Catalyst: standard.

Transmission: Front-wheel drive; five-speed manual gearbox. Automatic, not available. Top gear speed at 1000 rpm: 22.6 mph (36.4 km/h).

Suspension: Front, independent, wishbones and coil springs; anti-roll bar. Rear, torsion beam axle on trailing arms with Panhard rod; varying rate coil springs.

Steering: Rack and pinion. Power assistance: standard. **Brakes:** Vented discs front, solid discs rear. ABS: optional. **Tyres:** 195/65 HR 15. **Fuel tank:** 16.9 Imp. gall (77 litres). **Unladen weight:** 3064 lb (1390 kg).

Dimensions: Length 174.3 in (4429 mm), width 70.6 in (1795 mm), height 71.0 in (1805 mm), wheelbase 101.5 in (2580 mm).

Performance *Autocar & Motor* test: Maximum speed 116 mph (187 km/h); 0 to 60 mph (97 km/h) 9.4 sec; 80 mph (130 km/h) 16.7 sec. Fuel consumption at constant 75 mph (120 km/h): 26.2 mpg; overall test, 19.9 mpg.

Features: Espace V6 is available with RT or the more luxurious RXE trim. Both have remote central locking; RXE has twin tilting sunroofs which are optional for RT. **Summary:** All versions of the Espace come with two rows of individual seats, ingeniously made to be removable or serve as tables; additional two seats in rear are optional. Versatile and extremely comfortable multi-seater, now fast as well.

Identity: At Geneva 1992, a revised version of the former GTA V6 Turbo was introduced, following preview at Barcelona 1991. The new model has a more powerful engine, now 3-litre capacity and giving 250 PS, and a lot of the weight has been moved forward to improve stability.

Engine: Mid-mounted longitudinal V6-cylinder with alloy block and heads. Chain-driven ohc each bank. Fuel injection and Garrett T3 turbocharger with intercooler. Bore 93.0 mm, stroke 73.0 mm; capacity 2975 cc. Power 250 PS (184 kW) at 5750 rpm; torque 253 lb ft (350 Nm) at 2900 rpm. Compression 7.6-to-1. Catalyst: standard.

Transmission: Rear-wheel drive; five-speed manual gearbox. Automatic, not available. Top gear speed at 1000 rpm: 27.2 mph (43.8 km/h).

Suspension: Front, independent, wishbones with coil spring and damper units bearing on to upper wishbones; anti-roll bar. Rear, independent, wishbones with coil spring and damper units bearing on to upper wishbones; anti-roll bar.

Steering: Rack and pinion. Power assistance: standard. **Brakes:** Vented discs front and rear. ABS: standard. **Tyres:** 205/45 R 16 front; 245/45 R 16 rear. **Fuel tank:** 17.6 Imp. gall (80 litres). **Unladen weight:** 3130 lb (1420 kg).

Dimensions: Dimensions: Length 173.8 in (4415 mm), width 69.4 in (1762 mm), height 46.8 in (1188 mm), wheelbase 92.1 in (2340 mm).

Performance Works: Maximum speed 165 mph (265 km/h); 0 to 62 mph (100 km/h) 5.7 sec. Fuel consumption: no data.

Features: Unusual interior with elaborate audio equipment and luxurious appearance; electric window lifts and alloy wheels. **Summary:** Previously the GTA V6 was atrociously unstable due to the excess of weight at the rear, but Renault have now tried to rectify this. The Alpine name is reserved by Chrysler, so the official name is the 'A610 from Alpine'.

RJD   (GB, USA)   **Tempest**

Identity: Launched at the end of December 1990, Tempest results from an attempt to produce the best and fastest two-seater sports car so far. It is the work of former Panther founder Robert Jankel and his company Robert Jankel Design. It is developed from the Chevrolet Corvette L98.

Engine: Front-mounted longitudinal V8-cylinder with alloy heads and block. Carroll supercharger, and water injection. Tuned-port fuel injection. Bore 105.5 mm, stroke 95.3 mm; capacity 6665 cc. Power 535 PS (394 kW) at 5250 rpm; torque 608 lb ft (841 Nm) at 4000 rpm. Compression 10.0-to-1. Catalyst: standard.

Transmission: Rear-wheel drive; six-speed manual gearbox. Automatic, optional extra. Top gear speed at 1000 rpm: 29.6 mph (47.6 km/h).

Suspension: Front, independent, forged aluminium upper and lower control arms and transverse monoleaf spring; anti-roll bar. Rear, independent, five-link location and monoleaf filament-wound carbon fibre composite spring. Gas-filled dampers with three-position electronic ride control.

Steering: Rack and pinion. Power assistance: standard. **Brakes:** Vented discs front and rear. ABS: standard. **Tyres:** P275-40 17 (front); P315-35 17 (rear). **Fuel tank:** 20.0 Imp. gall (91 litres). **Unladen weight:** 3270 lb (1483 kg).

Dimensions: Length 176.5 in (4483 mm), width 71.0 in (1803 mm), height 46.7 in (1186 mm), wheelbase 96.2 in (2444 mm).

Performance Works: Maximum speed 200 mph (322 km/h); 0 to 60 mph (97 km/h) 3.3 sec; 120 mph (193 km/h) 12.0 sec. Fuel: no data.

Features: Very comprehensive specification, including climate control air conditioning, top level Bose audio system, and Connolloy hide upholstery or other materials to choice. **Summary:** Hailed as a 'new statement in sports car performance', this is certainly a most exciting specification, well thought-out and brilliantly designed. UK price at launch was £98,000.

ROLLS-ROYCE (GB) Silver Spirit II

Identity: With the important changes announced for Motorfair 1989, including the introduction of Automatic Ride Control, all Rolls-Royce models took the 'II' designation, which was not applied to Bentley cars. Many subtle changes to the world's most distinguished car were made at the same time.

Engine: Front-mounted longitudinal V8-cylinder with alloy block and heads, and pushrod ohv; hydraulic tappets. Bosch K-Motronic fuel injection. Bore 104.1 mm, stroke 99.1 mm; capacity 6750 cc. Power and torque: no data released. Compression 8.0-to-1. Catalyst: optional.

Transmission: Rear-wheel drive; three-speed GM automatic, with R-R column-mounted control. Speed at 1000 rpm: 30.0 mph (48.3 km/h).

Suspension: Front, independent, wishbones and coil springs with compliant controlled upper levers and electronic damper control; anti-roll bar. Rear, independent, semi-trailing arms; coil springs and self-levelling struts with electronically controlled dampers; anti-roll bar.

Steering: Rack and pinion. Power assistance: standard. **Brakes:** Vented discs front, solid discs rear. ABS: standard. **Tyres:** 235/70 R 15. **Fuel tank:** 23.5 Imp. gall (107 litres). **Unladen weight:** 5180 lb (2350 kg).

Dimensions: Length 207.4 in (5268 mm), width 74.0 in (1879 mm), height 58.5 in (1485 mm), wheelbase 120.5 in (3061 mm).

Performance *Autocar & Motor* test: Maximum speed 126 mph (203 km/h); 0 to 60 mph (97 km/h) 10.4 sec; 80 mph (130 km/h) 17.9 sec. Fuel consumption at 75 mph (120 km/h): 17.6 mpg; overall test, 13.8 mpg.

Features: Redesigned facia with new warning module, improved air conditioning, and still better audio system were among the many 1989 improvements to an already superb car. **Summary:** Big efforts are being made to keep the Rolls-Royce abreast of latest developments, such as remote control anti-theft alarm, now standard. Perhaps we might look forward to out-of-sight parking for the windscreen wipers.

ROVER (GB) 218 SLD Turbo

Identity: Although Rover have their own Perkins-adapted diesel engine, as used in the Montego, they sensibly adopted the much more refined Peugeot diesel engines for the 200 and 400 series in March 1991. The 218 SD has the non-turbo 1.9-litre unit, but all other models are as the 218 SLD, with the excellent 1.8-litre turbo unit.

Engine: Front-mounted transverse four-cylinder with alloy head, single ohc, and KKK turbocharger with intercooler. Lucas fuel injection. Bore 80 mm, stroke 88 mm; capacity 1769 cc. Power 88 PS (65 kW) at 4300 rpm; torque 133 lb ft (180 Nm) at 2500 rpm. Compression: 22-to-1. Catalyst: not required.

Transmission: Front-wheel drive; five-speed manual gearbox. Automatic, not available. Top gear speed at 1000 rpm: 26.0 mph (41.8 km/h).

Suspension: Front, independent, MacPherson struts, anti-roll bar. Rear, independent, wishbones with compensating trailing arm, coil springs, anti-roll bar.

Steering: Rack and pinion. Power assistance: standard. **Brakes:** Vented discs front, drums rear. ABS: optional. **Tyres:** 175/70 TR 14. **Fuel tank:** 12.1 Imp. gall (55 litres). **Unladen weight:** 2612 lb (1185 kg).

Dimensions: Length 166.1 in (4220 mm), width 66.1 in (1680 mm), height 55.0 in (1400 mm), wheelbase 100.4 in (2550 mm).

Performance Works: Maximum speed 106 mph (171 km/h); 0 to 60 mph (97 km/h) 11.8 sec; 80 mph (130 km/h) 23.0 sec. Fuel consumption at constant 75 mph (120 km/h): 46.5 mpg.

Features: This model has the five-door hatchback body, but same specification is available in the saloon as 418 SLD or GSD. Good equipment. **Summary:** Excellent mid-range business car offering comfortable travel for long journeys with outstanding fuel economy, yet performance is also very acceptable. A quiet, satisfying and well-specified diesel car.

ROVER (GB)   420 GSi Sport

Identity: Widening the spread and appeal of the 400 saloon range, Rover announced four new versions called the 420, with the 2-litre M16 engine and PG1 gearbox, in November 1991. Top model is the Sport, priced the same as the 420 GSi Executive at launch. All have the same generous 140 PS power.

Engine: Front-mounted transverse four-cylinder with alloy head and twin ohc working four valves per cylinder. Lucas multi-point injection. Bore 84.5 mm, stroke 89.0 mm; capacity 1994 cc. Power 140 PS (103 kW) at 6000 rpm; torque 130 lb ft (180 Nm) at 4500 rpm. Compression 10.0-to-1. Catalyst: standard.

Transmission: Front-wheel drive; five-speed manual gearbox. Automatic, not available. Top gear speed at 1000 rpm: 20.7 mph (33.3 km/h).

Suspension: Front, independent, MacPherson struts, anti-roll bar. Rear, independent, wishbones with compensating trailing arm, coil springs, anti-roll bar.

Steering: Rack and pinion. Power assistance: standard. **Brakes:** Vented discs front, drums rear. ABS: optional. **Tyres:** 185/55 VR 15. **Fuel tank:** 12.1 Imp. gall (55 litres). **Unladen weight:** 2612 lb (1185 kg).

Dimensions: Length 171.8 in (4365 mm), width 66.1 in (1680 mm), height 55.0 in (1400 mm), wheelbase 100.4 in (2550 mm).

Performance Works: Maximum speed 127 mph (204 km/h); 0 to 60 mph (97 km/h) 7.9 sec; 80 mph (130 km/h) 13.7 sec. Fuel consumption at constant 75 mph (120 km/h): 36.4 mpg.

Features: The Sport has leather-trimmed sports seats and special steering wheel; car interior in flint grey. Spoilers on boot and at front; rear wheel arch spats and rubbing strips. **Summary:** Good combination of high power output and compact overall dimensions make this a responsive and eager car to drive; although rather expensive it compares well with rivals.

ROVER (GB) 820i

Identity: Revised and greatly improved Rover 800 range was launched in November 1991 (not at Motorfair because Rover did not participate). When prices were announced, the 820i emerged as outstandingly good value for an impressively well-furnished and comfortable executive car.

Engine: Front-mounted transverse four-cylinder with alloy head, twin ohc, and four valves per cylinder. Multi-point fuel injection. Bore 84.5 mm, stroke 89.0 mm; capacity 1994 cc. Power 136 PS (100 kW) at 6000 rpm; torque 136 lb ft (188 Nm) at 2500 rpm. Compression 10.0-to-1. Catalyst: standard.

Transmission: Front-wheel drive; five-speed manual gearbox. Automatic, optional extra, four-speed. Top gear speed at 1000 rpm: 22.5 mph (36.2 km/h).

Suspension: Front, independent, wishbones and coil springs; anti-roll bar. Rear, independent, struts, coil springs; anti-roll bar.

Steering: Rack and pinion. Power assistance: standard. **Brakes:** Vented discs front, solid discs rear. ABS: optional. **Tyres:** 195/65 VR 15. **Fuel tank:** 15.0 Imp. gall (68 litres). **Unladen weight:** 2985 lb (1355 kg).

Dimensions: Length 192.1 in (4880 mm), width 68.1 in (1730 mm), height 54.7 in (1390 mm), wheelbase 108.9 in (2766 mm).

Performance *Autocar & Motor* test: Maximum speed 125 mph (201 km/h); 0 to 60 mph (97 km/h) 9.2 sec; 80 mph (130 km/h) 15.9 sec. Fuel consumption at constant 75 mph (120 km/h): 38.8 mpg; overall test, 27.4 mpg.

Features: For the basic model of the new 800 range, equipment is good and includes remote central locking, winding glass sunroof, and electric action for mirrors and front windows. **Summary:** Suspension is slightly on the soft side, but ride is extremely smooth and handling very reasonable. This new 820i is a very pleasant, relaxing and comfortable car to ride in or to drive.

ROVER (GB)   825SLD

Identity: As indicated when the new 800 range was launched in November 1991, the turbo diesel version did not become available until February 1992. It uses the Italian VM four-cylinder turbo diesel engine, and is available with standard, S, or SL trim. Low exhaust emissions.

Engine: Front-mounted transverse four-cylinder with individual alloy heads, indirect injection; turbocharger and intercooler. Bore 92.0 mm, stroke 94.0 mm; capacity 2500 cc. Power 118 PS (86 kW) at 4200 rpm; torque 194 lb ft (268 Nm) at 2100 rpm. Compression 22.1-to-1. Catalyst: not required.

Transmission: Front-wheel drive; five-speed manual gearbox. Automatic, not available. Top gear speed at 1000 rpm: 29.0 mph (46.7 km/h).

Suspension: Front, independent, wishbones and coil springs; anti-roll bar. Rear, independent, struts, coil springs, anti-roll bar.

Steering: Rack and pinion. Power assistance: standard. **Brakes:** Vented discs front, solid discs rear. ABS: standard. **Tyres:** 195/65 VR 15. **Fuel tank:** 15.0 Imp. gall (68 litres). **Unladen weight:** 3175 lb (1970 kg).

Dimensions: Length 192.1 in (4880 mm), width 68.1 in (1730 mm), height 54.8 in (1393 mm), wheelbase 108.9 in (2766 mm).

Performance Works: Maximum speed 118 mph (190 km/h); 0 to 60 mph (97 km/h) 10.5 sec. Fuel consumption at constant 75 mph (120 km/h): 43.9 mpg.

Features: Equipment levels are the same as for the equivalent petrol model; SLD gets alloy wheels and such luxuries as powered seat adjustment. **Summary:** An excellent choice for the thinking executive looking for a fuel-efficient car, but able to run to a luxury specification; the 825SD is perhaps even better value, though. Unusually, prices were announced in November 1991, well ahead of the 1992 launch.

ROVER (GB)

Metro 1.1C

Identity: 1990 was a busy year for Rover, and one of the most significant launches came in May. The Metro appeared then in much-improved form, with restyled body and an eight-valve version of the K-Series all-alloy engine. Best value seemed at the bottom of the range, in this 1.1C.

Engine: Front-mounted transverse four-cylinder with all-alloy construction and belt-driven single ohc; eight valves, and KIF carb. Bore 75.0 mm, stroke 63.0 mm; capacity 1120 cc. Power 60 PS (44 kW) at 3500 rpm; torque 66 lb ft (91 Nm) at 3500 rpm. Compression 9.75-to-1. Catalyst: optional.

Transmission: Front-wheel drive; four-speed manual gearbox (five-speed optional). Automatic, not available. Top gear speed at 1000 rpm: 16.1 mph (25.9 km/h); fifth: 19.9 mph (32.0 km/h).

Suspension: Front, independent, wishbones and Hydragas spring-damper units linked front to rear. Rear, independent, trailing arms and Hydragas linked spring-damper units.

Steering: Rack and pinion. Power assistance: not available. **Brakes:** Solid discs front, drums rear. ABS: not available. **Tyres:** 155/65 R 13. **Fuel tank:** 7.7 Imp. gall (35.5 litres). **Unladen weight:** 1795 lb (815 kg).

Dimensions: Length 138.6 in (3521 mm), width 69.8 in (1775 mm), height 54.2 in (1377 mm), wheelbase 89.3 in (2269 mm).

Performance _Autocar & Motor_ test: Maximum speed 97 mph (156 km/h); 0 to 60 mph (97 km/h) 13.7 sec; 80 mph (130 km/h) 27.2 sec. Fuel consumption at constant 75 mph (120 km/h): 45.8 mpg; overall test, 31.9 mpg.

Features: Equipment is fairly simple at this base level, with even rear wash/wipe listed as an option and no audio as standard; choice of three- or five-door body. **Summary:** Performance is very respectable, showing the efficiency of the K-Series engine, and maximum speed is in fourth. The five-speed gearbox comes with lower ratio, so fifth is not much higher than fourth on the four-speed model.

ROVER (GB)   Mini Cooper 1.3i

Identity: After the twenty-fifth anniversary of the Mini there was a revival of interest in the once so popular little two-door marvel. This was further encouraged by Rover's introduction of the sprightly Cooper version, which even progressed to injection and catalyst in October 1991.

Engine: Front-mounted transverse four-cylinder with pushrod ohv, fuel injection and catalyst as standard. City and Mayfair models also continue. Bore 70.6 mm, stroke 81.3 mm; capacity 1275 cc. Power 61 PS (45 kW) at 5550 rpm; torque 66 lb ft (91 Nm) at 3000 rpm. Compression 10.3-to-1. Catalyst: standard.

Transmission: Front-wheel drive; four-speed manual gearbox. Automatic, not available (Mayfair only). Top gear speed at 1000 rpm: 18.6 mph (29.9 km/h).

Suspension: Front, independent, wishbones and rubber cone springs. Rear, independent, trailing arms and rubber cone springs; anti-roll bar.

Steering: Rack and pinion. Power assistance: not available. **Brakes:** Solid discs front, drums rear. ABS: not available. **Tyres:** 145/70 R 12. **Fuel tank:** 7.5 Imp. gall (34 litres). **Unladen weight:** 1556 lb (706 kg).

Dimensions: Length 120.3 in (3054 mm), width 55.5 in (1410 mm), height 53.3 in (1353 mm), wheelbase 80.1 in (2035 mm).

Performance *Autocar & Motor* test: Maximum speed 97 mph (156 km/h); 0 to 60 mph (97 km/h) 11.0 sec; 80 mph (130 km/h) 22.7 sec. Fuel consumption at constant 75 mph (120 km/h): 38.8 mpg; overall test, 26.5 mpg.

Features: Cooper badges, special steering wheel and sports wheels enhance the appearance. Wheel-arch extensions accommodate the larger wheels. **Summary:** Although still offering the nippiness which made the Mini legendary in its day, the car is now very dated and its appeal diminishes when you sit in the driving seat.

ROVER (GB)   Sterling Coupé

Identity: Eye-catching new models launched Geneva 1992 were the Cabriolet version of the 200, and this elegant Coupé based on the 800 Series, shown here as the Sterling. It has flowing lines and 16 in alloy road wheels. The Sterling is available only with automatic, although 827 models have a no-cost manual transmission option.

Engine: Front-mounted transverse V6-cylinder with alloy block and heads; PGM-F1 multi-point fuel injection and programmed ignition. Bore 87.0 mm, stroke 75.0 mm; capacity 2675 cc. Power 169 PS (124 kW) at 5900 rpm; torque 163 lb ft (225 Nm) at 4500 rpm. Compression 9.0-to-1. Catalyst: standard.

Transmission: Front-wheel drive; automatic, standard, four-speed. Top gear speed at 1000 rpm: 21.3 mph (34.3 km/h).

Suspension: Front, independent, wishbones and coil springs; anti-roll bar. Rear, independent, struts, coil springs; anti-roll bar.

Steering: Rack and pinion. Power assistance: standard. **Brakes:** Vented discs front, solid discs rear. ABS: standard. **Tyres:** 205/55 VR 16. **Fuel tank:** 15.0 Imp. gall (68 litres). **Unladen weight:** 3175 lb (1440 kg).

Dimensions: Length 192.2 in (4882 mm), width 68.1 in (1730 mm), height 54.8 in (1393 mm), wheelbase 108.9 in (2766 mm).

Performance *Autocar & Motor* test (saloon): Maximum speed 130 mph (209 km/h); 0 to 60 mph (97 km/h) 9.3 sec; 80 mph (130 km/h) 16.2 sec. Fuel consumption at constant 75 mph (120 km/h): 31.3 mpg; overall test, 21.3 mpg.

Features: Lavishly furnished, and magnificent equipment specification; this new version moves up near the top of the executive class. **Summary:** Performance figures quoted above are for the saloon model: the new Coupé should give much the same performance although wind flow is slightly better (drag factor 0.29). A rewarding luxury car.

ROVER (GB)   Vitesse

Identity: Added to the 800 range from February this year, the Vitesse effectively replaces the former 820 Turbo, and has the new body with turbocharged version of the four-cylinder T-Series engine. It is available with saloon or fastback body style, and is fastest model of the range.

Engine: Front-mounted transverse four-cylinder with alloy head and twin ohc working four valves per cylinder. Turbocharger and intercooler. Bore 84.5 mm, stroke 89.0 mm; capacity 1994 cc. Power 180 PS (132 kW) at 6100 rpm; torque 156 lb ft (216 Nm) at 2000 rpm. Compression 8.5-to-1. Catalyst: standard.

Transmission: Front-wheel drive; five-speed manual gearbox. Automatic, not available. Top gear speed at 1000 rpm: 22.5 mph (36.2 km/h).

Suspension: Front, independent, wishbones and coil springs; anti-roll bar. Rear, independent, struts, coil springs, anti-roll bar.

Steering: Rack and pinion. Power assistance: standard. **Brakes:** Vented discs front, solid discs rear. ABS: standard. **Tyres:** 205/55 VR 16. **Fuel tank:** 15.0 Imp. gall (68 litres). **Unladen weight:** 3075 lb (1395 kg).

Dimensions: Length 192.2 in (4882 mm), width 68.1 in (1730 mm), height 54.8 in (1393 mm), wheelbase 108.9 in (2766 mm).

Performance *Autocar & Motor* test (820 Turbo): Maximum speed 135 mph (217 km/h); 0 to 60 mph (97 km/h) 9.0 sec; 80 mph (130 km/h) 13.5 sec. Fuel consumption at constant 75 mph (120 km/h): 34.7; overall test, 20.8 mpg.

Features: Vitesse gets Recaro sports seats, 16 in Roversport alloy wheels and sports suspension. Fastback version has a spoiler on the tailgate. **Summary:** Last year I enjoyed driving the 820 Turbo, which proved much better able to deliver its formidable power and torque through the front wheels without wheelspin than the MG Montego Turbo. With the improvements of the new body, this successor should prove very desirable.

Identity: At Frankfurt 1991, Saab presented a much-improved model range centred on the five-door hatchback body: the 9000CS, with choice of 2-litre or 2.3-litre engine and with or without turbo, making a choice of four power units. A visit to Sweden to try the new CS before the Show left me very impressed.

Engine: Front-mounted transverse four-cylinder with counter-rotating balance shafts, twin ohc, 16 valves, and Garrett T25 turbocharger; intercooler. Bore 90.0 mm, stroke 90 mm; capacity 2290 cc. Power 203 PS (149 kW) at 5000 rpm; torque 244 lb ft (337 Nm) at 2000 rpm. Compression 8.5-to-1. Catalyst: standard.

Transmission: Front-wheel drive; five-speed manual gearbox. Automatic, optional extra, four-speed. Top gear speed at 1000 rpm: 21.6 mph (34.8 km/h).

Suspension: Front, independent, MacPherson struts, anti-roll bar. Rear, dead beam axle on trailing arms with Panhard rod; coil springs.

Steering: Rack and pinion. Power assistance: standard. **Brakes:** Vented discs front, solid discs rear. ABS: standard. **Tyres:** 205/60 VR 15. **Fuel tank:** 14.5 Imp. gall (66 litres). **Unladen weight:** 3014 lb (1370 kg).

Dimensions: Length 187.4 in (4761 mm), width 69.4 in (1764 mm), height 55.9 in (1420 mm), wheelbase 105.2 in (2672 mm).

Performance *Autocar & Motor* test (1990 model): Maximum speed 140 mph (225 km/h); 0 to 60 mph (97 km/h) 7.5 sec; 80 mph (130 km/h) 11.5 sec. Fuel consumption at constant 75 mph (120 km/h): 31.4 mpg; overall test, 19.7 mpg.

Features: Generous equipment includes such features as electrically heated front seats, headlamps wash/wipe, and ABS; extra equipment on S version. Interior design much more attractive. **Summary:** Elimination of many of the irritating features of the previous model has made the 9000CS a much more likeable car. Still a poor automatic, and rather a lot of work for the front wheels to do, but now much more refinement.

SAAB (S)   9000CS 2.3 Carlsson

Identity: In 1990, the Saab Carlsson graduated to a more powerful version of the 2.3-litre turbo engine, giving 223 PS, and this was continued for 1992 with addition of the extensive body revisions made inside and out for the 9000CS. The model is named after Saab's long-serving ambassador and former rally driver, Eric Carlsson.

Engine: Front-mounted transverse four-cylinder with counter-rotating balance shafts, twin ohc, 16 valves, and Garrett T25 turbocharger; intercooler. Bore 90 mm, stroke 90 mm; capacity 2290 cc. Power 223 PS (164 kW) at 5200 rpm; torque 246 lb ft (340 Nm) at 2000 rpm. Compression 8.5-to-1. Catalyst: standard.

Transmission: Front-wheel drive; five-speed manual gearbox. Automatic, optional extra, four-speed. Top gear speed at 1000 rpm: 24.4 mph (39.3 km/h).

Suspension: Front, independent, MacPherson struts, anti-roll bar. Rear, dead beam axle on trailing arms with Panhard rod; coil springs.

Steering: Rack and pinion. Power assistance: standard. **Brakes:** Vented discs front, solid discs rear. ABS: standard. **Tyres:** 205/55 ZR 16. **Fuel tank:** 14.5 Imp. gall (66 litres). **Unladen weight:** 3085 lb (1400 kg).

Dimensions: Length 187.4 in (4761 mm), width 69.4 in (1764 mm), height 55.9 in (1420 mm), wheelbase 105.2 in (2672 mm).

Performance Works: Maximum speed 145 mph (233 km/h); 0 to 60 mph (97 km/h) 7.4 sec; 80 mph (130 km/h) 11.3 sec. Fuel consumption at constant 75 mph (120 km/h): 31.4 mpg.

Features: Although most things are standard with the lavishly equipped Carlsson, you still have to pay extra for air conditioning. **Summary:** Final drive and gearbox ratios are the same as for the standard 9000CS Turbo, but the bigger wheels give more relaxed cruising at speed with fewer revs, while the extra power compensates, to make this an outstanding car for long, fast journeys.

SAAB (S) CDS 2.0i

Identity: Improvements for the Saab range in September 1991 concentrated on the 9000 hatchback model, but the CD saloon also comes with the full range of engines: 2.0 or 2.3, with and without turbo, as well as the high performance Carlsson version. Many of the details here for the 2.0 apply also to the 9000 in cheapest form.

Engine: Front-mounted transverse four-cylinder with alloy head, twin ohc, 16 valves, and Bosch LH-Jetronic fuel injection. Bore 90.0 mm, stroke 78.0 mm; capacity 1985 cc. Power 132 PS (97 kW) at 6000 rpm; torque 126 lb ft (174 Nm) at 3750 rpm. Compression 10.1-to-1. Catalyst: standard.

Transmission: Front-wheel drive; five-speed manual gearbox. Automatic, optional extra, four-speed. Top gear speed at 1000 rpm: 22.5 mph (36.2 km/h).

Suspension: Front, independent, MacPherson struts, anti-roll bar. Rear, dead beam axle on four longitudinal links with Panhard rod; coil springs, anti-roll bar.

Steering: Rack and pinion. Power assistance: standard. **Brakes:** Vented discs front, solid discs rear. ABS: standard. **Tyres:** 195/60 VR 15. **Fuel tank:** 13.7 Imp. gall (62 litres). **Unladen weight:** 2870 lb (1304 kg).

Dimensions: Length 188.1 in (4777 mm), width 69.4 in (1764 mm), height 55.9 in (1420 mm), wheelbase 105.2 in (2672 mm).

Performance *Autocar & Motor* test: Maximum speed 122 mph (196 km/h); 0 to 60 mph (97 km/h) 9.3 sec; 80 mph (130 km/h) 16.2 sec. Fuel consumption at constant 75 mph (120 km/h): 32.8 mpg; overall test, 24.8 mpg.

Features: Impressive interior finish with extensive use of polished walnut, but even at CD level there is still quite a lengthy options list.
Summary: Comfortable and attractively appointed car, and even in this least powerful format, the Saab offers vigorous performance, since the engine has four valves per cylinder. Turbo or 2.3-litre are available if more acceleration is needed.

Identity: MCL Group, which handles Mazda imports to Britain, formed Automotive Holdings in 1991 to look for new marketing business, and launched the Kia Pride, followed in June by this car, the Sao Penza. It is basically the Mazda 323 built by the South African Motor Corporation (Samcor).

Engine: Front-mounted transverse four-cylinder with alloy head and single ohc; eight valves. Two-stage downdraught carb. Bore 71.0 mm, stroke 83.6 mm; capacity 1324 cc. Power 65 PS (48 kW) at 5500 rpm; torque 74 lb ft (103 Nm) at 3300 rpm. Compression 9.4-to-1. Catalyst: not available.

Transmission: Front-wheel drive; five-speed manual gearbox. Automatic, not available. Top gear speed at 1000 rpm: 19.6 mph (31.5 km/h).

Suspension: Front, independent, MacPherson struts, anti-roll bar. Rear, torsion beam axle with struts; anti-roll bar.

Steering: Rack and pinion. Power assistance: not available. **Brakes:** Vented discs front, drums rear. ABS: not available. **Tyres:** 155/70 SR 13. **Fuel tank:** 12.5 Imp. gall (57 litres). **Unladen weight:** 2072 lb (940 kg).

Dimensions: Length 165.2 in (4195 mm), width 64.8 in (1645 mm), height 54.7 in (1390 mm), wheelbase 94.5 in (2400 mm).

Performance Works: Maximum speed 92 mph (148 km/h); no acceleration times quoted. Fuel consumption at constant 75 mph (120 km/h): 41.5 mpg.

Features: Equipment is fairly basic but includes automatic choke and locking fuel flap, and there is a Clarion radio/cassette for the saloon. **Summary:** Model choice is saloon (dimensions and data above apply) or five-door hatchback. For those who don't mind buying a slightly dated model, the Penza is a way of getting a Mazda 323 with nearly £2,000 off the price.

SEAT (E)   Ibiza 1.5 SXi

Identity: Always good performers in relation to their engine size, SEAT cars were joined by the new injection model in July 1989, offering 100 PS output in the small Ibiza three-door body. Special alloy wheels and SXi badge on front are identity features. Restyled body introduced Geneva 1991.

Engine: Front-mounted transverse four-cylinder with alloy head and belt-driven ohc operating eight valves. Bosch LE2 multi-point fuel injection. Bore 83.0 mm, stroke 67.5 mm; capacity 1461 cc. Power 100 PS (72 kW) at 5900 rpm; torque 94 lb ft (128 Nm) at 4700 rpm. Compression 11.0-to-1. Catalyst: not available.

Transmission: Front-wheel drive; five-speed manual gearbox. Automatic, not available. Top gear speed at 1000 rpm: 19.9 mph (32.0 km/h).

Suspension: Front, independent, MacPherson struts, anti-roll bar. Rear, independent, lower wishbones and transverse leaf spring.

Steering: Rack and pinion. Power assistance: not available. **Brakes:** Vented discs front, drums rear. ABS: not available. **Tyres:** 185/60 SR 14. **Fuel tank:** 11.0 Imp. gall (50 litres). **Unladen weight:** 2039 lb (925 kg).

Dimensions: Length 143.2 in (3638 mm), width 63.3 in (1610 mm), height 54.8 in (1394 mm), wheelbase 96.3 m (2443 mm).

Performance *Autocar & Motor* test: Maximum speed 107 mph (172 km/h); 0 to 60 mph (97 km/h) 10.3 sec; 80 mph (130 km/h) 19.4 sec. Fuel consumption at constant 75 mph (120 km/h): 40.9 mpg; overall test, 34.9 mpg.

Features: Quite a lot of extra equipment is included with the SXi package, including electric front windows and central locking, but no sunroof. **Summary:** Lively performance for a 1.5-litre, accompanied by a harsh snarl of exhaust when accelerating hard. But the red-on-black instruments are not easy to read, and steering very heavy.

SEAT (E) Toledo 2.0 GTi

Identity: Competitive pricing was promised when I first drove the new Toledo at Barcelona 1991, and it lived up to the claim when it was launched in Britain at Motorfair. Roomy hatchback with appearance of a saloon, available with 1.6-, 1.8- or 2.0-litre engines, plus 1.9 diesel.

Engine: Front-mounted transverse four-cylinder with alloy head and single ohc; eight valves. Digifant fuel injection and ignition. Bore 82.5 mm, stroke 92.8 mm; capacity 1984 cc. Power 115 PS (85 kW) at 5400 rpm; torque 122 lb ft (166 Nm) at 3200 rpm. Compression 10.0-to-1. Catalyst: optional.

Transmission: Front-wheel drive; five-speed manual gearbox. Automatic, optional extra, four-speed. Top gear speed at 1000 rpm: 22.2 mph (35.7 km/h).

Suspension: Front, independent, MacPherson struts, anti-roll bar. Rear, trailing arms and torsion beam axle; coil springs and anti-roll bar.

Steering: Rack and pinion. Power assistance: standard. **Brakes:** Vented discs front, solid discs rear. ABS: Standard. **Tyres:** 185/60 R 14. **Fuel tank:** 11.0 Imp. gall (50 litres). **Unladen weight:** 2436 lb (1105 kg).

Dimensions: Length 170.1 in (4321 mm), width 65.4 in (1662 mm), height 56.1 in (1424 mm), wheelbase 97.3 in (2471 mm).

Performance *Autocar & Motor* test: Maximum speed 123 mph (198 km/h); 0 to 60 mph (97 km/h) 10.6 sec; 80 mph (130 km/h) 17.8 sec. Fuel consumption at constant 75 mph (120 km/h): 35.8 mpg; overall test, 31.8 mpg.

Features: Equipment is generous, with electric windows all round, sunroof, and a good radio/cassette unit all included; air conditioning is to be optional later. **Summary:** A very practical car, the Toledo has an unusually roomy boot, with folding rear seats. Interior finish is good—emulating Volkswagen standards—and the 2.0 GTi is a brisk, responsive and reassuring car to drive.

SKODA (CS)   **Favorit Estate LS**

Identity: At Birmingham 1990, Skoda showed the prototype for a new estate car version of the 136LS hatchback, predicted to become available later. It went on sale in Britain in June 1991, offering generous carrying capacity in relation to its price. The first Skoda estate since the Octavia ceased production in 1971.

Engine: Front-mounted transverse four-cylinder with all-alloy construction and pushrod ohv. Pierburg twin-choke carb. Bore 75.5 mm, stroke 72.0 mm; capacity 1289 cc. Power 57 PS (42 kW) at 5000 rpm; torque 69 lb ft (95 Nm) at 3000 rpm. Compression 8.8-to-1. Catalyst: not available.

Transmission: Front-wheel drive; five-speed manual gearbox. Automatic, not available. Top gear speed at 1000 rpm: 21.5 mph (34.5 km/h).

Suspension: Front, independent, MacPherson struts. Rear, semi-independent, trailing arms and torsion beam; coil springs.

Steering: Rack and pinion. Power assistance: not available. **Brakes:** Solid discs front, drums rear. ABS: not available. **Tyres:** 165/70 SR 13.
Fuel tank: 10.3 Imp. gall (47 litres). **Unladen weight:** 1852 lb (840 kg).

Dimensions: Length 163.8 in (4160 mm), width 63.8 in (1620 mm), height 56.1 in (1425 mm), wheelbase 96.5 in (2450 mm).

Performance Works: Maximum speed 87 mph (140 km/h); 0 to 60 mph (97 km/h) 14.0 sec; 80 mph (130 km/h) 33.2 mpg sec. Fuel consumption at constant 75 mph (120 km/h): 36.2.

Features: Two-piece rear parcels shelf, divided rear seat, pop-up glass sunroof and alloy wheels are among the quite generous equipment.
Summary: A little basic inside, with very much the plastic look, but there are many good features such as the neat little rechargeable torch at the back. Performance is reasonable, and load-carrying very capable.

SUBARU (J)

Identity: Small car for those who have to tackle tricky going and don't want to get stuck, the Justy has front-wheel drive in normal running but adds rear drive when a button on top of the gear lever is pressed. Interesting addition for Motorfair 1989 was the availability of continuously variable automatic transmission with electronic control.

Engine: Front-mounted transverse three-cylinder with alloy head and belt-driven ohc working three valves per cylinder. Twin-choke carb. Bore 78.0 mm, stroke 83.0 mm; capacity 1189 cc. Power 67 PS (49 kW) at 5600 rpm; torque 71 lb ft (98 Nm) at 3600 rpm. Compression 9.1-to-1. Catalyst: not available.

Transmission: Four-wheel drive; five-speed manual gearbox. Automatic, optional extra. Automatic is of ECVT type, using continuously variable belts and pulleys under electronic control. Top gear speed at 1000 rpm: 17.6 mph (28.3 km/h).

Suspension: Front, independent, MacPherson struts, anti-roll bar. Rear, independent, wishbones and coil springs; anti-roll bar.

Steering: Rack and pinion. Power assistance: not available. **Brakes:** Vented discs front, drums rear. ABS: not available. **Tyres:** 165/65 R 13. **Fuel tank:** 7.7 Imp. gall (35 litres). **Unladen weight:** 1874 lb (850 kg).

Dimensions: Length 145.5 in (3695 mm), width 60.4 in (1534 mm), height 55.9 in (1420 mm), wheelbase 90.0 in (2285 mm).

Performance *Autocar & Motor* test: Maximum speed 90.0 mph (145 km/h); 0 to 60 mph (97 km/h) 14.4 sec; 80 mph (130 km/h) 31.0 sec. Fuel consumption at constant 75 mph (120 km/h): 35.3 mpg; overall test, 31.0 mpg.

Features: Choice of three- or five-door body; equipment is reasonable for this class of car, and interior materials appear durable. **Summary:** The combination of four-wheel drive (easily engaged at the touch of a switch), with optional automatic transmission is unique to Subaru; economy is claimed to be as good, or better, with the automatic version.

SUBARU (J)   Legacy 2.0 4-cam Turbo 4WD

Identity: During the summer of 1991 I used a Legacy estate car for a towing job and was well pleased by its roominess, traction and performance. It was overshadowed at Motorfair, however, by the new model with four camshafts and turbocharger, extracting nearly 200 PS.

Engine: Front-mounted longitudinal horizontally-opposed four-cylinder with twin ohc on each bank of cylinders; 16 valves. All-alloy construction. IHI turbocharger and intercooler. Bore 92.0 mm, stroke 75.0 mm; capacity 1994 cc. Power 197 PS (147 kW) at 6000 rpm; torque 193 lb ft (262 Nm) at 3600 rpm. Compression 8.0-to-1. Catalyst: standard.

Transmission: Four-wheel drive; five-speed manual gearbox. Automatic, not available for turbo. Top gear speed at 1000 rpm: 23.4 mph (37.7 km/h).

Suspension: Front, independent, MacPherson struts, anti-roll bar. Rear, independent, struts, transverse links and trailing arms; coil springs and anti-roll bar.

Steering: Rack and pinion. Power assistance: standard. **Brakes:** Vented discs front and rear. ABS: standard. **Tyres:** 205/60 VR 15. **Fuel tank:** 13.2 Imp. gall (60 litres). **Unladen weight:** 3120 lb (1415 kg).

Dimensions: Length 177.6 in (4510 mm), width 66.5 in (1690 mm), height 55.1 in (1400 mm), wheelbase 101.6 in (2580 mm).

Performance *Autocar & Motor* test (estate): Maximum speed 133 mph (214 km/h); 0 to 60 mph (97 km/h) 7.0 sec; 80 mph (130 km/h) 12.3 sec. Fuel consumption at constant 75 mph (120 km/h): 31.4 mpg; overall test, 21.8 mpg.

Features: Very comprehensive specification includes alloy wheels, spoiler on boot, headlamp washers, and low-level fog lamps. **Summary:** Test figures for the estate car show this to be one of the fastest load carriers, and with the added advantage of four-wheel drive it is in a class where there are few competitors. Saloon is claimed to be even faster, with 143 mph top speed.

SUZUKI (J)   Vitara JLX SE Estate

Identity: New in the Suzuki range of cross-country vehicles at Birmingham 1988, Vitara offered a larger and more powerful 1.6-litre engine, with selectable four-wheel drive. Automatic transmission option was added April 1990, and at Motorfair 1991, this five-door estate version with more powerful engine was shown.

Engine: Front-mounted longitudinal four-cylinder with alloy head and single ohc; 16 valves. Electronic multi-point fuel injection. Bore 75.0 mm, stroke 90.0 mm; capacity 1590 cc. Power 96 PS (71 kW) at 5600 rpm; torque 98 lb ft (132 Nm) at 4000 rpm. Compression 9.5-to-1. Catalyst standard.

Transmission: Rear-wheel drive plus selectable front drive; five-speed manual gearbox. Automatic, optional extra, four-speed with electronic control. Top gear speed at 1000 rpm: 17.8 mph (28.6 km/h).

Suspension: Front, independent, MacPherson struts, anti-roll bar. Rear, independent, trailing links with centre wishbone; coil springs.

Steering: Ball and nut. Power assistance: optional. **Brakes:** Solid discs front, drums rear. ABS: not available. **Tyres:** 195 SR 15. **Fuel tank:** 9.5 Imp. gall (43 litres). **Unladen weight:** 2634 lb (1195 kg).

Dimensions: Length 158.7 in (4030 mm), width 64.2 in (1630 mm), height 66.9 in (1700 mm), wheelbase 97.6 in (2480 mm).

Performance Works: Maximum speed 87 mph (140 km/h); 0 to 60 mph (97 km/h) 14.5 sec; 80 mph (130 km/h) 34.7 sec. Fuel consumption at constant 75 mph (120 km/h): 27.2 mpg; overall test, 24.2 mpg.

Features: Rear seats divide 60/40 and fold; electric windows front and rear, and central locking, as well as height-adjustable steering column and electric mirror adjustment, all now standard. **Summary:** Inadequate information from the manufacturer gives no idea of performance, so figures for the previous open model, which was lighter but less powerful, are given above. This promises to be the most civilised Suzuki off-roader yet.

Identity: At the launch in Germany in September 1991, I was tremendously impressed by the quietness and smoothness of the new Camry V6. The Camry was launched at Frankfurt, and on the UK market from Motorfair. As well as the V6, there is a four-cylinder 2.2-litre GL.

Engine: Front-mounted transverse V6-cylinder with alloy heads, each with twin ohc working four valves per cylinder; L Jetronic fuel injection. Bore 87.5 mm, stroke 82.0 mm; capacity 2959 cc. Power 188 PS (138 kW) at 5400 rpm; torque 188 lb ft (260 Nm) at 4400 rpm. Compression 9.6-to-1. Catalyst: standard.

Transmission: Front-wheel drive; automatic, four-speed standard. Top gear speed at 1000 rpm: 25.6 mph (41.2 km/h).

Suspension: Front, independent, MacPherson struts, anti-roll bar. Rear, independent, struts and twin transverse arms; coil springs and anti-roll bar.

Steering: Rack and pinion. Power assistance: standard. **Brakes:** Vented discs front, solid discs rear. ABS: standard. **Tyres:** 205/65 R 15. **Fuel tank:** 15.4 Imp. gall (70 litres). **Unladen weight:** 3120 lb (1515 kg).

Dimensions: Length 186.0 in (4725 mm), width 69.7 in (1770 mm), height 55.1 in (1400 mm), wheelbase 103.1 in (2620 mm).

Performance Works: Maximum speed 134 mph (216 km/h); 0 to 60 mph (97 km/h) 8.8 sec; 80 mph (130 km/h) 14.2 sec. Fuel consumption at constant 75 mph (120 km/h): 26.9 mpg.

Features: Comprehensive equipment includes air-conditioning and such refinements as electric sunroof. Superb audio unit. **Summary:** Very comfortable and relaxing car to drive, spoilt only by an automatic transmission selector which can too easily be knocked into neutral when on the move, but it has an overdrive cut-out switch to select third.

TOYOTA (J) — Celica 2.0 GT-Four

Identity: Fifth generation to carry the Celica name was launched November 1989, with sleek styling, and again with pop-up headlamps and choice of front- or four-wheel drive. Mechanically much as before but with a better and stronger body, making use of galvanealed steel.

Engine: Front-mounted transverse four-cylinder with alloy head and twin ohc working four valves per cylinder. Electronic injection and turbocharger with air-air inter-cooler. Bore 86.0 mm; stroke 86.0 mm; capacity 1998 cc. Power 204 PS (150 kW) at 6000 rpm; torque 199 lb ft (275 Nm) at 3200 rpm. Compression 8.8-to-1. Catalyst: standard.

Transmission: Four-wheel drive; five-speed manual gearbox. Automatic, not available. Top gear speed at 1000 rpm: 28.5 mph (45.9 km/h).

Suspension: Front, independent, MacPherson struts, anti-roll bar. Rear, independent, MacPherson struts, anti-roll bar.

Steering: Rack and pinion. Power assistance: standard. **Brakes:** Vented discs front, solid discs rear. ABS: standard. **Tyres:** 215/50 VR 15. **Fuel tank:** 13.2 Imp. gall (60 litres) **Unladen weight:** 4166 lb (1890 kg).

Dimensions: Length 174.4 in (4430 mm), width 68.7 in (1745 mm), height 51.2 in (1300 mm), wheelbase 99.4 in (2525 mm).

Performance *Autocar & Motor* test (4 × 2): Maximum speed 132 mph (212 km/h); 0 to 60 mph (97 km/h) 8.1 sec; 80 mph (130 km/h) 13.9 sec. Fuel consumption at constant 75 mph (120 km/h): 37.1 mpg; overall test, 22.5 mpg.

Features: Exciting appearance, and very well-equipped car including air conditioning and an advanced audio system. **Summary:** My last and perhaps most exciting overseas test drive of 1989 was in the Celica GT-Four in France; I also enjoyed the standard front-drive model (test figures above), which is available with automatic, but the enthusiast will appreciate the superb handling and performance of the turbocharged GT-Four.

164

TOYOTA (J) Corolla GTi 16v

Identity: In the new Corolla range at Frankfurt 1987 was, as usual, a performance model, now called the GTi 16v. It has similar 16-valve engine to the Executive, but with fuel injection. This is the 4A-GE engine, giving very lively performance. Many other changes to make the GTi more sporting.

Engine: Front-mounted transverse four-cylinder with alloy head and twin ohc operating four valves per cyl. Bosch D-Jetronic fuel injection. Bore 81.0 mm, stroke 77.0 mm; capacity 1587 cc. Power 123 PS (90 kW) at 6600 rpm; torque 107 lb ft (148 Nm) at 5000 rpm. Compression 10.0-to-1. Catalyst: not available.

Transmission: Front-wheel drive; five-speed manual gearbox. Automatic, not available. Top gear speed at 1000 rpm: 19.9 mph (32.0 km/h).

Suspension: Front, independent, MacPherson struts, anti-roll bar. Rear, independent, MacPherson struts, anti-roll bar.

Steering: Rack and pinion. Power assistance: standard. **Brakes:** Vented discs front, solid discs rear. ABS: not available. **Tyres:** 185/60 HR 14. **Fuel tank:** 11.0 Imp. gall (50 litres). **Unladen weight:** 2083 lb (945 kg).

Dimensions: Length 165.9 in (4215 mm), width 65.1 in (1655 mm), height 53.7 in (1365 mm), wheelbase 95.6 in (2430 mm).

Performance *Autocar & Motor* test: Maximum speed 121 mph (195 km/h); 0 to 60 mph (97 km/h) 9.2 sec; 80 mph (130 km/h) 15.6 sec. Fuel consumption at constant 75 mph (120 km/h): 36.2 mpg; overall test, 35.1 mpg.

Features: GTi gets much extra equipment such as electric adjustment for door mirrors. Extra spoilers and side sills reveal identity. **Summary:** Impressively lively car to drive, with exceptionally good handling and general road behaviour. Excellent controls. Rather noisy, but not out of keeping with its sporting character. A good 'fun' car.

Identity: Toyota offer the Lexus as a separate brand, but it seems to belong more amongst the Ts than the Ls, despite being a very individual and luxurious car. Good though Toyotas are, Lexus marked a major adventure into a very different field – as a new rival for Jaguar and Mercedes – when it was launched here in May 1991.

Engine: Front-mounted longitudinal V8-cylinder with alloy block and heads, and twin ohc each bank working four valves per cylinder; electronic fuel injection. Bore 87.5 mm, stroke 82.5 mm; capacity 3969 cc. Power 241 PS (177 kW) at 5400 rpm; torque 258 lb ft (357 Nm) at 4400 rpm. Compression 10.0-to-1. Catalyst: standard.

Transmission: Rear-wheel drive; four-speed automatic, standard. Top gear speed at 1000 rpm: 27.1 mph (43.6 km/h).

Suspension: Front, independent, wishbones and coil springs, anti-roll bar. Rear, independent wishbones and coil springs, anti-roll bar.

Steering: Rack and pinion. Power assistance: standard. **Brakes:** Vented discs front and rear. ABS: standard. **Tyres:** 205/65 ZR 15. **Fuel tank:** 18.7 Imp. gall (85 litres). **Unladen weight:** 3890 lb (1765 kg).

Dimensions: Length 196.6 in (4995 mm), width 71.6 in (1820 mm), height 56.1 in (1425 mm), wheelbase 110.8 in (2815 mm).

Performance *Autocar & Motor* test: Maximum speed 147 mph (237 km/h); 0 to 60 mph (97 km/h) 8.3 sec; 80 mph (130 km/h) 13.2 sec. Fuel consumption at constant 75 mph (120 km/h): 27.4 mpg; overall test, 19.7 mpg.

Features: In any list of standard features, the Lexus scores 'full house', having everything from the neat remote central locking, with sender built into the key, to air conditioning. **Summary:** Quietness and refinement are what I chiefly remember from driving the Lexus. It also stood out as a very fast car, always trying to go soaring into three-figure speeds, and a very safe one as well. I thoroughly enjoyed testing it.

TOYOTA (J)

MR2 2.0 GT T-Bar

Identity: Sleek, purposeful and eye-catching styling came to the mid-engined Toyota sports GT in April 1990, when the new version with much more rounded body shape was introduced. Engine size was increased to 2-litre, and there is a choice of two power output levels, standard or GT. The T-Bar body is available only with GT engine.

Engine: Mid-mounted transverse four-cylinder with twin ohc working four valves per cylinder and varying induction, by altering lift and opening time of valves. Electronic fuel injection. Bore 86.0 mm, stroke 86.0 mm; capacity 1998 cc. Power 160 PS (118 kW) at 6600 rpm; torque 140 lb ft (194 Nm) at 4800 rpm. Compression 10.0-to-1. Catalyst: standard.

Transmission: Rear-wheel drive; five-speed manual gearbox. Automatic, optional extra on standard model only; not available on GT. Top gear speed at 1000 rpm: 21.2 mph (34.1 km/h).

Suspension: Front, independent, MacPherson struts, anti-roll bar. Rear, MacPherson struts, anti-roll bar.

Steering: Rack and pinion. Power assistance: not available. **Brakes:** Vented discs front and rear. ABS: not available. **Tyres:** 195/60 R 14 85V (front); 205/60R 14 88V (rear). **Fuel tank:** 12.1 Imp. gall (55 litres). **Unladen weight:** 2810 lb (1275 kg).

Dimensions: Length 164.6 in (4180 mm), width 66.9 in (1700 mm), height 48.8 in (1240 mm), wheelbase 94.5 in (2400 mm).

Performance *Autocar & Motor* test (fixed head): Maximum speed 137 mph (220 km/h); 0 to 60 mph (97 km/h) 6.7 sec; 80 mph (130 km/h) 9.9 sec. Fuel consumption at constant 75 mph (120 km/h): 37.7 mpg; overall test, 27.2 mpg.

Features: Complex seven-way adjustment of driving seat is provided, and top-level audio is fitted. T-Bar gets removable glass roof panels and has leather upholstery as standard. **Summary:** Accommodation is a bit restricted, but the MR2 is adequate for two, and offers a small luggage space at each end. Exceptional roadholding and an exciting car to drive.

TOYOTA (J) Previa 2.4

Identity: Cleverly designed replacement for the Spacecruiser, launched in UK Birmingham 1990, Previa has its engine mid-mounted beneath the floor, with ancillaries such as the alternator shaft-driven at the front. Spacious and comfortable eight-seater, yet relaxing to drive.

Engine: Mid-mounted longitudinal four-cylinder with twin overhead camshafts and 16 valves; fuel injection. Bore 95.0 mm, stroke 86.0 mm; capacity 2438 cc. Power 134 PS (99 kW) at 5000 rpm; torque 152 lb ft (210 Nm) at 4000 rpm. Compression 9.3-to-1. Catalyst: not available.

Transmission: Rear-wheel drive; five-speed manual gearbox. Automatic, optional extra. Top gear speed at 1000 rpm: 22.1 mph (35.6 km/h).

Suspension: Front, independent, MacPherson struts; anti-roll bar. Rear, independent, wishbones and coil springs.

Steering: Rack and pinion. Power assistance: standard. **Brakes:** Vented discs front and rear. ABS: not available. **Tyres:** 215/65 R15 96H. **Fuel tank:** 16.5 Imp. gall (75 litres). **Unladen weight:** 3968 lb (1800 kg).

Dimensions: Length 187.0 in (4750 mm), width 70.9 in (1800 mm), height 71.3 in (1810 mm), wheelbase 112.6 in (2860 mm).

Performance *Autocar & Motor* test: Maximum speed 109 mph (175 km/h); 0 to 60 mph (97 km/h) 12.9 sec; 80 mph (130 km/h) 22.9 sec. Fuel consumption at constant 75 mph (120 km/h): 24.1 mpg; overall test, 21.6 mpg.

Features: Sliding side door and large tailgate; pop-up front sunroof and electric sliding roof over centre of vehicle. Generous equipment.
Summary: Futuristic fascia design and sleek appearance give a very modern look to this advanced multi-seater. Centre row of seats has reach adjustment and rear seats fold against the sides for extra load space. Most impressive design.

TOYOTA (J)

Supra 3.0i Turbo

Identity: Following the launch of the completely new Supra in 1986, a very fast turbocharged model was added in early 1989. In this form, Supra can challenge the world's fastest cars, and it presents an exciting appearance with its flat deck front, rear wing, and removable roof panels.

Engine: Front-mounted longitudinal six-cylinder with all-alloy construction and belt-driven twin ohc working four valves per cylinder. Multi-point fuel injection. Turbocharger and inter-cooler. Bore 83.0 mm, stroke 91.0 mm; capacity 2954 cc. Power 232 PS (173 kW) at 5600 rpm; torque 254 lb ft (345 Nm) at 3200 rpm. Compression 8.4-to-1. Catalyst: standard.

Transmission: Rear-wheel drive; five-speed manual gearbox. Automatic, optional extra. Top gear speed at 1000 rpm: 25.7 mph (41.4 km/h).

Suspension: Front, independent, wishbones and coil springs; anti-roll bar. Rear, independent, wishbones and coil springs; anti-roll bar.

Steering: Rack and pinion. Power assistance: standard. **Brakes:** Vented discs front, and rear. ABS: standard. **Tyres:** 225/50 VR 16. **Fuel tank:** 15.4 Imp. gall (70 litres). **Unladen weight:** 3470 lb (1575 kg).

Dimensions: Length 181.9 in (4620 mm), width 68.7 in (1745 mm), height 51.6 in (1310 mm), wheelbase 102.4 in (2600 mm).

Performance *Autocar & Motor* test: Maximum speed 144 mph (232 km/h); 0 to 60 mph (97 km/h) 6.9 sec; 80 mph (130 km/h) 11.4 sec. Fuel consumption at constant 75 mph (120 km/h): 27.4 mpg; overall test, 18.8 mpg.

Features: Excellent standard equipment including air conditioning, leaving automatic transmission as about the only extra listed. **Summary:** Extremely fast and competent 2+2 to rival some of the world's top super-cars, although its interior finish and standards of furnishing are not up to the same level.

TVR (GB)

Griffith 4.0

Identity: Eye-catching new shape on the TVR stand at Birmingham in 1990 was the completely new Griffith. TVR say it was developed to meet market demand for a very high-performance V8 model, and it evolved in conjunction with the TVR racing programme. In production from Motorfair 1991.

Engine: Front-mounted longitudinal V8-cylinder with alloy block and heads, and pushrod ohv. Electronic fuel injection. Bore 94.0 mm, stroke 71.1 mm; capacity 3947 cc. Power 240 PS (177 kW) at 6250 rpm; torque 270 lb ft (373 Nm) at 2600 rpm. Compression 10.5-to-1. Catalyst: optional.

Transmission: Rear-wheel drive; five-speed manual gearbox. Automatic, not available. Top gear speed at 1000 rpm: 26.8 mph (43.2 km/h).

Suspension: Front, independent, wishbones and coil springs; anti-roll bar. Rear, independent, semi-trailing arms with coil springs and anti-roll bar.

Steering: Rack and pinion. Power assistance: not available. **Brakes:** Vented discs front, solid discs rear. ABS: not available. **Tyres:** 215/60 XR 15. **Fuel tank:** 11.8 Imp. gall (53.6 litres). **Unladen weight:** 2095 lb (950 kg).

Dimensions: Length 152.8 in (3882 mm), width 67.0 in (1701 mm), height 46.1 in (1172 mm), wheelbase 90.6 in (2300 mm).

Performance Works: Maximum speed 148 mph (238 km/h); 0 to 60 mph (97 km/h) 4.9 sec; 80 mph (130 km/h) 8.6 sec. Fuel consumption: no data.

Features: Semi-frameless electric windows and folding rear-quarter hood with removable targa roof panel. Trim in ambla, leather optional. **Summary:** After its Birmingham appearance, the show car was stripped down preparatory to setting up for production, but the Griffith is expected to be as fast as its exciting looks and preliminary figures suggest.

VAUXHALL (B, GB, D)   Astra 1.4i GLS

Identity: Launched Frankfurt 1991, and in Britain from Motorfair, the new Astra is a tremendous all-round improvement over its predecessor. All engines have exhaust catalyst and fuel injection. Choice of three- or five-door hatchback; saloon added April 1992. Merit, LS, GLS or CD trim.

Engine: Front-mounted transverse four-cylinder with alloy head and single ohc; eight valves. Electronic multi-point fuel injection. Bore 77.6 mm, stroke 73.4 mm; capacity 1398 cc. Power 82 PS (60 kW) at 5800 rpm; torque 83 lb ft (113 Nm) at 3400 rpm. Compression 9.8-to-1. Catalyst: standard.

Transmission: Front-wheel drive; five-speed manual gearbox. Automatic, optional extra from end-1992, four-speed. Top gear speed at 1000 rpm: 22.2 mph (35.7 km/h).

Suspension: Front, independent, MacPherson struts, anti-roll bar. Rear, torsion beam compound crank axle with coil springs and anti-roll bar.

Steering: Rack and pinion. Power assistance: standard. **Brakes:** Solid discs front, drums rear. ABS: optional. **Tyres:** 175/65 R 14. **Fuel tank:** 11.4 Imp. gall (52 litres). **Unladen weight:** 2233 lb (1015 kg).

Dimensions: Length 159.5 in (4051 mm), width 66.5 in (1688 mm), height 55.5 in (1410 mm), wheelbase 99.0 in (2515 mm).

Performance *Autocar & Motor* test: Maximum speed 106 mph (170 km/h); 0 to 60 mph (97 km/h) 12.8 sec; 80 mph (130 km/h) 25.0 sec. Fuel consumption at constant 75 mph (120 km/h): 41.5 mpg; overall test, 34.7 mpg.

Features: Functional interior design with neat layout of instruments and minor controls. Separate radio and time display above the radio/cassette player, in the console. **Summary:** Suspension is on the soft side, but the Astra handles well and gives a very comfortable ride without float on undulations. Getting expensive for a 1.4, but a very pleasing and attractive small car.

VAUXHALL (B, GB, D)

Astra 2.0i CD

Identity: As the new Vauxhall Astra moved up the market a little in terms of size, and a long way in design appeal, it was a logical step to make a 2-litre 'junior executive' version available as well. It has the top CD trim, or a sporty SRi version is offered, both having the 115 PS engine.

Engine: Front-mounted transverse four-cylinder with alloy cross-flow head and single ohc; eight valves. Bosch M1.5 Motronics. Bore 86.0 mm, stroke 86.0 mm; capacity 1998 cc. Power 115 PS (85 kW) at 5400 rpm; torque 125 lb ft (170 Nm) at 2600 rpm. Compression 9.2-to-1. Catalyst: standard.

Transmission: Front-wheel drive; five-speed manual gearbox. Automatic, not available. Top gear speed at 1000 rpm: 26.4 mph (42.5 km/h).

Suspension: Front, independent, MacPherson struts, anti-roll bar. Rear, torsion beam compound crank axle with coil springs and anti-roll bar.

Steering: Rack and pinion. Power assistance: standard. **Brakes:** Solid discs front, drums rear. ABS: standard. **Tyres:** 185/60 R 14. **Fuel tank:** 11.4 Imp. gall (52 litres). **Unladen weight:** 2446 lb (1112 kg).

Dimensions: Length 159.5 in (4051 mm), width 66.5 in (1688 mm), height 55.5 in (1410 mm), wheelbase 99.0 in (2515 mm).

Performance Works: Maximum speed 121 mph (195 km/h); 0 to 60 mph (97 km/h) 9.5 sec. Fuel consumption at constant 75 mph (120 km/h): 38.7 mpg.

Features: Standard equipment on the CD includes sliding glass sunroof, front electric windows, electrically adjusted/heated door mirrors, and alloy wheels. **Summary:** Although the less sporting model of the pair, the CD is better than the SRi for fast cruising as it is a lot higher geared, with economical benefit as well. Very pleasing small to medium car; available also as saloon.

VAUXHALL (B, GB, D)   Astra 2.0i GSi 16v

Identity: As with the previous Astra, there's a high-performance 'hot hatch' version of the newcomer, with the same 16-valve 150 PS engine as fitted in the Calibra 16v. Available only with three-door body. The engine has advanced injection control, claimed to give better response during warm-up.

Engine: Front-mounted transverse four-cylinder with alloy cross-flow head and twin ohc; 16 valves. Bosch M2.5 Motronics. Bore 86.0 mm, stroke 86.0 mm; capacity 1998 cc. Power 150 PS (110 kW) at 6000 rpm; torque 145 lb ft (196 Nm) at 4800 rpm. Compression 10.5-to-1. Catalyst: standard.

Transmission: Front-wheel drive; five-speed manual gearbox. Automatic, not available. Electronic traction control (ETC). Top gear speed at 1000 rpm: 21.9 mph (35.2 km/h).

Suspension: Front, independent, MacPherson struts, anti-roll bar. Rear, torsion beam crank axle with coil springs and twin anti-roll bars.

Steering: Rack and pinion. Power assistance: standard. **Brakes:** Vented discs front, solid discs rear. ABS: standard. **Tyres:** 205/50 VR 15. **Fuel tank:** 11.4 Imp. gall (52 litres). **Unladen weight:** 2490 lb (1132 kg).

Dimensions: Length 160.9 in (4087 mm), width 66.5 in (1688 mm), height 55.5 in (1410 mm), wheelbase 99.0 in (2515 mm).

Performance *Autocar & Motor* test: Maximum speed 130 mph (209 km/h); 0 to 60 mph (97 km/h) 7.2 sec; 80 mph (130 km/h) 12.6 sec. Fuel consumption at constant 75 mph (120 km/h): 38.2 mpg; overall test, 26.4 mpg.

Features: Stiffer spring rates and rear suspension lowered by 15 mm, plus gas-filled dampers, give a tauter ride; electronic traction control is standard. **Summary:** Terrific performance, as shown by the acceleration figures, but the problem is getting so much power through the front wheels without excessive wheelspin; hence the ETC provision. An excitingly fast car but needs to be handled with respect.

VAUXHALL (D)   Calibra 4 × 4 Turbo

Identity: Special high-efficiency version of the Calibra was launched Frankfurt 1991, and shown the following month at Motorfair, although without any price or positive news about planned availability. The engine has high torque output, and a new GM six-speed gearbox is fitted.

Engine: Front-mounted transverse four-cylinder with alloy head, twin ohc working 16 valves, and special pistons. Turbocharger integral with exhaust manifold. Bore 86.0 mm, stroke 86.0 mm; capacity 1998 cc. Power 204 PS (150 kW) at 5600 rpm; torque 203 lb ft (280 Nm) at 2400 rpm. Compression 9.0-to-1. Catalyst: standard.

Transmission: Four-wheel drive; six-speed manual gearbox. Automatic, not available. Top gear speed at 1000 rpm: 26.5 mph (42.7 km/h).

Suspension: Front, independent, MacPherson struts, anti-roll bar. Rear, independent, semi-trailing arms with self-steering provision in suspension bushes; anti-roll bar.

Steering: Rack and pinion. Power assistance: standard. **Brakes:** Vented discs front, solid discs rear. ABS: standard. **Tyres:** 205/55 R 16. **Fuel tank:** 14.3 Imp. gall (65 litres). **Unladen weight:** 3010 lb (1365 kg).

Dimensions: Length 176.8 in (4490 mm), width 66.9 in (1700 mm), height 55.1 in (1400 mm), wheelbase 102.4 in (2600 mm).

Performance Works: Maximum speed 152 mph (245 km/h); 0 to 62 mph (100 km/h) 6.8 sec. Fuel consumption at constant 75 mph (120 km/h): 34.0 mpg.

Features: Four-spoke sports steering wheel and leather-trimmed gear lever knob; alloy wheels. Roof-mounted rear aerial with booster.
Summary: Picture shows the Opel version, since the Vauxhall Calibra Turbo had not appeared at time of going to press. GM make a big feature of the efficiency of this new engine with its fully integrated turbocharger.

174

VAUXHALL (D)

Carlton 2.6i CDX

Identity: Improved model in the Vauxhall range, launched Birmingham 1990, is the Carlton CDX. It has a new engine, enlarged to 2.6-litre capacity, and features the same 'dual ram' induction system as first introduced by GM on the Senator 3.0i-24v. All Carltons now have ABS.

Engine: Front-mounted longitudinal six-cylinder with cylinders in-line and alloy head; single ohc working eight valves. Dual-stage induction, changing at 4,000 rpm. Bosch M1.5 injection and ignition system. Bore 88.8 mm, stroke 69.8 mm; capacity 2594 cc. Power 150 PS (110 kW) at 5600 rpm; torque 162 lb ft (224 Nm) at 3800 rpm. Compression 9.2-to-1. Catalyst: twin, standard.

Transmission: Rear-wheel drive; five-speed manual gearbox. Automatic, optional extra. Top gear speed at 1000 rpm: 23.2 mph (37.3 km/h); auto 27.8 mph (44.7 km/h).

Suspension: Front, independent, MacPherson struts with triangular control arms; anti-roll bar. Rear, independent, semi-trailing arms with transverse diagonal link each side; mini-block progressive rate coil springs and anti-roll bar.

Steering: Recirculating ball. Power assistance: standard. **Brakes:** Vented discs front, solid discs rear. ABS: standard. **Tyres:** 195/65 VR 14. **Fuel tank:** 16.5 Imp. gall (75 litres). **Unladen weight:** 3163 lb (1435 kg).

Dimensions: Length 184.5 in (4686 mm), width 69.8 in (1773 mm), height 57.8 in (1468 mm), wheelbase 107.5 in (2731 mm).

Performance Works: Maximum speed 134 mph (216 km/h); 0 to 62 mph (100 km/h) 9.8 sec. Fuel consumption at constant 75 mph (120 km/h): 30.1 mpg.

Features: Many improvements were made to the whole Carlton range at the same time as the 2.6 was introduced, and the CDX gets electrically heated seats and the ingenious Vauxhall computer. **Summary:** The company car tax limit for Band 4 (£19,250) makes the 2-litre limit irrelevant and this smooth new 2.6-litre takes advantage of the fact.

VAUXHALL (B, D, GB)   Cavalier 2.0i 4 × 4

Identity: New adventure for GM in this range was introduction of a four-wheel drive version, on the market November 1988. It was initially packaged as a 'working' car for business use, with L specification, but later up-rated to GL trim.

Engine: Front-mounted transverse four-cylinder with alloy head and single belt-driven ohc. Bosch Motronic injection/ignition. Bore 86.0 mm, stroke 86.0 mm; capacity 1998 cc. Power 130 PS (95 kW) at 5600 rpm; torque 129 lb ft (175 Nm) at 4600 rpm. Compression 10.0-to-1. Catalyst: not available.

Transmission: Four-wheel drive; five-speed manual gearbox. Automatic, not available. Top gear speed at 1000 rpm: 20.3 mph (32.7 km/h).

Suspension: Front, independent, MacPherson struts, anti-roll bar. Rear, independent, semi-trailing arms with multi-axis support brackets; double-conical miniblock coil springs and twin-tube telescopic dampers; anti-roll bar.

Steering: Rack and pinion. Power assistance: standard. **Brakes:** Vented discs front, solid discs rear. ABS: optional. **Tyres:** 175/70 TR 14. **Fuel tank:** 13.4 Imp. gall (61 litres). **Unladen weight:** 2668 lb (1210 kg).

Dimensions: Length 174.4 in (4429 mm), width 66.9 in (1699 mm), height 55.1 in (1400 mm), wheelbase 102.4 in (2601 mm).

Performance *Autocar & Motor* test: Maximum speed 123 mph (198 km/h); 0 to 60 mph (97 km/h) 8.6 sec; 80 mph (130 km/h) 15.0 sec. Fuel consumption at constant 75 mph (120 km/h): 38.7 mpg, overall test, 28.3 mpg.

Features: Equipment is largely the same as for the front-drive models with GL specification; 2-litre gets power steering as standard. **Summary:** The 4 × 4 model is available only with saloon body and not as hatchback. Major improvement is the use of independent suspension at the rear, and when I first drove the new range I considered this model to be best of all.

VAUXHALL (D)   Cavalier GSi 2.0i 16v 4 × 4

Identity: Although I was able to include details of the Cavalier 16V in the 1989 edition, based on the mechanically similar Opel Vectra, it did not arrive on the British market until September that year. Impressive combination of very high performance with safety, and good equipment.

Engine: Front-mounted transverse four-cylinder with alloy head and twin belt-driven ohc operating four valves per cyl. Bosch Motronic injection/ignition system. Bore 86.0 mm, stroke 86.0 mm; capacity 1998 cc. Power 150 PS (110 kW) at 6000 rpm; torque 145 lb ft (196 Nm) at 4800 rpm. Compression 10.5-to-1. Catalyst: standard.

Transmission: Four-wheel drive; five-speed manual gearbox. Automatic, not available. Top gear speed at 1000 rpm: 22.1 mph (35.6 km/h).

Suspension: Front, independent, MacPherson struts, anti-roll bar. Rear, independent, semi-trailing arms with transverse link each side; mini-block coil springs; anti-roll bar.

Steering: Rack and pinion. Power assistance: standard. **Brakes:** Vented discs front, solid discs rear. ABS: standard. **Tyres:** 205/55 VR 15. **Fuel tank:** 14.3 Imp. gall (65 litres). **Unladen weight:** 2890 lb (1311 kg).

Dimensions: Length 174.4 in (4430 mm), width 66.9 in (1700 mm), height 55.1 in (1400 mm), wheelbase 102.4 in (2600 mm).

Performance *Autocar & Motor* test: Maximum speed 128 mph (206 km/h); 0 to 60 mph (97 km/h) 8.5 sec; 80 mph (130 km/h) 14.8 sec. Fuel consumption at constant 75 mph (120 km/h): 34.9 mpg; overall test, 24.0 mpg.

Features: This was the first Vauxhall to have catalyst as standard, and it is also generously equipped, with such features as deadlocks, and electric sunroof. **Summary:** Vauxhall also offer the very powerful 16-valve engine with front-drive only, but four-wheel drive is well worth the extra for the added stability, making this a very fast yet extremely safe car to drive.

VAUXHALL (GB)   Frontera 2.3 TD Estate

Identity: New adventure into cross-country motoring by GM was first revealed at Geneva 1991, and on British market from Motorfair. Model palette begins with the 2-litre three-door Sport, and there are five-door estate cars with choice of 2.4-litre petrol or this turbo-charged diesel.

Engine: Front-mounted transverse four-cylinder with alloy head; single camshaft mounted in head, working eight valves. KKK turbocharger. Bore 92.0 mm, stroke 85.0 mm; capacity 2260 cc. Power 100 PS (74 kW) at 4200 rpm; torque 159 lb ft (215 Nm) at 2200 rpm. Compression 23.0-to-1. Catalyst: not required.

Transmission: Rear-wheel drive plus selectable front drive; five-speed manual gearbox. Automatic, not available. Low-ratio transfer gearbox. Top gear speed at 1000 rpm: 21.8 mph (35.1 km/h).

Suspension: Front, independent, wishbones and torsion bars; anti-roll bar. Rear, live axle on leaf springs.

Steering: Recirculating ball. Power assistance: standard. **Brakes:** Vented discs front, drums rear. ABS: not available. **Tyres:** 225/75 R 15. **Fuel tank:** 17.6 Imp. gall (80 litres). **Unladen weight:** 3925 lb (1784 kg).

Dimensions: Length 176.4 in (4480 mm), width 68.0 in (1728 mm), height 67.5 in (1715 mm), wheelbase 108.7 in (2760 mm).

Performance *Autocar & Motor* test: Maximum speed 83 mph (133 km/h); 0 to 60 mph (97 km/h) 18.1 sec; 80 mph (130 km/h): too slow to time. Fuel consumption at constant 75 mph (120 km/h): 25.2 mpg; overall test, 22.8 mpg.

Features: Free-wheeling front hubs reduce drag when 4 × 4 is not engaged. Low ratio and four-wheel drive are controlled by the same lever. **Summary:** Ride is a bit harsh with this basic form of suspension, and the engine is rather rough and noisy. Clumsy rear door arrangement with spare wheel carried on a swinging arm which must be moved back every time for the rear window to be opened.

VAUXHALL   (D, GB)   Lotus Carlton

Identity: Revealed at Geneva 1989 as the Lotus Omega (illustrated), this special version of the Carlton came to Britain at Birmingham 1990. Vauxhall provided a half-hearted launch, and talked rather unenthusiastically about a product which not long ago might have seemed a great achievement.

Engine: Front-mounted longitudinal six-cylinder with alloy head and twin ohc; four valves per cylinder. Distributorless ignition, three coils. Two Garrett T25 turbochargers. Bore 95.0 mm, stroke 85.0 mm; capacity 3615 cc. Power 381 PS (281 kW) at 5200 rpm; torque 419 lb ft (579 Nm) at 4200 rpm. Compression 8.2-to-1. Catalyst: standard.

Transmission: Rear-wheel drive; six-speed manual gearbox. Automatic, not available. Top gear speed at 1000 rpm: 44.1 mph (71.0 km/h).

Suspension: Front, independent, MacPherson struts with gas-filled dampers; anti-roll bar. Rear, independent, multi-link layout with coil springs and gas-filled dampers; anti-roll bar.

Steering: Recirculating ball. Power assistance: standard. **Brakes:** Vented discs front, solid discs rear. ABS: stamdard. **Tyres:** 235/45 ZR 17 (front); 265/40 ZR 17 (rear). **Fuel tank:** 16.5 Imp. gall (75 litres). **Unladen weight:** 3640 lb (1650 kg).

Dimensions: Length 187.7 in (4768 mm), width 76.1 in (1933 mm), height 56.5 in (1435 mm), wheelbase 107.5 in (2730 mm).

Performance *Autocar & Motor* test: Maximum speed 164 mph (264 km/h); 0 to 60 mph (97 km/h) 5.1 sec; 80 mph (130 km/h) 7.8 sec. Fuel consumption at constant 75 mph (120 km/h): 27.5 mpg; overall, 14.3 mpg.

Features: Luxury interior trim and equipment, with upholstery all in Connolly leather, but some of the features one might expect for the money (such as electric seat adjustments) are not provided. **Summary:** Given more distance, this special Carlton might score a true 170 mph, and the fact that it achieved 164 mph on a 1.8-mile runway shows its magnificent performance, not to mention the superb brakes.

179

VAUXHALL (E)

Nova 1.5TD

Identity: A few months after the Nova turbo diesel was launched at Motorfair 1988, the industrious new Vauxhall press manager asked me to see if I could get 100 mph and 100 mpg out of it. With RAC supervision I had a go, and the car managed it easily: 103 miles in the hour, and 105 miles on a gallon (obviously not at the same time!).

Engine: Front-mounted transverse four-cylinder with alloy head and single ohc; eight valves, and water-cooled turbocharger. Bore 76.0 mm, stroke 82.0 mm; capacity 1488 cc. Power 67 PS (49 kW) at 4600 rpm; torque 99 lb ft (135 Nm) at 2600 rpm. Compression 22.5-to-1. Catalyst: not required.

Transmission: Front-wheel drive; five-speed manual gearbox. Automatic, not available. Top gear speed at 1000 rpm: 24.2 mph (38.9 km/h).

Suspension: Front, independent, MacPherson struts. Rear, independent, compound crank with miniblock coil springs; anti-roll bar.

Steering: Rack and pinion. Power assistance: not available. **Brakes:** Solid discs front, drum rear. ABS: not available. **Tyres:** 165/70 R 13. **Fuel tank:** 9.2 Imp. gall (42 litres). **Unladen weight:** 1874 lb (850 kg).

Dimensions: Length 142.6 in (3622 mm), width 60.4 in (1534 mm), height 53.7 in (1363 mm), wheelbase 92.2 in (2342 mm).

Performance *Autocar & Motor* test: Maximum speed 101 mph (163 km/h); 0 to 60 mph (97 km/h) 12.2 sec; 80 mph (130 km/h) 24.2 sec. Fuel consumption at constant 75 mph (120 km/h): 50.4 mpg; overall test, 43.8 mpg.

Features: Nova 1.5TD comes only with Merit trim level and three-door hatchback body, but equipment is not too basic. One-piece rear seats fold for extra load space. **Summary:** With rather more mileage behind it, my car for the economy test went better than the road test figures suggest; it consistently lapped at over 104 mph, to give an average of 103.8 miles in the hour average speed from a standing start. A good commuting car.

VAUXHALL (D)　　　　　Senator CD 3.0i 24v

Identity: Launched Germany in August 1988, and on UK market from mid-November 1988, the revised Senator has the same Dual Ram engine as the Carlton GSi 3000, with many improvements. Small 24v badge and rectangular exhaust pipes identify the new Senator.

Engine: Front-mounted longitudinal six-cylinder with alloy head and twin ohc working 24 valves. Bosch Motronic ignition/injection, with separate induction pipes in groups of three, linked above 4,000 rpm. Bore 95.0 mm, stroke 69.6 mm; capacity 2969 cc. Power 204 PS (150 kW) at 6000 rpm; torque 199 lb ft (275 Nm) at 3600 rpm. Compression 10.0-to-1. Catalyst: standard.

Transmission: Rear-wheel drive; four-speed automatic, standard; five-speed manual is no-cost option. Top gear speed at 1000 rpm: 27.6 mph (44.4 km/h); manual: 24.4 mph (39.3 km/h).

Suspension: Front, independent, MacPherson struts with triangular controls arms and pendulum stabiliser. Rear, independent, semi-trailing arms with transverse diagonal link each side; mini-block progressive rate coil springs; anti-roll bar.

Steering: Recirculating ball. Power assistance: standard. **Brakes:** Vented discs front, solid discs rear. ABS standard. **Tyres:** 205/65 ZR 15. **Fuel tank:** 16.5 Imp. gall (75 litres) **Unladen weight:** 3404 lb (1544 kg).

Dimensions: Length 190.7 in (4844 mm), width 69.4 in (1763 mm), height 57.0 in (1448 mm), wheelbase 107.5 in (2731 mm).

Performance *Autocar & Motor* test: Maximum speed 139 mph (224 km/h); 0 to 60 mph (97 km/h) 9.1 sec; 80 mph (130 km/h) 14.3 sec. Fuel consumption at 75 mph (120 km/h): 31.4 mpg; overall test, 21.4 mpg.

Features: Available with leather trim, or at lower price with velour; choice of analogue or digital instruments. Lavish equipment including air conditioning, electric sunroof, and selectable suspension firmness. **Summary:** Extremely fast yet very docile, quiet and comfortable car. The 'Dual Ram' feature reflects the switchover effect at 4,000 rpm.

VENTURI (F)

260 Coupé

Identity: France's impressive sports car came to the British market at Motorfair 1991, imported through a new company, Raptor UK. There is a choice of four models, coupé or cabriolet, with turbocharged V6 of PRV origin in 2.6- or 2.8-litre size, identified as the 210 and the 260.

Engine: Mid-mounted longitudinal V6-cylinder with alloy block and heads; chain-driven ohc, 12 valves. Garrett T3 turbocharger with air-air intercooler. Bore 91.0 mm, stroke 73.0 mm; capacity 2849 cc. Power 260 PS (191 kW) at 5500 rpm; torque 318 lb ft (440 Nm) at 2000 rpm. Compression 8.2-to-1. Catalyst: standard.

Transmission: Rear-wheel drive; five-speed manual gearbox. Automatic, optional extra, four-speed (non-turbo only). Top gear speed at 1000 rpm: 27.7 mph (44.6 km/h).

Suspension: Front, independent, wishbones and coil springs; anti-roll bar. Rear, independent, five-link layout with coil springs and anti-roll bar.

Steering: Rack and pinion. Power assistance: standard. **Brakes:** Vented discs front and rear. ABS not available. **Tyres:** Front, 205/55 ZR 16; rear, 245/45 ZR 16. **Fuel tank:** 19.8 Imp. gall (90 litres). **Unladen weight:** 2766 lb (1255 kg).

Dimensions: Length 161.0 in (4089 mm), width 66.9 in (1699 mm), height 46.0 in (1168 mm), wheelbase 94.5 in (2400 mm).

Performance Works: Maximum speed 168 mph (270 km/h); 0 to 62 mph (100 km/h) 5.3 sec. Fuel consumption at constant 75 mph (120 km/h): 29.6 mpg.

Features: High security anti-theft system is standard; air conditioning and leather upholstery are options. Electric seat adjustment. **Summary:** Venturi aims high, and is well finished, but it suffers the usual problems of mid-engined cars—poor rear three-quarter visibility and luggage accommodation severely restricted. When imports started, the dearest model was the 210 Cabriolet, at just over £55,000.

VOLKSWAGEN (D)   Caravelle GL

Identity: After years of using rear-drive for the van and personnel carrier, Volkswagen launched the new front-drive model at Paris 1990. Choice of four-cylinder 2-litre engine, or five-cylinder 2½-litre; there is also a five-cylinder 2.3-litre diesel. Details follow for the 2½-litre GL.

Engine: Front-mounted transverse five-cylinder with single ohc and two valves per cylinder. Electronic fuel injection. Bore 81.0 mm, stroke 95.5 mm; capacity 2450 cc. Power 110 PS (81 kW) at 4500 rpm; torque 137 lb ft (190 Nm) at 2200 rpm. Compression 8.5-to-1. Catalyst: standard.

Transmission: Front-wheel drive; five-speed manual gearbox. Automatic, optional extra (from late 1991). Top gear speed at 1000 rpm: 21.4 mph (34.4 km/h).

Suspension: Front, independent, wishbones with longitudinal torsion bars. Rear, independent, semi-trailing arms and coil springs.

Steering: Rack and pinion. Power assistance: standard. **Brakes:** Solid discs front, drums rear. ABS: optional. **Tyres:** 195/70 R 15. **Fuel tank:** 17.6 Imp. gall (80 litres). **Unladen weight:** 3836 lb (1740 kg).

Dimensions: Length 183.3 in (4655 mm), width 72.6 in (1845 mm), height 72.4 in (1840 mm), wheelbase 115.0 in (2920 mm).

Performance Works: Maximum speed 100 mph (161 km/h). Acceleration: no data. Fuel consumption at constant 75 mph (120 km/h): 21.1 mpg.

Features: Wide choice of body styles and two wheelbase lengths to seat from six to as many as 12. One sliding side door standard, two optional. **Summary:** Although good in some respects, the former rear-drive Caravelle always lacked directional stability. It is to be hoped that the new one will handle much better, but at time of writing there had been no opportunity to drive it, although the Caravelle went on sale in UK May 1991.

VOLKSWAGEN (D)   Corrado G60

Identity: G-charger is the name given to Volkswagen's ingenious scroll-type supercharger, belt-driven from the front of the engine, which boosts the charge and increases the power. It makes this version of the Corrado a very responsive and fast coupé, with much more power than the 16-valve version.

Engine: Front-mounted transverse four-cylinder with cross-flow alloy head and single ohc; eight valves. Supercharger and Digifant electronic fuel injection. Bore 81.0 mm, stroke 86.4 mm; capacity 1781 cc. Power 160 PS (118 kW) at 5600 rpm; torque 165 lb ft (225 Nm) at 4000 rpm. Compression 8.0-to-1. Catalyst: standard.

Transmission: Front-wheel drive; five-speed manual gearbox. Automatic, not available. Top gear speed at 1000 rpm: 21.3 mph (34.3 km/h).

Suspension: Front, independent, MacPherson struts, anti-roll bar. Rear, torsion beam trailing arms with track-correcting mountings; coil springs, anti-roll bar.

Steering: Rack and pinion. Power assistance: standard. **Brakes:** Vented discs front, solid discs rear. ABS: standard. **Tyres:** 195/50 VR 15. **Fuel tank:** 12.0 Imp. gall (55 litres). **Unladen weight:** 2459 lb (1115 kg).

Dimensions: Length 159.3 in (4048 mm), width 65.9 in (1674 mm), height 51.9 in (1318 mm), wheelbase 97.2 in (2470 mm).

Performance *Autocar & Motor* test: Maximum speed 137 mph (221 km/h); 0 to 60 mph (97 km/h) 8.9 sec; 80 mph (130 km/h) 14.5 sec. Fuel consumption at constant 75 mph (120 km/h): 36.2 mpg; overall test, 22.0 mpg.

Features: Alloy wheels, snug sports seats, and neat but rather sombre interior finish. Trip computer also standard, as is electric sunroof. **Summary:** Only one thing spoilt the Corrado for me, and that was the ridiculous arrangement which makes the rear spoiler elevate, partly obstructing rear view, at only 45 mph. In Germany it does not come up until 75 mph. Otherwise a sporty, fun car with excellent handling.

VOLKSWAGEN (D)

Golf 2.8 VR6

Identity: New generation Golf was launched Frankfurt 1991, and although it was also unveiled at Motorfair, it did not come on the British market until February this year. Top model is the VR6, with narrow angle V6 2.8-litre engine, giving smooth, vigorous performance without effort.

Engine: Front-mounted transverse V6-cylinder with single alloy head covering both cylinder banks; single ohc, 12 valves; Bosch Motronics. Bore 81.0 mm, stroke 90.3 mm; capacity 2792 cc. Power 174 PS (128 kW) at 5800 rpm; torque 170 lb ft (235 Nm) at 4200 rpm. Compression 10.0-to-1. Catalyst: standard.

Transmission: Front-wheel drive; five-speed manual gearbox. Automatic, optional extra, four-speed. Top gear speed at 1000 rpm: 23.4 mph (37.7 km/h).

Suspension: Front, independent, MacPherson struts, anti-roll bar. Rear, torsion beam axle, coil spring struts; anti-roll bar.

Steering: Rack and pinion. Power assistance: standard. **Brakes:** Ventilated discs front, solid discs rear. ABS: standard. **Tyres:** 205/50 VR 15. **Fuel tank:** 12.1 Imp. gall (55 litres). **Unladen weight:** 2546 lb (1155 kg).

Dimensions: Length 158.3 in (4020 mm), width 67.3 in (1710 mm), height 55.3 in (1405 mm), wheelbase 97.4 in (2475 mm).

Performance *Autocar & Motor* test: Maximum speed 138 mph (222 km/h); 0 to 60 mph (97 km/h) 7.1 sec; 80 mph (130 km/h) 11.9 sec. Fuel consumption at constant 75 mph (120 km/h): 31.7 mpg; overall test, 24.0 mpg.

Features: VR6 badge on grille identifies this top model of the new Golf range. A little plain inside, but good equipment. **Summary:** *Autocar & Motor* rated the VR6 better than the BMW 325i. I am inclined to agree with the verdict in favour of the precise handling, vigorous performance and low noise level of this new six-cylinder Golf.

185

VOLKSWAGEN (D)   Passat GL 2.8 VR6

Identity: First appearance of the new Volkswagen narrow-angle V6 engine was at Geneva 1991, later to become top engine for the new Golf as well. Passat is a solid, well-engineered car with a feeling of longevity about the way it is built.

Engine: Front-mounted transverse V6-cylinder with single alloy head covering both cylinder banks; single ohc, 12 valves; Bosch Motronics. Bore 81.0 mm, stroke 90.3 mm; capacity 2792 cc. Power 174 PS (128 kW) at 5800 rpm; torque 174 lb ft (240 Nm) at 4200 rpm. Compression 10.0-to-1. Catalyst: standard.

Transmission: Front-wheel drive; five-speed manual gearbox. Automatic, not available. Top gear speed at 1000 rpm: 23.5 mph (37.8 km/h).

Suspension: Front, independent, MacPherson struts, anti-roll bar. Rear, independent, semi-trailing arms with struts; anti-roll bar.

Steering: Rack and pinion. Power assistance: standard. **Brakes:** Vented discs front, solid discs rear. ABS: standard. **Tyres:** 185/65 R 14T. **Fuel tank:** 15.4 Imp. gall (70 litres). **Unladen weight:** 2920 lb (1325 kg).

Dimensions: Length 180.1 in (4575 mm), width 67.0 in (1705 mm), height 56.3 in (1430 mm), wheelbase 103.4 in (2625 mm).

Performance Works: Maximum speed 139 mph (224 km/h); 0 to 62 mph (100 km/h) 8.2 sec. Fuel consumption at constant 75 mph (120 km/h): 31.4 mpg.

Features: Generous equipment for this VR6 version of the Passat includes a differential lock for added low-speed traction, alloy wheels and leather-trimmed steering wheel. **Summary:** This very roomy saloon always deserved a better engine, and in the new 2.8-litre form it is a lot more responsive, giving easy, relaxed cruising at speed. Variant estate car version also available.

VOLKSWAGEN (D)

Polo G40

Identity: At first it seemed that the belt-driven supercharger made the 1.3-litre engine develop almost too much power for such a small car, but on longer appraisal I came to be delighted by the terrific response of this little hatchback, and enjoyed it greatly.

Engine: Front-mounted transverse four-cylinder with cross-flow alloy head and belt-driven supercharger; eight valves. Digifant electronic fuel injection. Bore 75.0 mm, stroke 72.0 mm; capacity 1272 cc. Power 113 PS (83 kW) at 6000 rpm; torque 111 lb ft (150 Nm) at 3600 rpm. Compression 8.0-to-1. Catalyst: standard.

Transmission: Front-wheel drive; five-speed manual gearbox. Automatic, not available. Top gear speed at 1000 rpm: 21.7 mph (34.9 km/h).

Suspension: Front, independent, MacPherson struts, anti-roll bar. Rear, dead beam axle on trailing arms from torsion beam; anti-roll bar.

Steering: Rack and pinion. Power assistance: not available. **Brakes:** Vented discs front, drums rear. ABS: not available. **Tyres:** 175/60 R 13 H. **Fuel tank:** 9.2 Imp. gall (42 litres). **Unladen weight:** 1830 lb (830 kg).

Dimensions: Length 146.7 in (3725 mm), width 62.6 in (1590 mm), height 52.2 in (1325 mm), wheelbase 91.9 in (2335 mm).

Performance *Autocar & Motor* test: Maximum speed 119 mph (191 km/h); 0 to 60 mph (97 km/h) 8.4 sec; 80 mph (130 km/h) 14.3 sec. Fuel consumption at constant 75 mph (120 km/h): 37.2 mpg; overall test, 30.1 mpg.

Features: Alloy wheels are fitted, and there are sports seats with good wraparound, but otherwise the equipment is not over-generous. **Summary:** You pay for the performance, and that is certainly what you get in this wonderfully vigorous three-door hatchback. G40 badge on the grille and red line along the bumpers identify the pocket rocket Polo.

VOLKSWAGEN (D)

Vento 2.0 GL

Identity: Saloon version of the Golf, launched Geneva 1992 (UK in October). The Vento is available with 1.8- or 2.0-litre engine, as well as the V6 (see Golf VR6) and 1.9-litre diesel engines, with or without turbo. There is a GT, with same trim as the VR6. Best intermediate model seemed this version, the GL, with 115 PS. UK will also get Vento 1.4.

Engine: Front-mounted transverse four-cylinder with alloy head and single ohc working eight valves; Digifant fuel injection. Bore 82.5 mm, stroke 92.8 mm; capacity 1984 cc. Power 115 PS (85 kW) at 5400 rpm; torque 120 lb ft (166 Nm) at 3200 rpm. Compression 10.4-to-1. Catalyst: standard.

Transmission: Front-wheel drive; five-speed manual gearbox. Automatic, optional extra, four-speed. Top gear speed at 1000 rpm: 22.0 mph (35.4 km/h).

Suspension: Front, independent, MacPherson struts. Rear, semi-independent, spring struts and torsion beam axle.

Steering: Rack and pinion. Power assistance: standard. **Brakes:** Vented discs front, solid discs rear. ABS: not available. **Tyres:** 185/60 R 14. **Fuel tank:** 12.1 Imp. gall (55 litres). **Unladen weight:** 2400 lb (1090 kg).

Dimensions: Length 172.4 in (4380 mm), width 66.7 in (1695 mm), height 55.7 in (1415 mm), wheelbase 97.4 in (2475 mm).

Performance Works: Maximum speed 123 mph (198 km/h); 0 to 62 mph (100 km/h) 10.4 sec. Fuel consumption at constant 75 mph (120 km/h): 37.7 mpg.

Features: Significant development of the Vento is the introduction of an air bag restraint system for both front occupants, as an option. **Summary:** Easy to drive, comfortable and roomy saloon, with big boot, folding rear seats (which are individually lockable), and generous interior space for its size. Low noise level. Rather thick screen pillars obstruct vision on tight bends.

VOLVO (S) 460GLi

Identity: When the saloon model of the 440 hatchback was launched at Brussels 1990, it was pitched higher up the market – well-equipped, but rather expensive. When it came to the British market in March 1990, this version, with injection engine, seemed to offer best value of the range.

Engine: Front-mounted transverse four-cylinder with alloy head and single ohc; eight valves. Electronic fuel injection. Bore 81.0 mm, stroke 83.5 mm; capacity 1721 cc. Power 102 PS (75 kW) at 5600 rpm; torque 105 lb ft (145 Nm) at 3900 rpm. Compression 10.0-to-1. Catalyst: standard.

Transmission: Front-wheel drive; five-speed manual gearbox. Automatic, optional extra. Top gear speed at 1000 rpm: 21.5 mph (34.6 km/h).

Suspension: Front, independent, MacPherson struts, anti-roll bar. Rear, dead beam axle on longitudinal Watts linkage with Panhard rod; coil springs.

Steering: Rack and pinion. Power assistance: optional. **Brakes:** Vented discs front, solid discs rear. ABS: optional. **Tyres:** 175/70 HR 14. **Fuel tank:** 10.6 Imp. gall (48 litres). **Unladen weight:** 2153 lb (977 kg).

Dimensions: Length 173.4 in (4405 mm), width 66.5 in (1690 mm), height 54.3 in (1380 mm), wheelbase 98.5 in (2503 mm).

Performance *Autocar & Motor* test: Maximum speed 109 mph (175 km/h); 0 to 60 mph (97 km/h) 11.1 sec; 80 mph (130 km/h) 21.5 sec. Fuel consumption at constant 75 mph (120 km/h): 38.0 mpg; overall test, 26.4 mpg.

Features: All British imports of the 460 get electric sunroof as standard; but it is surprising that power steering is an option for this rather expensive car. **Summary:** Pleasant and refined to drive, the 460GLi appeals to the more traditional motorist looking for quality in a compact car. The Turbo version is available for those wanting more lively performance.

VOLVO (NL)   480 Turbo

Identity: There always seems to be an inordinate delay before new Volvos reach the UK market, but 480 in turbocharged form arrived February 1989. Performance not all that much greater, but a little more in keeping with the sporty appeal of the 480 coupé.

Engine: Front-mounted transverse four-cylinder with alloy head and wet cylinder liners; electronic fuel injection. Water-cooled turbocharger with inter-cooler. Bore 81.0 mm, stroke 83.5 mm; capacity 1721 cc. Power 120 PS (88 kW) at 5400 rpm; torque 127 lb ft (175 Nm) at 4600 rpm. Compression 8.1-to-1. Catalyst: optional.

Transmission: Front-wheel drive; five-speed manual gearbox. Automatic, not available. Top gear speed at 1000 rpm: 21.3 mph (34.3 km/h).

Suspension: Front, independent, MacPherson struts, with eccentric coil springs; anti-roll bar. Rear, dead beam axle on longitudinal links with Panhard rod, coil springs; anti-roll bar.

Steering: Rack and pinion. Power assistance: standard. **Brakes:** Vented discs front, solid discs rear. ABS: standard. **Tyres:** 185/60 HR 14. **Fuel tank:** 10.1 Imp. gall (46 litres). **Unladen weight:** 2165 lb (982 kg).

Dimensions: Length 167.7 in (4260 mm), width 67.3 in (1710 mm), height 52.0 in (1320 mm), wheelbase 98.5 in (2502 mm).

Performance *Autocar & Motor* test: Maximum speed 124 mph (200 km/h); 0 to 62 mph (100 km/h) 9.6 sec; 80 mph (130 km/h) 15.0 sec. Fuel consumption at constant 75 mph (120 km/h): 34.9 mpg; overall test, 22.5 mpg.

Features: Turbo version gains oil-pressure gauge and colour-matched bumpers. Anti-lock brakes are an option for both models in some markets. **Summary:** This very attractive GT offers wider appeal in turbo form, though it's still very much an elegant coupé rather than a GT or sports car. However, performance in this turbo form is good for a 1.7.